Lecture Notes in Computer Science 1183

Edited by G. Goos, J. Hartmanis and J. van Leeuwen

Springer
Berlin
Heidelberg
New York
Barcelona
Budapest
Hong Kong
London
Milan
Paris
Santa Clara
Singapore
Tokyo

Andreas Wierse   Georges G. Grinstein
Ulrich Lang   (Eds.)

Database Issues for Data Visualization

IEEE Visualization '95 Workshop
Atlanta, Georgia, USA, October 28, 1995
Proceedings

 Springer

Series Editors

Gerhard Goos, Karlsruhe University, Germany

Juris Hartmanis, Cornell University, NY, USA

Jan van Leeuwen, Utrecht University, The Netherlands

Volume Editors

Andreas Wierse
Ulrich Lang
Universität Stuttgart, Rechenzentrum
Allmandring 30, D-70550 Stuttgart, Germany
E-mail: (wierse/lang)@rus.uni-stuttgart.de

Georges G. Grinstein
University of Massachusetts Lowell
Institute of Visualization and Perception Research
1 University Avenue, Lowell, MA 01854, USA
E-mail: grinstein@cs.uml.edu

Cataloging-in-Publication data applied for

Die Deutsche Bibliothek - CIP-Einheitsaufnahme

Database issues for data visualization : proceedings / IEEE
Visualization '95 Workshop, Atlanta, Georgia, USA, October
28, 1995. Andreas Wierse ... (ed.). - Berlin ; Heidelberg ; New
York ; Barcelona ; Budapest ; Hong Kong ; London ; Milan ;
Paris ; Santa Clara ; Singapore ; Tokyo : Springer, 1996
  (Lecture notes in computer science ; Vol. 1183)
  ISBN 3-540-62221-7
NE: Wierse, Andreas [Hrsg.]; Visualization Workshop <2, 1995, Atlanta,
  Ga.>; Institute of Electrical and Electronics Engineers; GT

CR Subject Classification (1991): H.2, H.5, I.6.8, E.1

ISSN 0302-9743
ISBN 3-540-62221-7 Springer-Verlag Berlin Heidelberg New York

© Springer-Verlag Berlin Heidelberg 1996
Printed in Germany

Typesetting: Camera-ready by author
SPIN 10550015   06/3142 – 5 4 3 2 1 0   Printed on acid-free paper

Preface

Database Issues for Data Visualization: the word data occurs twice in this title and thus clearly shows the emphasis of these proceedings. Databases and visualizations both deal with data. But each of these fields typically deals with its data independently from the other. Visualization features found in today's database management systems are far from what are provided by visualization systems. And today's visualization systems provide very primitive data access and manipulation tools compared to those that a well developed database management system offers.

It is obvious that both groups will benefit significantly from close cooperation. The ever increasing amount of data stored in databases demands new, comfortable ways of access and manipulation. The amount of data that is produced daily by satellites and sent back to Earth to be stored in huge databases require interactive visual support to provide more efficient data management and other tasks. Visual exploration of data stored in databases offers new ways of accessing and interpreting this data.

There are many other applications providing examples for the need to integrate databases and visualization. The data that is currently dealt with and visualized in supercomputing environments has grown in step with the ever increasing size of the numerical problems that can currently be computed and solved. The results of time-dependent numerical simulations can easily reach gigabytes in size. To allow a useful interpretation of these results it is important that the data can be accessed and managed efficiently, and thus visualized.

On October 28, 1995, the second workshop on Database Issues for Data Visualization was held during the IEEE Visualization '95 conference in Atlanta, Georgia. Two years after the first and very successful workshop (proceedings of which are available in Lecture Notes in Computer Science Volume 871), researchers from the areas of databases and visualization met again to discuss and share their problems, needs, and goals. The second workshop topics included data modeling and access, object modeling, user interface construction, dataflow and program module storage and retrieval, the composition and manipulation of graphical representations, and the integration of knowledge bases and rule-based systems, all in a visualization context.

These proceedings offer a snapshot of current research in this field and together with the proceedings of the first workshop offer a way to see the progress of this emerging area. The proceedings also provide a survey of the problems that must be addressed now and in the future towards the integration of database management systems and data visualization.

With these proceedings, the reader is presented with a treatment of a wide range of issues, top to bottom, of the research areas and problems facing the integration of database and visualization systems. We hope to further stimulate research activity in this field, and look forward to the realization of truly integrated systems that accommodate end-user requirements in terms of models, services, displays, and interaction capabilities. We also hope the reader will find the reports and papers as invigorating as the discussion sessions during the workshop.

October 1996, Stuttgart and Lowell

Andreas Wierse
Georges G. Grinstein
Ulrich Lang

Table of Contents

Workshop Description

The second workshop on database issues for data visualization took place in Atlanta in 1995. Two years after the first workshop (1993 in San Jose) it gave the opportunity to analyze and discuss the current situation in this field and the progress achieved in the meantime.

The basic problem is still that current data visualization environments offer minimal support for database management and data interrogation methods. Although in the research area a lot of work has been done, the results of this work are not yet available for a broader range of users. The visual presentation of data still predominates over all other system functions. While the graphical modeling and rendering issues are addressed sufficiently by these systems, the underlying problems of data modeling, data access, and dialog design are not yet handled as efficiently.

In contrast to the first workshop,however,the submissions show a much larger share of descriptions of existing systems that try to address some of these problems. These systems have also reached a very high level of functionality, giving hope that these achievements will soon be found in commercially available systems.

This development confirms our opinion that the application of database management system (DBMS) technology to data visualization for scientific discovery brings powerful data access methods in addition to the standardization of data models and access interfaces. The ever increasing amount of data (produced by satellites or the new generations of parallel supercomputers) makes it mandatory to have an efficient data management.

Related to this is a field that crystallized during the workshop: data mining. While the submitted papers only marginally touch this topic, the discussions held during the workshop quickly showed that the problems related to data mining are very similar to those encountered in bringing visualization and databases together. In fact they are basically the same. For the next workshop (to be held parallel to Visualization '97) data mining will be an important part of the topics to be discussed.

1 Workshop Goals

As in the first workshop, the primary goal was to provide an open forum for interested researchers to discuss the important issues concerning the integration of database systems and data visualization systems. Of course the developments during the two years since the last workshop were of special interest. The progress was evaluated and new fields of interest were established, based upon this evaluation.

The exchange of information and discussion between the researchers from different fields was very important, with the aim of establishing a communication that survives the end of the workshop. Although this cross-fertilization was better than two years ago, it can still be improved in the future.

This book is another goal of the workshop, collecting research papers from scientists working in these fields and giving them the opportunity to publish their latest results as well as outlining the problems of current interest and guiding researchers into new activities.

2 Workshop Format

The papers were solicited in the Call for Participation. The working subgroups during the workshop were chosen accordingly. After a short introduction each participant had the opportunity to sketch his work, so that each participant could get an impression about the others. Following these presentations a discussion was held to collect topics to be discussed in the subgroups. These topics were distributed into three subgroups: Scientific Data Modeling, Supporting Interactive Database Exploration, and Metadata, and the participants worked on these topics. The key research issues that were worked out can be found in the subgroup reports that form the first part of this book. The contributions of the participants describing their work can be found in the second part.

3 Contents Overview

The three workshop subgroup reports summarize the discussion sessions held by the participants. The content of these reports was determined by the subgroup participants based upon the topics agreed upon by all workshop participants. Naturally the style of these reports depends on the subgroup members, there was no general guideline for their appearance. It is also clear that the fields pointed out by the subgroups are not completely distinct, but overlap to a certain degree. So the three reports should not be viewed as independent articles but as a whole intended to describe the current research field of database issues for data visualization.

In contrast to the first book the articles are not grouped according to the subgroups. Since the subgroups were formed during the workshop and not based on the submissions it is not possible to assign every article to an appropriate subgroup. Instead the articles are ordered in a way that leads the reader from a general overview via some theoretical papers to case studies of existing systems.

The first three papers (Lee, Grinstein, and Mukherjea) are more general overviews of the field of visualization and databases. Some concepts are introduced and explained and interesting directions are examined. The papers from Hibbard and Kao take a look at the mathematical basics of data and its structure. Beginning with Wittenbrink's paper the section of system description starts. All these articles present a software system and an application. The authors describe their systems, their advantages and disadvantages and why they are written the way they are.

4 The Editors

Andreas Wierse is a doctoral candidate at the University of Stuttgart. He is employed at the Institute for Computer Applications, Department for Computer Simulation and Visualization. He is fully integrated into the Visualization Department of the Computing Center at the University of Stuttgart. Here he is engaged in research on collaborative work, distributed visualization systems, and the data management of these systems. He received his Diploma in Mathematics in 1991 at Bonn University. He co-organized the second Database Issues for Data Visualization Workshop in Atlanta in 1995.

His research interests include distributed visualization environments, distributed data management, and computational steering.

Georges Grinstein is a full time Professor of Computer Science at University of Massachusetts Lowell, Director of the Graphics Research Laboratory, and Director of the Institute for Visualization and Perception Research. He is also a Principal Engineer with the MITRE Corporation. He received his B.S. from the City College of N.Y. in 1967, his M.S. from the Courant Institute of Mathematical Sciences of New York University in 1969 and his Ph.D. in Mathematics from the University of Rochester in 1978. Dr. Grinstein is a member of IEEE's Technical Committee on Computer Graphics and on the editorial board of several journals including Computers and Graphics and the Eurographics Society's Computer Graphics Forum. He was vice-chair of the executive board of IFIP WG 5.10 (Computer Graphics) and was co-chair of the IFIP Conference on Experimental Workstations held in Boston in 1989. He was panels co-chair of Visualization '90 (San Francisco), program co-chair for Visualization '91 (San Diego), conference co-chair for Visualization '92 (Boston) and for Visualization '93 (San Jose), co-chair of the IFIP 1993 Workshop on Cognitive and Psychological Issues in Visualization, and co-chair for the Database and Visualization Issues Workshop. He has chaired several committees for the American National Standards Institute (ANSI) and the International Standards Organization (ISO). He is co-chair for the SPIE '95 Visual Data Exploration and Analysis Conference.

His areas of research include graphics, imaging, sonification, virtual environments, user interfaces, data mining, and interaction, with a very strong interest in the visualization of complex systems.

Ulrich Lang is head of the Visualization Department at the University of Stuttgart Computing Center, which is the First German Academic Supercomputing Center. He received his University Diploma (Dipl.-Ing.) in 1979 and his Ph.D. (Dr.-Ing.) in Mechanical Engineering in 1988, both from the University of Stuttgart. He was a Visiting Scientist at the Center for High Performance Computing of the University of Texas System in 1989. Dr. Lang is a member of the steering committee of the German Computer Society Group on Imaging and Visualization Techniques, member of the organization committee of Eurographics Workshops on Visualization in Scientific Computing, member of the program committee of the Eurographics Workshops on Parallel Visualization, International Liaison Co-Chair of IEEE Visualization conferences, and reviewer for international visualization journals. He is project leader of multiple European and national research, development, and industrial cooperation projects. He is heading the development of a distributed collaborative visualization environment (COVISE) specifically oriented towards High Performance Computer and Network usage.

His areas of activities include distributed software environments, visualization, virtual environments, and interaction, with special emphasis on the handling of large volumes of complex data.

Acknowledgements

We would like to thank all those who participated in the workshop and assisted us by providing timely submissions of extended papers. Special thanks go to David Kao and John Peter Lee for leading the subgroup report writing activity. We also wish to thank Alfred Hofmann, Editor, Springer-Verlag, for his continued support in making these im-portant proceedings available to the research community within the Lecture Notes in Computer Science series.

October 1996   Andreas Wierse
                                                       Georges G. Grinstein
                                                            Ulrich Lang

Workshop Participants

The following people participated in the workshop:

R. Daniel Bergeron, University of New Hampshire, Durham
rdb@cs.unh.edu

Harvey Davies, CSIRO, Melbourne
hld@dar.csiro.au

June M. Donato, Oak Ridge National Laboratory
donato@msr.epm.ornl.gov

Eve Edelson, University of California, Berkeley
eve@garnet.berkeley.edu

Georges Grinstein, University of Massachusetts, Lowell
grinstein@cs.uml.edu

Bill Hibbard, University of Wisconsin-Madison
whibbard@macc.wisc.edu

David T. Kao, University of New Hampshire
dtk@cs.unh.edu

Daniel Keim, University of Munich
keim@informatik.uni-muenchen.de

Ulrich Lang, University of Stuttgart
lang@rus.uni-stuttgart.de

John Peter Lee, University of Massachusetts, Lowell
jlee@cs.uml.edu

Sougata Mukherjea, Georgia Tech Station, Atlanta
sougata@cc.gatech.edu

Bernice Rogowitz, IBM T.J. Watson Research Center, Hawthorne
rogowtz@watson.ibm.com

Walter Schmeing, VISTEC Software GmbH, Berlin
walt@vistec.FTA-Berlin.de

Bhavani Thuraisingham, MITRE Corporation, Bedford
thura@mitre.org

XIV

Aravindan Veerasamy, Georgia Tech Station, Atlanta
veerasam@cc.gatech.edu

Andreas Wierse, University of Stuttgart
wierse@rus.uni-stuttgart.de

Craig M. Wittenbrink, Hewlett-Packard Laboratories
craig_wittenbrink@hpl.hp.com

Workshop Subgroup Reports

Database Issues for Data Visualization: Scientific Data Modeling

William L. Hibbard[1], David T. Kao[2], Andreas Wierse[3]

[1] University of Wisconsin, Madison, WI, U.S.A.
[2] University of New Hampshire, Durham, NH, U.S.A.
[3] University of Stuttgart, Germany

Abstract. Visualization is one of the most important activities involved in modern *exploratory data analysis*. Traditional database data models, in their current forms, are inadequate to satisfy the data modeling need of exploratory data analysis in general and visualization in particular. A comprehensive *scientific data model* is required for seamless integration of various components of a *scientific database system* which includes visualization, data analysis, and data management.

This paper identifies the criteria of a comprehensive scientific data model and discusses the implementation aspect of such a model based on existing DBMS. Recent research in scientific data modeling and various issues raised in the workshop subgroup are also presented.

1 Introduction

General-purpose visualization systems have proven to be valuable tools for scientific research in various disciplines. As scientific data grow in size and complexity, it becomes apparent that data management capability should be incorporated into the visualization systems. Many commercial visualization systems have already been equipped with some data management tools. However, most of them are *ad hoc* implementations tuned for specific visualization systems. The other trend is to integrate visualization systems with existing general-purpose database management systems. The challenge of this approach lies in developing an effective and streamlined interface between the visualization system and database system.

As useful as these systems currently are, they support very little formalism for modeling scientific data. Traditional data models developed for database systems can not be readily adapted to the scientific data visualization and analysis environment [BCH+94]. The absence of a formal *scientific data model* results in incompatibility among different systems and platforms, to say the least. More importantly, without a formal mathematical model, it would be hard to validate and justify the results derived from visualization and data analysis.

The objective of visualization is to explore hidden relationships, patterns, or characteristics of data with the aid of human visual perception. From a wider perspective, visualization only plays a part – a very important one, nonetheless

– in modern *exploratory data analysis*[†]. A comprehensive scientific data model should not only facilitate visualization but also general exploratory data analysis process. Thus, we distinguish *scientific data models* from those pure *visualization data models*, which have a relatively narrower scope.

This report summarizes the issues proposed and discussed by the data model subgroup of the Second IEEE Workshop on Database Issues for Data Visualization. No attempts were made to make this report comprehensive, covering all the important issues of scientific data modeling. Instead, we focus on those problems which are of particular interest to the attendees of the workshop as well as this subgroup.

A lot of discussion in the subgroup was originated from the fundamental question: *What is the definition of scientific data?* There are no easy or common answers. It seems that most researchers have their own ideas. Here follows a list of characteristics of scientific data as suggested by subgroup members:

1. Interrelationships in scientific data are fundamentally more implicit and difficult to capture than relationships in most other database applications.
2. Scientific data are mostly the results of finite and discrete sampling with finite accuracy of inherently infinite continuous objects.
3. Most scientific data are multi-dimensional in nature.

Short of a formal definition, the above characteristics do illustrate the problems that scientific data models have to address.

This report is organized as follows. Section 2 introduces the basic ideas of data models, the taxonomy of data models, and their relationships to database systems. Section 3 presents the issues to be addressed by a comprehensive scientific data model. Recent research efforts in this area are also summarized. Section 4 identifies the challenges of implementing a scientific data model based on existing database data models in a scientific database system. Several issues raised in the subgroup meeting are presented in Section 5. Section 6 contains concluding remarks.

2 Data Models and Database

In the broadest sense, a data model is just an abstraction of data. A good abstraction lets us focus on the essences of data without the distractions from unimportant details. However, what are the essences of data? The answer is very much depending on applications. Different applications might have different needs and thus require different data models. It is clear that the development of a single model for handling all our data processing need is neither feasible nor desired. Instead, we should study the data analysis process of applications with similar goals to develop a uniform data model for them.

[†] The term, *exploratory data analysis*, was probably first formally introduced in [Tuk77].

Traditionally, the study of data models is a strict database issue. For general database applications, *efficient data storage* and *easy data access* are important. Thus, data models for database applications have to address these two problems specifically. For convenience, let us call this group of data models as *database data models*. In database terminology, database data models can be classified into three categories based on the level of data abstraction – *conceptual, implementation*, and *physical*.

Conceptual data models provide concepts that are close to the way users perceive data. They provide a high-level abstraction of the real world entities. The *Entity-Relationship (ER) model* and *enhanced-ER (EER) model* are the two most widely used conceptual data models. A *conceptual schema* is the description of a database at the conceptual level using a particular conceptual data model. For instance, a STUDENT database for managing student information can be defined as a conceptual schema in any conceptual data model. It can be defined as an ER diagram based on the ER model or, for example, as an EER diagram based on the EER model.

Physical data models provide concepts that describe the low level details of how data is stored in the computer. Physical data models are usually invisible to database users. It is the database system designer's job to define the physical data model and how it is implemented. Common physical data models include *B-tree, B^+-tree, B^*-tree, R-tree*, etc.

Between the two extremes is a class of *implementation data models*, which provide concepts at an intermediate level of abstraction still understandable by users but with enough details to define the way data is logically organized within the computer. Common implementation data models include *relational, network, hierarchical*, and *object-oriented*. An *implementation schema* is the description of a database at the implementation level using a particular implementation data model. For instance, given a conceptual schema (in either the ER or EER model) of the STUDENT database, the implementation schema can be defined as a relational schema in the relational model or an object-oriented schema in the object-oriented model.

Unfortunately, the scientific data model defined in our context does not fit too well with the traditional three layer data model taxonomy based on levels of abstraction for DBMS. In the pure database environment, the three layers are perfectly separated. However, a scientific data model is likely to encompass more than one level of abstractions in the pure database sense.

Nonetheless, in order to utilize the existing database systems, we may have to define scientific data models based on database data models. If this is the case, the scientific data models would be built upon the implementation database data models, although they would be totally different from conceptual database data models like ER or EER diagrams. The possibility of designing scientific data models based on object-oriented database systems will be studied in Section 4.

3 Scientific Data Models

There are a lot more issues needed to be addressed by scientific data models than database data models. In addition to the two basic requirements of a database data model, a visualization data model should also satisfy the following criteria:

1. The exploratory data analysis process, visualization in particular, involves the inevitable trial-and-error component – the exploratory part. During this stage, lots of intermediate data are generated and stored. In other words, the data set is constantly evolving rather than static. Thus, a visualization data model has to have the flexibility to model evolving data sets. *Temporal* and *version* mechanisms should be incorporated.

2. Visualization data models should facilitate common visualization operations. For instance, a large collection of visualization operations require processing data sequentially based on the adjacency of data points in the physical space. Thus, it is sensible to make this kind of locality-based access efficient.

3. Scientific data models shall facilitate *hierarchical data representations*, since visualizations of the same data set at different resolutions are often required. This is particularly important when extremely large data sets are concerned.

The most well known scientific data model is the *fiber bundle data model* [HLC91], based on the idea that the input data for scientific visualization are often functions over differentiable manifolds, sampled at regular or irregular grids. The term *lattice data model* has been used for two different data models. The first one is proposed by Bergeron and Grinstein [BG89, KBS94]. It is based on the idea that data are values of functions sampled on regular lattices of points in n-dimensional space. The major goal of both the fiber bundle data model and the first lattice is to capture the adjacency interrelationship among sampled data points.

The other lattice data model proposed by Hibbard et al. employs a very different approach [HDP94, Hib95]. It is based on the idea that scientific data objects are usually approximations to mathematical objects, and that data objects can be ordered according to the precision of that approximation. A lattice is a kind of ordered set; according to the first definition of lattice data model, the order relation exists between points in the function domain of a single data object. According to the second definition of lattice data model, the order relation exists between different data objects.

Although none of these scientific models is comprehensive, they represent significant research effort in bringing mathematical formalism into scientific data modeling. Since only models based on formal mathematics can be validated and verified, we believe these researches are on the right track.

4 Scientific Database Systems

In the broad sense, *scientific database systems* are database systems with integrated support for applications, such as visualization, that make extensive use of quantitative analysis. A scientific database system provides a comprehensive environment for exploratory data analysis.

Designing a scientific database system from scratch with a particular scientific data model embedded is a very costly project. Most likely, a scientific database system will be implemented as an infra-structure consisting of visualization subsystem, analysis components, and traditional database systems which are based on traditional database data models. From the data model aspect, the challenge lies in implementing a scientific data model with traditional database data models. Since the physical database data model is hidden from the application interface of database systems, a scientific data model is to be implemented on implementation database data models such as relational, network, hierarchy, or object-oriented.

In this aspect, object-oriented or *extended relational* models seem to be the better choices. With object-oriented DML's (Data Manipulation Languages), both object-oriented and extended relational database systems can have data processing functions defined as part of a data object. This capability is essential in implementing a scientific data model. Through those encapsulated functions, the data integrity and structure of a scientific data model can be enforced. Thus, a scientific data model would be a class equipped with its access functions in the database sense.

It is in areas such as data evolution and user extensibility, that object-oriented DBMS truly excel. With class inheritance, it provides the necessary mechanism to implement data evolution. As promising as it may sound, implementing a comprehensive scientific data model on object-oriented DBMS is not an easy task.

In order to deal with complex scientific data without actually implementing a scientific data model in a class definition, some database systems treat large and complicated scientific data sets as BLOB's (Binary Large Objects) [EEC92]. Only metadata of a data set is actually stored in the database. This approach hides the data model information from the database system and it is up to the users to retrieve metadata from the database to interpret those BLOB's. Without building a data model into the class hierarchy, it is almost impossible to maintain a consistent data model among data sets (i.e., BLOB's). While this practice is quite popular in current scientific community, we believe that a comprehensive scientific data model should be built on class level to fully utilize the potential of database systems.

5 Research Issues

Various research issues and open questions are raised and discussed in the data model subgroup. This section summarizes some of those discussions.

5.1 Discrete Approximation of Continuous Objects

The traditional database data models assume that data represent discrete objects in the real world, such as people, addresses, dollar amounts and department names, and are primarily concerned with relations between discrete objects. For such applications, the finite accuracy a computer can process is generally not a problem. However, most scientific data represent continuous objects in the real world, such as real numbers and functions over n-dimensional real spaces. There is a need for data models that integrate these two views.

The problem of modeling real numbers in computers is of particular interest. Instead of specifying the points of the real line **R**, it is common to specify *sets of points* and to regard such a set as approximation to all of its elements [Sco70, ML70, Gia93]. Recent advances in *domain theory* and *topology* [Smy92] provide solid theoretical background for data models of this type [Sün94].

5.2 Mathematical Models of Perceptions and Display

Properties of human perception can be expressed by mathematical structures. For example, the perceptual distance between stimuli can be quantized in terms of "just perceptible" differences. Experiments can determine pairs of colors that people can distinguish such that a closer pair of colors can not be distinguished. This can be used to define a metric on color space as the minimum number of such pairs connecting any two colors [CIE78, RO88]. Similar metrics can be defined for textures [LR95] and for other stimuli. Such metrics give mathematical structure to sets of displays (stimuli).

Human perception is a very subjective and personal matter. We all know those contour images where you can see two things – for instance, either a young girl or an old woman, depending on what region your brain perceives as the foreground. This also does not take into account whether the mood influences our perception. There is a difference in perception whether you are wide awake or half asleep, or whether you are in a hurry or have plenty of time. This is part of the reasons that each witness of a crime might come out with a very different account of the villain.

However, we can argue that *objective perception*, the one which can be modeled mathematically, is invariant to translation in location and time – seeing a display at a different time should not change the way we perceive it. This allows us to define a mathematical symmetry group of transformations on sets of displays. Other symmetries, such as spatial rotation, are possible although open to debate.

Visualization can be viewed as a mapping from a set of data objects to a set of displays. Mathematical structures on these sets provide a rigorous basis for defining conditions on visualization mappings. For example, metric structures on data and display models let us define the condition that the visualization mapping is isometric. That is, the mapping preserves distances so that perceptual distance represents data distance.

We can also define a repertoire of visualization mappings, which is a set of mappings implemented by some system (or the set of mappings regarded as useful). Given a symmetry group on a display model, we can define a condition on the repertoire that it be invariant to composition with transformations in a symmetry group of transformations on displays. This provides a mathematical way to express the idea that perception is invariant to certain transformations of displays. In general we can say that if the mathematical models of data and display are consistent, a whole range of mathematical tools can be applied to our advantage.

5.3   Data Models of GIS

Advanced GIS (Geographical Information System) combine traditional DBMS data models with geographical data models that include points, lines and regions in 2-D space. Queries can combine traditional DBMS queries with geometrical predicates about location, borders, containment, etc. However, while geographical data are an example of scientific data, they are not a general model for scientific data.

The whole spectrum of scientific data is much wider and there is not much that can be taken from 2-D to 3-D without significant effort. Nonetheless, part of the current GIS can be utilized as a base for the management of *time series* data, since many GIS data are temporal by nature (e.g., images collected by LanSat's).

5.4   User Extensibility

Since data models may be quite abstract, and since they are the basis for implementing data analysis and display functions in visualization systems, the best approach may be to define data models that are sufficiently general that users do not need to extend them.

If sufficiently general data models are developed, users can specialize these and apply them to real world data. Object oriented technology might come in naturally here. Subclasses could be used for specialization depending on the data, delivering good flexibility together with reuse of higher level methods and existing code. It also guarantees consistency for a certain set of methods. However, this might also lead away from the extensibility of data models to the implementation level. To make an abstract data model extensible will prove difficult. Either the extension is straightforward, then it could be said that it is already contained in the data model, or it is unpredictable and then it would be very problematic to prepare for extension other than in a very general fashion.

6   Conclusions

In this report, we recognize the need for a scientific data model to support exploratory data analysis in general and visualization in particular. The criteria of a comprehensive scientific data model is proposed and the relation between scientific data model and database data model is examined. Various other questions are also raised in the subgroup discussion. While there were no conclusive results for answering all those questions, we believe data modeling is a proper and important research area which deserves further investigation and contribution from visualization researchers in various fields.

Acknowledgments

The issues raised in this paper were clarified during the stimulating discussions of the data model group of the Second IEEE Workshop on Database Issues for Data Visualization. All members of the group contributed substantially to the discussions which lead to the writing of this report. In addition to the group members, which include Harvey Davies, William L. Hibbard, David T. Kao, Walter Schmeing, and Andreas Wierse, the authors are also in debt to R. Daniel Bergeron who provided numerous suggestions in preparing this report.

References

[BCH+94] R. D. Bergeron, W. Cody, W. Hibbard, D. T. Kao, K. D. Miceli, L. A. Treinish, and S. Walther. Database Issues for Data Visualization: Developing a Data Model. In J. P. Lee and G. G. Grinstein, editors, *Database Issues for Data Visualization*, number 871 in Lecture Notes in Computer Science, pages 3–15. Springer-Verlag, 1994.

[BG89] R. D. Bergeron and G. G. Grinstein. A Reference Model for the Visualization of Multi-dimensional Data. In *Proceedings of Eurographics '89*, Hamburg, F. R. G., September 1989. North Holland Publishing Company.

[CIE78] CIE. CIE Recommendations on Uniform Color Spaces – Color Difference Equations, Psychometric Color Terms. Bureau Central de la CIE, Paris, France, 1978. CIE Publication No. 15 (E-13.1) 1971 / (TC-1.3) 1978, Supplement No. 2, 9-12.

[EEC92] EECS Department, University of California, Berkeley, California. *The POSTGRES 4.0 References*, 1992.

[Gia93] P. Di Gianantonio. *A Functional Approach to Computability on Real Numbers*. PhD thesis, University of Pisa, 1993.

[HDP94] W. L. Hibbard, C. R. Dyer, and B. E. Paul. A Lattice Model for Data Display. In *Proceedings of IEEE Visualization '94*, Washington D.C., October 1994.

[Hib95] W. L. Hibbard. *Visualizing Scientific Computations: A System Based on Lattice Structured Data and Display Models*. PhD thesis, Department of Computer Science, University of Wisconsin, Madison, 1995. Tech Report 1226.

[HLC91] R. B. Haber, B. Lucas, and N. Collins. A Data Model for Scientific Visualization with Provisions for Regular and Irregular Grids. In *Proceedings of IEEE Visualization '91*, San Diego, California, October 1991.

[KBS94] D. T. Kao, R. D. Bergeron, and T. M. Sparr. An Extended Schema Model for Scientific Data. In J. P. Lee and G. G. Grinstein, editors, *Database Issues for Data Visualization*, number 871 in Lecture Notes in Computer Science, pages 69–82. Springer-Verlag, 1994.

[LR95] R. Li and P. K. Robertson. Towards Perceptual Control of Markov Randon Field Textures. In G. G. Grinstein and H. Levkowitz, editors, *Perceptual Issues in Visualization*, pages 83–94. Springer-Verlag, 1995.

[ML70] P. Martin-Löf. *Notes on Constructive Mathematics*. Almqvist and Wiksell, Stockholm, Sweden, 1970.

[RO88]   P. K. Robertson and J. F. O'Callaghan. The Application of Perceptual
          Color Spaces to the Display of Remotely Sensed Imagery. *IEEE Trans-
          actions on Geoscience and Remote Sensing*, 26(1):49–59, 1988.

[Sco70]   D. S. Scott. Outline of a Mathematical Theory of Computation. In *4th
          Annual Princeton Conference on Information Sciences and Systems*, pages
          169–176, 1970.

[Smy92]   M. B. Smyth. Topology. In S. Abramsky, D. M. Gabbay, and T. S. E.
          Maibaum, editors, *Handbook of Logic in Computer Science, Volume 1, Back-
          ground: Mathematical Structures*, Oxford Science Publication. Clarendon
          Press, Oxford, England, 1992.

[Sün94]   P. Sünderhauf. *Discrete Approximation of Spaces: A Uniform Approach to
          Topological Structured Datatypes and their Function Spaces.* PhD thesis,
          Technische Hochschule Darmstadt, 1994.

[Tuk77]   J. D. Tukey. *Exploratory Data Analysis.* Addison-Wesley Publishing Com-
          pany, Reading, Massachusetts, 1977.

Database Issues for Data Visualization: Supporting Interactive Database Exploration

Daniel A. Keim[1], John Peter Lee[2], Bhavani Thuraisinghaman[3], Craig Wittenbrink[3]

[1] Institute for Computer Science, University of Munich
[2] University of Massachusetts, Lowell
[3] The MITRE Corporation, Bedford MA
[4] University of California, Santa Cruz

1 Introduction

A recurrent theme from the Second Database Issues for Data Visualization workshop was the importance of interactively exploring databases using numerous tools and techniques. Database exploration is a discovery process where relevant information or knowledge is identified and extracted from data. It is related to the field of Knowledge Discovery in Databases (KDD), and emphasizes the *process* of knowledge discovery: the development of hypotheses about the data, and the validation of those hypotheses. Discovery is not only possible from analytic tools, but also from graphical, textual, numeric, and tabular presentations of data. Flexibility in data processing and output presentation are fundamental requirements of any data exploration environment. A shared sentiment among workshop participants was that database exploration requires the cooperation of database management, data analysis and data visualization facilities, as shown in Figure 1.

Interaction is also central to database exploration. The user must *interact with data* to discover information. User-data interactions must, then, be supported by an integrated exploration system. Because of the potential complexity of such a system, interactions occur at many levels between the data, system and user. These include interactions among software modules and user-data interfaces. Process management will play a larger role in the development of adequate exploration environments, because such environments will be integrations of numerous types of systems that focus on smaller aspects of the overall problem. If we are to realize any benefits from such an integration, the whole must be greater than the sum of the components.

1.1 Goals of the report

To build useful data exploration and analysis systems, we must bring the disciplines of database management, data analysis and data visualization together and examine the importance of interaction in this context. This will pose new problems and conditions resulting from the additional capabilities of the integrated system. The primary goal of this report is to look at interactions in database

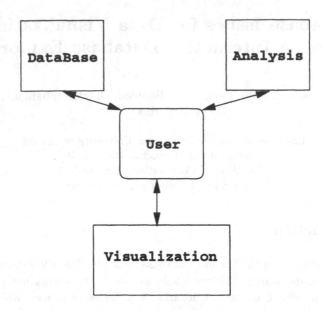

Fig. 1. Interactions between the user, Database, Visualization, and Ana lysis The components of scenarios in user interaction explored in the report

exploration, from a system and user perspective. The ultimate research goal is to effectively support user-data interactions in both the underlying data models and high-level data interfaces. The two primary focus areas are:

1. **Interactions Between System Components** - What are the system components, and how do they interact/communicate with each other? What are the duties and responsibilities of each component? What constraints must be considered to integrate the components?
2. **Interactions Between User and System** - What does the user interact with and how does the user interact with each system component? What additional constraints does the user impose on the system, or what constraints are placed on the user by the system?

In this report we describe the system components and outline several research issues necessary to make the visualization component the interface to the analysis, database, and visualization. Figure 2 shows the user interacting directly with the visualization, which then acts as an intermediary to the other systems. This changes the user from being surrounded by many tools, to one using and interacting with a single tool, but managing the same sophistication of analysis, data-mining, knowledge discovery, and visualization. Visualization's effective human communication qualities enable it to play this important role.

1.2 Definitions of Important Terms

This domain has an ever increasing number of terms that often mean the same thing, and the fundamental definitions in this domain are fairly broad. We distil

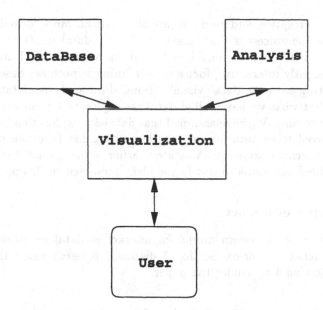

Fig. 2. User primarily interacting with the visualization to access the other system elements.

the following from the universe of definitions to suit our discussions:

data analysis - The computation of quantitative deductions from data. This is the broadest defintion, and often the ultimate goal of any database exploration process. Data analysis can have numeric, symbolic or graphical, etc., components.

data visualization - The graphical presentation of data, whether the data is base data, summary data, configuration data, or knowledge extracted from data. This is a type of visual data analysis, where the analytic component is offloaded to human perception. Often, qualitative deductions are performed from the visualization, and must be confirmed by quantitative data analysis.

knowledge discovery / data mining - The nontrivial, algorithmic, and predominantly autonomous extraction of previously unknown information (patterns, clusters, rules, etc.) from data. The primary focus here is on autonomous calculations and algorithms to extract structure from data. Data mining often specifically relates to the algorithms, and knowledge discovery often relates to the overall processes.

database exploration - The process of finding previously unknown information from a database, using database management, data analysis, data visualization, and data mining facilities. This places greater focus on the human user component of the knowledge discovery process. Since visualization is a critical component, user perception and guidance are also critical. More formally, database exploration is the process of finding subsets D' of a database D and hypotheses $H(D', U, C)$ which a user U considers "useful" in a context C. Database exploration is inherently interactive, focusing on refining hypotheses based on results from interacting with the data (visualizations, data analysis, database queries, etc.). Note that what we have called database exploration is also referred to by some as data mining. We have assumed that database exploration includes what we have referred to as data mining together with other functions such as data analysis, data visualization etc. As stated earlier, there are no standard terms. We have defined the terms to clarify the ideas presented in this paper.

1.3 Overview of Report

Section 2 describes a system model for interactive database exploration, and system interaction scenarios. Section 3 discusses research issues that must be addressed. Section 4 concludes the paper.

2 Overview of an Interactive Data Exploration System

Database exploration is a complex process that cannot adequately be described in terms of database, analysis, or visualization domains alone. An empirical study [Spri92] developed a taxonomy of data analysis tasks, most of which are not adequately supported by current software environments. These tasks encompass all three domains we are considering, and exist at a very low level. A higher level description of the knowledge discovery process [Brac96] emphasized the human component and highlighted the process as iterative, protracted over time, and requiring a great deal of bookeeping. Sequences of task iterations have been modeled in various forms for some time [Nich83, Carr86, Oldf88, Vell90, Youn91], usually to help manage the data analysis process, but not to analyze or exploit it. Exploitation of interaction histories are outlined in [Lee90], and provide the impetus for analyzing database explorations for improvements in system performance and user modeling. There has been little, if any, research done, however, to model and exploit the database exploration process.

In this section, we describe the primary components of a prototypical interactive database exploration system, the inter-component interactions, and the user-component interactions.

2.1 System Components

An effective data exploration system has three principal components: database management, data analysis, and data visualization. There is also a user component that must be supported by the system as shown in Figure 2. This is an incremental, evolutionary approach towards an effective database exploration environment. We envision these three separate system components to be tightly integrated in some way in the future, but currently can only develop interfaces between them, due to their complexities. Knowledge gained from research into this integration will help drive the design of next-generation database exploration, analysis, and visualization environments.

The database management component provides persistent data storage, data integrity and concurrency. It possesses a formal data model with well-defined access functions. A data manipulation language (DML) is avaliable to specify the selection of data. The data model is most often relational, though object-oriented and object-relational models are gaining popularity. Database management systems rely heavily on the user to pose queries and manipulate query results. Database management systems may manage centralized databases or distributed databases. The databases may also be heterogeneous in nature. Furthermore, heterogeneity could be with respect to data models, query processing, query languages, and transaction management algorithms. Most of the commercial database management systems have been geared toward OLTP (online transaction processing) applications. However, due to the large quantities of heterogeneous information, there is a need for many applications to process complex queries. As a result, data warehouses are not being developed. A data warehouse extracts data from multiple databases depending on the queries to be posed and stores the data in a single logical location so that a user need to query only the warehouse. Data warehouses are developed for OLAP (online applications processing) and decision support. Data exploration techniques can be used to extract information from the warehouse. Queries that update data warehouses are extremely application dependent, so an application analysis is necessary in order to abstract out the relevant queries for further analyses.

The data analysis component performs statistical operations over data distributions, transformations into new data, and provides discovery functions such as clustering, regressions and pattern matching. Some have used data mining for data analysis. However, we have defined data analysis as computing some derived data from the data in the database. Application-specific computations such as fluid dynamics and finite element methods are also supported by this component. The data model is often based on matrices and arrays. Typical analysis systems are most often file-oriented systems with some means for accessing data stored in relational databases, or data warehouses. Automatic discovery algorithms determine interesting and significant pattern classifications from this data with minimal user intervention. A more human-centered approach is exemplified by On-Line-Analytic-Processing (OLAP) systems, where data is organized into hierarchies of different resolutions, and a "drill-down" capability is used to access lower-level data from retrieved summary data. Other data navigation aids are used such as cross-tabulations of numeric and categoric data. Aside from comparing graphs, a popular method for analyzing data graphically is to link data displays together, and brush one display to see the effects on a different display [Buja91, Buja96].

The visualization component is primarily concerned with data presentation in the form of graphical displays. A secondary concern is providing an adequate user interface to map data and operations to intuitive forms for the user to interact with data. It is both an output and input component, providing results and facilitating graphical interactions. The data model is often a structural model having connectivity and topologic constraints. The visualization field has yielded many techniques for portraying data in 2D and 3D spaces, with animations where time is a variable. They place the discovery burden upon the user, who can apply graphical probes or alter the display parameters (such as opacity, thresholds, data ranges and viewing orientation). They encourage more "intimate" data interactions because data is mapped into a comprehensible (graphical) format for presentation. Visualization systems, however, are file-oriented, and lack robust data selection or data analysis capabilities.

The user component drives the discovery process by formulating hypotheses, testing hypotheses (issue query, transform and analyze result, compute new data, construct presentations, etc.) and drawing conclusions. The user usually has some knowledge of the application domain, and perhaps some knowledge of the exploration system and its internal data representations. The user performs sequences of linked interactions that serve to isolate relevant portions of the database, to generate and validate hypotheses about the data. There exist elements of navigation through data spaces, comparisons and annotations of important results and processes that must be supported by the exploration system components.

2.2 System Component Interactions

Data Analysis - Database Management: Most database systems are not used for data analysis, only data selection, so the analysis component must operate over retrieved data subsets. The analysis might produce new data, that might need to be inserted back into the database. Also, having a drill-down feature at the analysis component would necessitate queries to be issued to the database from the analysis component. It might be easy to transform between data models, because a matrix is rather similar to a relational table. Some analyses might need special data structures, so a mapping is required to a possibly more complex format. If the database system supports analysis, it would probably serve some needs well, as autonomous agents can continually scour the base data for interesting information, or extremely large databases can be analyzed in-place, without the need to transfer data to and from another tool.

We have worked on several projects that concern related issues of mapping data from the analysis packages to and from the database management systems. In REINAS the Real-Time Environmental Information Network and Analysis System [Long95] we have found that conceptualization of system components affects not only the performance and design, but the way in which users work with the system. Different user views of the data become embedded simply from experience with the tools, that in part coaches their interactions with the data. In other words, the mappings are experiential. And therefore an evolution of coexisting views of the data means that there are coexisting mappings. Even though the views are not mandated, they become important to the user in the training, conceptualizations, and expectations of what the system can and cannot do.

Database Management - Data Visualization: The visualization field is still very immature when considering data models and management. There are a multitude of data models, making translation to the database difficult. Most visualization data models are data format specifications, with little thought given to allowable operations over the data, as in the relational data model. Visualization often works in a batch mode, on huge numbers of records, so a cursor interface might not be appropriate for database-visualization interaction. By nature, the visualization component affords greater interactions with data because the graphical output may uncover relationships and information undetected by automated tools. Thus, there are visual probes and selections occuring that need to be mapped to the database. The querying and drill-down capability from visualization to database is being explored in the Exbase system [Lee94, Lee95, Lee96]. Exbase is a layered system that translates both data and interactions between database and visualization. We are currently exploring means for rapid data selection, such as dynamic queries [Albh92] for retrieved data, and to augment this with actual database queries.

Also, in traditional data base management systems there is no possibility to visualize the result of a query or the relevance of the data items with repsect to the query. New techniques directly presenting huge amounts of data to the user are needed if data visualization shall be used to support exploring large databases. An example for such techniques are the pixel-per-value techniques developed in the VisDB project [Keim94, Keim95, Keim95a]. The basic idea of pixel-per-value techniques is to map each data value to a colored pixel and present the data values belonging to each dimension in a separate window. This permits visualization of up to a million data values. The pixel-oriented techniques use different arrangements of pixels for different purposes. The user may use a query-independent visualization technique which sorts the data according to some dimension(s) and uses a screen-filling pattern to arrange the data values on the display. This is useful for data with a natural ordering according to one variable (e.g., time series data). However, if there is no natural ordering of the data and the main goal is an interactive exploration of the database, the user will be more interested in *feedback* of some query. In this case, the user may turn to the query-dependent visualization techniques which visualize the relevance of the data items with respect to a query. The query-dependent visualization techniques calculate the distances between data and query values, combine the distances for each data item into an overall distance, and visualize the distances for the dimensions and the overall distance, sorted by the overall distance. The arrangement of the data items centers the most relevant data items in the middle of the window, and disperses less relevant data items in a spiral-shape towards the outside of the window.

Data Analysis - Data Visualization: The data visualization component is critical to display the results produced by data analysis. This may be, for example, the visualization of summary data or the curves that represent portions of the data. On the other hand, the data analysis component may carry out further analysis from the visualization data produced by the data visualization component of the data in the database. Data analysis and computation actions are often performed over data to be visualized. Popular visualization dataflow environments often have a suite of analysis and compute modules to apply to data. These modules operate over the native data model of the visualization environment, so there is a tight integration of the two. In fact there are a large number of systems available that have explicit data analysis - data visualization capabilities, many developed from the initial theories of Tukey [Tukey77]. Examples include S Plus / Trellis [Beck88], XGobi [Sway92], and Data Desk [Vell92, Wilh95]. Direct interaction techniques, by not using a strict dataflow approach have also been developed such as used in the modular visualization environment of the *Spray Rendering* approach [Pang95]. Methods for evaluating visualizations have been researched in [Clev85].

2.3 User Interactions

A user should be free to interact with any of the three system components, to control their configuration and behavior. A user also may control the processes between components. For example, with respect to the data analysis and data visualization component interaction, a user may observe the results produced by the visualization component and guide the data analysis component as to the queries to be posed to the database management system. When the results produced by the database management system are visualized, the user again observes the results, and then guides the data analysis component again. In other words, a user could be a participant for every possible interaction. A worthwhile goal should be to effectively map the interactions at the user interface to the appropriate system action, so that the user is not burdened with unnecessary system details.

Data Visualization Component - User: The data visualization component enables a user to visualize, among other things, the database structure, base data in the database tables, database queries, query results and data analyses. Thus, it is the crucial component to support navigations through data spaces and the system components. Visualization allows the user to configure displays and control selection, analysis and display parameters by providing consistent and intuitive visual metaphors. It guides the exploration, and serves as the glue that holds the environment together. Visualizations of the data may also be used to generate new (qualitative) hypotheses and for confirming hypotheses, so there is a definite tight coupling between the visualization and the user.

Database Management - User: The data management system supports the user by providing persistent storage for both the base data under investigation and the metadata that is generated by the investigation. The metadata summarizes discoveries, and can be used for prediction and planning purposes. It also supports advanced users in directly posing complex queries using the database query language. The primary use of the DBMS is to satisfy queries that select data based on some criteria of interest. Other tasks include granting access priveledges, configuring access and storage parameters, and ensuring data integrity. Database interaction through a DML is often extremely difficult, so this must be shielded from the user to enable efficient querying with minimal effort.

Data Analysis - User: Data analysis aids the user in making deductions, performing data mining, and in decision support. This is primarily for quantitative data analysis to confirm a hypothesis, or to isolate data based on some rule that is not specifiable in the databases' DML. It may, however, also be useful for qualitative data analysis as a means of confirming stages of an exploration. Data must be supplied from either the database or visualization component, as the user directs some database subset or visualization portion to be analyzed. In many cases, the data analysis is visual, so means of comparing and computing over visualizations is necessary.

3 Database Exploration Research Issues

In practice, we usually do not find a database exploration system as described in Figures 1 or 2. In most cases, only a limited portion of the model is realized, usually being restricted to one system component and the user. As a consequence, the interactions between the system components is also restricted. Depending on the system component which is used in the model, three different classes of users may be distinguished:

1. **Statistics-oriented User** Statistics-oriented users perform a statistical analysis of the data for obtaining usually quantitative information about the data.
2. **Database-oriented User** Database-oriented users focus on exploring their databases by using the querying facilities of the database management system. The results may be of a qualitative or quantitative nature.
3. **Visualization-oriented User** Visualization-oriented users try to obtain new insight into the data by using different visualizations of the data. The results are usually qualitative in nature.

It is clear that all three interaction scenarios have their place in an integrated database exploration environment. For practical database exploration, the techniques employed in each of the domains have to be smoothly integrated. Also, an effective interaction between the system components as well as between the system components and the user has to be developed.

If data exploration tools from the different areas are used at all, it is usually the user who has to manually combine the different tools. The user might get some hypotheses about a subset of the database by using a visualization tool, s/he might retrieve the subset by using the database query lanuage, and finally s/he might try to confirm the hypotheses by using statistical analyses. In some other case, the user might get some initial hypotheses by using a statistical analysis tool and then turns to the database querying or visualization tool to confirm the hypotheses. Any sequence of using the different tools would be possible since there are many different techniques in either of the domains. A problem of the current situation, however, is that the interaction between the tools from the different domains is usually handled manually by the user. The user first obtains results by using one of the techniques and then decides which other techniques from the same or a different domain are suitable to continue the data exploration process. In our model, all three domains (statistical analysis, database querying, and visualization) are assumed to be fully integrated which, in our opinion, is necessary for an efficient and effective database exploration. A smooth integration however also raises many research issues which have to be solved to make the data exploration environment work.

We present several important research issues which we believe to be interesting, challenging and worthwhile. As mentioned previously, the integration of all three areas is important for effective data analysis. For example, because of the massive amounts of data being collected and archived into many DBMS's, any pruning, preprocessing, or discovery of important information by an analysis module as data is collected would be a great aid. Data mining alone will not determine interesting patterns and correlations that were unanticipated in its algorithms, but a visualization might portray such information easily. The synthesis of visualization with exploration of data bases will provide capabilities that would otherwise not be found, because of the capabilities of the people who use the tools we may develop.

An integrated system model: It is one issue to assemble the components such that they work together. This involves providing adequate data models and translation functions. It is another issue to provide an environment that exploits each component and the user exploration tasks at hand. This involves user-data interaction support, database subset manipulations and discovery representations and annotations. Having some intelligent retrieval mechanisms to access and analyze relevant discoveries from a knowledge base is an important aspect of this goal. An associated goal would be the ability to build rules from a visualization discovery, and insert these rules back into the knowledge base. We also need an interaction model, and a transaction model at the database. A complete model will not be realized until numerous system experiments are conducted, so this is probably the largest open research problem stated here.

Query formulation and refinement: Database exploration has two main goals: (1) to find important information within data, and (2) to find the important questions that (1) answers. The user often doesn't know what to look for, only that s/he must find *something* interesting. This implies that we not only need robust tools to explore and analyze the data, but also the means to express the results to others and to the integrated system. We need to have powerful knowledge representations and management, as well as the requisite user interfaces to enable efficient query specifications and interactions. Some promising research is described in [Brac93]. As the presentation of knowledge is refined, so is its specification. Improving query formulation and refinement requires research in defining an effective query, evaluation of users interacting with visualization and DBMS systems, and developing new interactive techniques and systems. For example, how can queries be specified from an immersive virtual environment? How can analyses or visualizations be specified in queries, or should they be left out?

Visualization for knowledge discovery: Visualization is inherently qualitative, but can be used in a quantitative manner as well. We need to know when it is most effective, for example, as a guidance mechanism to identify interesting regions of the data, for data reduction and exploration focus, or as a useful mechanism for in-depth comparative analysis. Again, the importance of experiments to determine when visualization is appropriate and can be relied upon for analysis is crucial. Little has been done on quantifying the effectiveness of visualization, as opposed to the underlying performance and system issues [Rush95].

Additional visualization discovery tools: The visualization component has incorporated into it aspects of database selection and data analysis, so these tasks must be supported by the visualization user interface. There is, then, a need for more visualization discovery tools, and visualization techniques for database exploration. For example, we have simple data probes, and can brush linked displays. But, what else can be used? Related work is represented by some developments in modular visualization environments, such as Spray Rendering [Pang95]. Direct manipulation interfaces will serve a useful purpose here. Dynamic query interfaces have been shown to be useful for data selection, but are limited to queries expressed as ranges over attributes. Visual programming is also being used to express queries to databases, but query networks are often more complicated than the SQL they support. Navigation through multidimensional data spaces is still an important issue deserving attention.

Cognitive models of data: The user has mental models of the data and the system. These need to be supported with a minimum of cognitive effort. Does the user need to interact with all components, or just one or two? It might seem natural for all user interaction to take place between the user and visualization system, and map data and interactions from the visualization to the other components. Though other workgroups investigated the modelling of data, the effects ripple through the interactions. The efficiency of any user task depends upon their knowledge of the system, the data, and the goals (tasks), and therefore chaining the model of the data and system may have a direct correlation to the task efficiency.

Data Exploration on the World Wide Web(WWW): There is now much work on interfacing database management systems with the WWW. SQL queries are now embedded into HTML home pages. This way users could access the multiple databases on WWW. Database exploration research should also include extracting the information from the WWW databases. What are the additional features that need to be added to HTML home pages? What is the impact on languages such as JAVA on data exploration? What are the appropriate data exploration techniques for digital libraries? Much research is needed.

Collaborative Database Exploration: Another important area is collaborative computing. The idea is for users to collaboratively work together to solve a problem, and the users could be at different locations. Since database exploration is a complex process, it may not be possible for one person to extract useful information in many cases. Therefore multiple individuals possibly at different locations may have to work together to collaboratively explore and extract useful information. Therefore, database exploration needs to be integrated with collaborative computing technology.

/em Performance Techniques: Of course, the demand for greater performance with larger and larger archives of data will continue to drive research. Techniques for parallelization and distributing of query execution, as well as for parallelization of the even more demanding data mining and knowledge discovery algorithms must be developed. Data mining is a batch application now, but if it were possible to make such computer intensive applications interactive, the capabilites for interactive data exploration would be tremendously improved.

4 Conclusions

In order for visualization to be ultimately useful as a knowledge discovery technique, it must be integrated into a system that also supports database and data analysis processes. We envision an evolution from monolithic visualization systems to integrated database exploration and knowledge discovery environments as outlined in this report. Once visulalization systems become more "data-centric", by offering data selection and analysis at the visualization interface, they will attain a more prominent status in knowledge discovery environments. Their greatest utility is in presentation and interaction affordances, and so they must seamlessly integrate with other tools that perform the core knowledge discovery tasks.

The interactions and metaphors for interaction determine in large part the success and usability of any database system. By focusing on the efforts necessary in combining visualization front ends with database engines, we have sought to clarify the research issues in pushing this field forward as quickly as possible. The possibility is there of a user interacting purely with a visualization front end to control the database, data mining, and data analysis investigations of very large datasets. Of course there are complications in connecting each of the modules together directly, and there are added complications in human interface choices. What we have shown is that the assumptions about where the user lies in relation to the system, and the tasks that a performed change the definition of the interaction, and add/change the necessary systems development. Direct graphics manipulation can be easily used for a high percentage of interactions with visualization from databases, but cannot handle all tasks. The open problem of how to map gestures to queries is intriguing from practical and theoretical standpoints. We hope that this group report serves to aid those in investigating this important area.

References

[Albh92] Albherg, C., C. Williamson, B. Schneiderman, "Dynamic Queries for Information Exploration: An Implementation and and Evaluation", *Proceedings of CHI'92*, pages 619-626, 1992.

[Beck88] Becker R., Chambers J. M., Wilks A. R.: 'The New S Language', Wadsworth and Brooks/Cole Advanced Books and Software, Pacific Grove, CA., 1988.

[Brac93] Brachman, R., P. Selfridge, L. Terveen, B. Altman, A. Borgida, F. Halper, T. Kirk, A. Lazar, D. McGuinness, L. Resnick, "Integrated Support for Data Archaeology", *International Journal of Intelligent and Cooperative Information Systems*, vol. 2, no. 2, pages 159-185, 1993.

[Brac96] Brachman, R., T. Anand, "The Process of Knowledge Discovery in Databases", in *Advances in Knowledge Discovery and Data Mining*, Fayyad, Piatetsky-Shapiro, Smyth, Uthurusamy, eds., MIT Press, pages 37-58, 1996.

[Buja91] Buja, A., J. MacDonald, J. Michalak, W. Stuetze, "Interactive Data Visualization Using Focusing and Linking", *Proceedings of Visualization'91*, pages 156-163, 1991.

[Buja96] Buja, A., D. Cook, D. Swayne, "Interactive High-Dimensional Data Visualization", *Journal of Compueational and Graphical Statistics*, vol. 5, number 1, pages 78-99, 1996.

[Carr86] Carr, D., W. Nicholson, P. Cowley, "Data Analysis Management - Goals and Experience", in *Proceedings of the American Statistical Society*, Stat. Comp. Section, pages 25-31, 1986.

[Clev85] Cleveland, William S., "The Elements of Graphing Data", Wadsworth, 1985.

[Keim94] Keim D. A., Kriegel H.-P., "VisDB: Database Exploration using Multidimensional Visualization", *Computer Graphics and Applications*, Sept.1994, pages 40-49.

[Keim95] Keim D. A., Kriegel H.-P., "VisDB: A System for Visualizing Large Databases", System Demonstra tion, *Proc. ACM SIGMOD Int. Conf. on Management of Data*, San Jose, CA, 1995.

[Keim95a] Keim A., Kriegel H.-P., Ankerst M.: 'Recursive Pattern: A Technique for Visualizing Very Large Amounts of Data', Proc. Visualization '95, Atlanta, GA, 1995, pp. 279-286.

[Keim96] Keim D. A., "Enhancing the Visual Clustering of Query-dependent Data Visualization Techniques using Screen-Filling Curves", *Proc. Int. Workshop on Database Issues in Data Visualization*, Atlanta, GA, 1995.

[Lee90] Lee, A., "A Taxonomy of Uses of Interaction History", *Proceedings of Graphics Interface'90*, pages 113-122, 1990.

[Lee94] Lee, J.P., G.G. Grinstein, "Data Exploration Interactions and the Exbase System", in *Database Issues for Data Visualization*, J.P. Lee and G.G. Grinstein, eds., *Lecture Notes in Computer Science*, Springer Verlag, volume 871, pages 118-137, 1994.

[Lee95] Lee, J.P, G.G. Grinstein, "An Architecture for Retaining and Analyzing Visual Explorations of Databases", *Proceedings of Visualization'95*, pages 101-109, 1995.

[Lee96]   Lee, J.P., G.G. Grinstein, "Describing visual interactions to the database: closing the loop between user and data", *Proceedings of SPIE: Data Exploration and Analysis III*, volume 2656, pages 93-103, 1996.

[Long95]   Long, D.D.E., Mantey, P.E., Wittenbrink,C. M, Haining, T.R., and Montague,.B.R., "The real-time environmental information network and analysis system", *Proceedings of COMPCON'95*, pages 482–487.

[Nich83]   Nicholson, W., "Analyzing Large Data Sets: A Challenge for Statistical Computing", *in Proceedings of the American Statistical Society*, Stat. Comp. Section, pages 194-199, 1983.

[Oldf88]   Oldford, R., S. Peters, "Statistical Analysis Maps", *University of Waterloo Technical Report STAT-88-21*, Department of Statistics and Actuarial Science, 1988.

[Pang95]   Pang, A., Wittenbrink, C., "Spray Rendering as a Modular Visualization Environment", *ACM Computer Graphics*, volume 29, number 2, pages 33 – 36, 1995.

[Rush95]   Rushmeyer, H., M. Botts, S. Uselton, J. Walton, D. Watson, H. Watkins, "Metrics and Benchmarks for Visualization", *Proceedings of Visualization'95*, Panel Discussion, pages 422-427, 1995.

[Spri92]   Springmeyer, R., Blattner, M., and N. Max, "A Characterization of the Scientific Data Analysis Process", *Proceedings of Visualization'92*, pages 235-242, 1992.

[Sway92]   Swayne D.F., Cook D., Buja A.: 'User's Manual for XGobi, a Dynamic Graphics Program for Data Analysis', Bellcore Technical Memorandum, 1992.

[Tukey77] Tukey, J.W., "Exploratory Data Analysis", Addison Wesley, 1977.

[Vell90]   Velleman, P., "Computing and Modern (Exploratory) Data Analysis", *Proceedings of the American Statistical Society*, Stat. Comp. Section, pages 46-54, 1990.

[Vell92]   Velleman P. F: 'Data Desk 4.2: Data Description', Ithaca, NY, 1992.

[Wilh95]   Wilhelm A., Unwin A.R., Theus M.: 'Software for Interactive Statistical Graphics - A Review', Proc. Int. Softstat '95 Conf., Heidelberg, Germany, 1995.

[Youn91]   Young, F., J. Smith, "Towards a Structured Data Analysis Environment: A Cognition-Based Approach", *in Computing and Graphics in Statistics*, A. Buja and P. Tukey eds., Springer Verlag, 1991.

Visualization Related Metadata

Ulrich Lang[1], Georges Grinstein[2], R. Daniel Bergeron[3]

[1] University of Stuttgart Computing Center, lang@rus.uni-stuttgart.de
[2] The MITRE Corporation and the University of Massachusetts at Lowell,grinstein@cs.uml.edu
[3] Department of Computer Science, University of NewHampshire, rdb@cs.unh.edu

Abstract: This Metadata Workgroup Report first overviews various metadata activities reported on the world wide web. The workgroup participant discussions and contributions are then summarized. A detailed discussion of metadata for scientific simulation and measurement handling has been selected. Different metadata architectures which depend on the relationship between the usage characteristics and goals of data and metadata are then described. Finally key research issues are identified. A specific emphasis of this paper is to present metadata discussion issues from the viewpoint of visualization and its integration with large scale simulation and data handling.

1 Introduction

During the Second Workshop on Database Issues for Data Visualization a series of topics for discussion were identified, and workgroups were established to permit in-depth coverage of each. The Metadata workgroup concentrated on identifying major issues, and postponed detailing the issues through email. As the Metadata workgroup was created spontaneously during the workshop, it could not immediately do any survey of previous and ongoing metadata oriented activities of other workshops and conferences; such a survey was added later, however, in the context of the workgroup discussion held during the workshop.

2 Survey of Metadata-Oriented Workshops and Conferences

In recent years a series of metadata oriented workshops have been held, beginning in August 1993 at the Center for High Performance Computing (Austin, Texas, see [1]), and followed by further workshops on metadata and data management issues. The IEEE Mass Storage Systems and Technology Committee has sponsored metadata workshops and maintains an information server on the WWW entitled „The Metadata and Data Management Information Page" (see [2]). Aims stated in the preamble are as follows.

Increasingly large amounts of scientific and technical data are being created and saved in digital data storage systems. There is a need to expedite access and use of this data. A variety of different data and formats need to be addressed, such as images, video, audio, tables, arrays, graphics, algorithms, procedures, and documents.

The purpose of the IEEE workshops is to bring together individuals with a common interest in managing and using large stores of scientific and technical data. The focus will be on defining a framework for metadata (data describing stored data). It is a particular goal of the specialist workshop series to produce a metadata reference model for scientific and technical data management.

The key difference between this workshop and the IEEE workshops is our intense focus on the relationship between metadata and data visualization, which the IEEE workshops did not cover specifically.

2.1 Initial Metadata Workshop

The initial metadata workshop provided a first structuring of the type of information that is represented by metadata. It stated that metadata is information about:

- stored information entities, such as semantics/information content, structural mapping to storage, type and encoding of elements, relationships among entities, format/structure/type, related data, inferential/derived data,

- storage management and administration, such as location/name, access time, method of access,

- use of storage and entities, such as permissions, usage, history.

A natural split occurred among the participants; one group focused on storage related issues, the other on application related issues of metadata.

2.2 White Paper on Data Management

As input for the second workshop in February 1994 Robyne Sumpter produced a white paper in which metadata is put into the framework of a data management system (see [3]). The National Storage Laboratory (NSL) at the Lawrence Livermore National Laboratory is more focused towards improving file storage environments.

Quoting:

Metadata promises to improve storage system-level performance through more efficient staging, migration and application-level performance by allowing users more informed choices.

System-level and application-level metadata are differentiated. System-level metadata is related to file system organization and management. Examples are access times, size, current location especially in storage hierarchies, storage methods, etc. Application-level metadata is related to user data, that helps to find, evaluate, access and manage data. This type of metadata could include text, graphics, audio or information describing relationship to other files.

It is assumed that metadata should be stored in the same hierarchical storage system environment as data, although additional requirements for metadata are necessary, such as access speed, which requires that metadata must never be migrated. No other limitations are imposed on metadata; it can be of any data type and can be of any size - - even larger than the original data it relates to.

High level system oriented metadata maintains information about access statistics. Many people have started to implement their own metadata management systems. There is an urgent need for a metadata reference model. It should define a common set of terms and an intellectual framework for discussion of data management solutions.

The Intelligent Archive (IA) project at Lawrence Livermore Laboratory is an example of the incorporation of metadata usage. It contains an intelligent interface to data on disk, in databases, mass storage and documents. It will use metadata to help users navigate in their data. User interface concepts are described together with unsolved metadata integration problems.

2.3 Reference Model for Metadata

The IEEE Workshop on Metadata for Scientific and Technical Data Management held May 15 through 18, 1994 at the National Archives in Washington, D.C., could be regarded as the third metadata workshop. Francis Bretherton presented work on a reference model for metadata for scientific and technical data management as an intellectual framework and guide for metadata (see [4]). Bretherton clearly differentiates between the requirements of a commercial and scientific or technical data management. Commercial DBMSs tend to have schemas that are relatively static, though the contents may be updated frequently, while scientific databases add not only more data, but also new types of data. Their operations are based on larger data volumes, such as entire datasets which are added or deleted.

The aim of the reference model is to provide a framework for specifying the logical structure of the external interfaces to a database with enough precision to be practically realizable in an efficient manner, yet deliberately independent of any particular implementation. Such a framework could then be used for specifying requirements and performance benchmarks in procurement of complete systems, hardware and software, and should permit explicit consideration of design and operational trade-offs in the light of evolving scientific understanding and technological innovation.

A metadata reference model should describe the structure of the interface of databases linked within a complete information system. The relevant communications within that system are between scientists and databases, and between databases themselves.

The latest metadata related event is the announced First IEEE Metadata conference (see [5]).

3 What is Metadata?

3.1 Definitions for the Term Metadata

A common definition is that metadata is data about data. Bretherton (see[4]), for example, adds that metadata is information required to make scientific data useful. For successful communication it is essential that parties share a common set of assumptions, i.e. have a common context, according to which the messages that pass are to be interpreted. Metadata provides such contextual information.

The interpretation of the meaning of metadata has evolved differently in the different application fields and is thus context dependent itself.

3.2 Usage of Metadata

Examples of metadata usage and interpretation such as those in the papers of the First IEEE Metadata Conference (see [5]) show considerable diversity. Data occurs in such diverse fields as social science, geospatial science, banking, insurance, scientific computing and simulation, measurements, image recording from satellites or medical (CT, MRI), and many more.

Metadata has to be generated in addition to the data it relates to - an effort that is only useful if metadata has a purpose. Metadata could thus be described as additional information that is required to provide or improve certain functionalities.

The aims and purposes of data use are, of course, as diverse as the application fields are. Structuring, volume, characteristics of operations in frequency, granularity, to cite a few, vary widely. To the extent that metadata is used, it is also subject to this diversity. To get a clearer view of metadata's meaning, purpose, and usage, it is useful to concentrate on a narrower application field and only later try to generalize from the findings about metadata in that field. We selected the scientific simulation and measurement field with its typically large datasets, where single data values seldom require distinct operations.

4 Metadata and Database Environment

Our more focused approach, aimed at improving our understanding of metadata, is applied here to the handling of scientific or technical problems using computers. We assume that data derives from simulations or from external measurement sources. We further assume that a software environment integrates the different processing steps together with the data handling functionalities.

Databases store data as well as metadata, which is derived data about the original data. A database management system should be an intrinsic part of any software environment that aims to attain insight into simulation models, measurement data or database content. A DBMS provides long-term data storage and data consistency, and coordinates data access.

A current area of strong development is data warehousing, where processing is performed to extract relevant information from different possibly distributed resources and bring the merged result to a form that allows immediate access to meaningful information for a certain field. A relevant part of the data in such a warehouse could be described as derived data or metadata.

5 Structuring of Metadata

Metadata can be structured based on different criteria. The relationship between data, metadata and models is one criterion. It is also possible to define different qualities and levels of metadata.

5.1 Relationship between Data, Metadata and Models

Metadata can be structured due to its relationship to data and models. The set of cases we have identified are as follows.

Metadata as Descriptive Information

Data + Descriptive Metadata -> Complete information

Descriptive metadata is required, otherwise it is not possible to interpret the data itself.

Examples are: dimensions of a matrix, number of pixels per row and column, physical dimensions, basic data type (e.g., integer).

Generation of descriptive metadata is independent of the data itself, as it adds information.

Metadata as Optional Information

Data + Optional Metadata -> Augmented information

Optional metadata adds information that augments the information content of the data.

Examples are: date and time of generation, author, annotations, origin, measurement equipment.

Generation of optional metadata is independent of the data itself, as it adds information.

Metadata as Derived Information

Data -> Metadata -> Information

Metadata as derived data extracts relevant parts of the original data or summarizes data which is stored as metadata.

Examples are: selection of regions with temperatures higher than 323K, mean temperature of the last 20 years in a certain region.

Generation of metadata results as a derivation from data. Metadata itself can be regarded again as data, possibly leading to multiple derivation steps.

Metadata and Meaning

Data + Procedural Metadata -> Insight

In most application fields data is only an intermediary representation. The original aim is to get insight into the behavior of a system or model. The process that starts with original data, adds descriptive metadata and arrives at some final insight is exploratory in nature. During the exploratory process metadata is used to maintain derived results and to store descriptions of the undertaken processing steps. Procedural metadata permits one to repeat and understand the steps taken to gain insight. The GRASPARC project (see [6]) is an example, where history recording and repetition of procedures was a major activity. See also Lee and Grinstein [7].

Examples are: description of processing steps, such as removal of irrelevant data, transformation into other representations, description of relationships between spatial and temporal behavior of certain data components.

During its generation procedural metadata is partially derived from data. Scripts or processing descriptions can be automatically processed for this purpose. The person who gains insight from the data and metadata may also add annotations or written descriptions.

5.2 Metadata in a Phased Processing Pipeline

Metadata can be characterized by the different phases of the processing pipeline in which it is generated. The processing pipeline (Figure 1) is a modified version of the visualization pipeline, with the additional assumption that intermediate processing states can be stored and reused as different types of metadata.

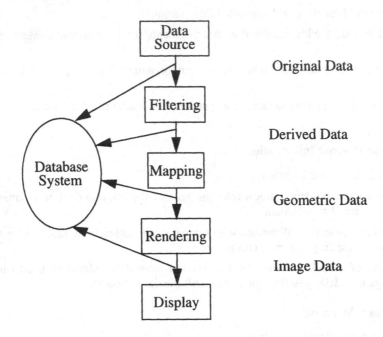

Fig. 1. Data in the Processing Pipeline

Data Source - Data originates from a simulation process, representing behavior modeled as algorithms in the simulation code, from measurement facilities locally or remote (e.g. satellite data), or from database extractions. Data in the database itself may originally have come from measurements or simulations. We assume that data from this phase is original data.

Filtering - The filtering step produces derived data, already a type of metadata. The interactive analysis process with visual representations of results at the end of the processing pipeline is typically interactive, with multiple loops based on combined alternative filtering and mapping steps. While from the visualization oriented viewpoint filtering is only a preparation step, from the database management oriented viewpoint it is called data analysis, as it automatically generates results and stores them. Resulting metadata after this step can either be stored explicitly as data in a database, or the processing procedure can be stored to regenerate the metadata from the original data. The results are the same. The alternatives, however, offer a trade-off between storage space and computing power.

Mapping - The mapping step produces a geometric representation, providing a visual representation of data, which can be regarded as another type of metadata. Storing this data in the database also reduces processing time in case of a repetition. Especially during the rendering step, repeated processing of the geometrical representations is required for visual interactions such as rotation or zooming.

Rendering - The rendering step produces images, which may be directly rendered into a framebuffer memory using graphics hardware. In this case the display step is integrated into the rendering step.

Display - Alternatively, pixel images generated in the rendering step can be transferred to the display step, which shows them optionally also as animated sequences. Separated display steps often receive images from a rendering step across a network.

5.3 Metadata in a Layered Processing Model

Metadata on a Database AbstractionLayer

In a database model the lowest layer of data representation describes data objects consisting of continuous fields of certain basic datatypes. Metadata is used to describe these data objects.

Such metadata guarantees a self-contained representation of a dataset or data object. This type of metadata adds specific information, such as the number of basic elements (e.g. dimensions of a matrix) or types of basic elements that allow the user to access and handle data objects properly on the data processing layer. Data itself, together with such metadata, allows for generation of self-contained data objects.

The basic metadata can be then be separated into a specific and a generic part. Generic metadata describes the context in which data itself is defined. Examples for context information are physical units, such as temperatures being measured in degrees Kelvin instead of Fahrenheit, or distances being given in meters instead of feet. Contextual metadata is applicable to a whole class of data objects. For data objects to be self-contained the specific as well as the contextual metadata needs to be stored with the data object. While some fundamental information is sufficient for basic data management purposes, additional information is needed for the data to have a proper meaning. In the case of measurement such additional information may be, e.g., data and place of measurement, and measurement equipment.

Metadata on a Physical Media Layer

At the higher database level the goal is self-contained complete descriptions of data objects containing data together with descriptive metadata. To manage huge amounts of data requires more elaborate, often hierarchical storage systems, and these cause large variations in access speed.

Thus on the storage management level operational performance is of major importance. Access to datasets stored off-line on a second level storage medium such as tapes takes much longer than access to disk storage. Where very large databases are stored on such tape archives, descriptive information typically must be stored apart from the data, because otherwise the selection process would have to parse through too many tapes. Accordingly descriptive metadata is stored separately in on-line repositories to allow faster selection processes.

This separation should be transparent to users. Extraction of datasets should, for example, combine the data coming from a tape with the descriptive metadata, to create a common data object.

Additional metadata typically stores information about processing characteristics to allow estimation of processing durations. Thus it is possible for users to design a query, get an estimation of the processing duration and costs, and then decide whether to initiate processing.

Metadata and the Information Extraction Process

Metadata can hold any extracted information. Representations of results can be arbitrary, such as data objects, images, 3D object scenes, audio, or video. For complex information processing chains with many human decision-based alternative branches, the specific information processing history is relevant and must be stored and linked with the results, as alternative processing chains might lead to different results or a reduced number of findings. In addition to completely describing the results of scientific analysis processes, history metadata and bookkeeping metadata permit the user to resume the analysis process at different points and to even reevaluate certain phases and decisions made there.

6 Conclusions

Further improvement in the handling of large, complex volumes of data and the speed-up and improvement in quality of data processing require a holistic approach. Software systems are needed that integrate database management, data analysis and visualization with data generation. Different incarnations of metadata are the glue at the interface layer between these components.

An important issue for further research is integration of knowledge from different fields of science, not just computer science (e.g., database management, scientific visualization) but also those from psychology (e.g., human perception and cognition) and various application domains. This integration will specialize the metadata and permit finer user responsive environments. It should have become clear for the reader, that metadata reference models and software architectures including metadata handling are still open research and development issues, which need contributions from all relevant fields.

7 Literature

[1] *Minutes of the First Metadata Workshop*, http://www.llnl.gov/liv_comp/metadata/minutes/minutes-1993-08.html

[2] *Metadata Working GroupHomepage*, http://www.llnl.gov/liv_comp/metadata/metadata.html

[3] Robyne M. Sumpter: *Whitepaper on DataManagement*. http://www.llnl.gov/liv_comp/metadata/papers/whitepaper-draft.ps

[4] Francis Bretherton: *A Reference Model ForMetadata*. http://www.llnl.gov/liv_comp/metadata/papers/whitepaper-bretherton.ps

[5] First IEEE Metadata Conference, NOAA Auditorium in the NOAAComplex in Silver Spring, Maryland, April 16-18, 1996, Proceedings:http://www.llnl.gov/ liv_comp/metadata/events/ieee-md.4-96.html

[6] Ken Brodlie, A. Poon, H. Wright, L. Brankin, G. Banecki, A.Gay:*"GRASPARC A Problem Solving Environment Integrating Computation and Visualization"*, Proceedings of IEEE Visualization'93, pages 102-109

[7] John Peter Lee, Georges G. Grinstein: *„An Architecture for Retaining and Analyzing Visual Explorations of Databases"*,Proceedings of IEEE Visualization '95, pages 101-108

[8] David T. Kao, R. Daniel Bergeron, Ted M. Sparr: *„AnExtended Schema Model for Scientific Data"*, Proceedings IEEE Workshop on Database Issues for Data Visualization inDatabase Issues for Data Visualization, J.P. Lee, G.G. Grinstein (eds), Springer Verlag LNCS v871, Oct. 1994, pages 69-82

Workshop Papers

Views, Visualization and Databases

John Peter Lee
Institute for Visualization and Perception Research
Computer Science Department
University of Massachusetts Lowell
jlee@cs.uml.edu

Abstract. We describe a database management - data visualization integration based on the *view* concept. In general, views are descriptions of data transformations that enable more efficient interactions between user and data. Our intent is to use the view concept as the unifying link between the two systems, thereby enabling database interaction to be closely coupled with data visualization. We discuss the types of views used to realize the integration, and their implementation in our environment.

1 Introduction

Modern relational databases contain vast amounts of data that can be analyzed to extract useful knowledge, and the ability of database management systems to support data analysis is highly desirable. Relational databases are not built for analysis, however, so they must be made part of a larger, integrated, knowledge discovery environment having data analysis and data visualization capabilities [Fayyad96]. Such an integration would support the real-world tasks a data analyst requires, provided the components can be used interactively [Brachman96].

Mapping the data models (data structures and operations) between relational databases and algorithmic and visual analysis tools must therefore be resolved to enable this integration. There are many approaches to this problem, with associated tradeoffs between modeling expressiveness, data manipulation facilities and ease of use to be considered. This paper describes one approach we are pursuing in the Exbase (Exploration of Databases) system at the University of Massachusetts Lowell [Lee94, Lee95, Lee96]. Our implementation revolves around a data model based on a relational query result, which we term a local database view. We focus on data modeling issues by describing the various view classes that facilitate the integration. Views are an unifying concept because they are fundamental constructs in both visualization and database domains. We are not considering analysis functions at this time.

Section 2 discusses the relevant integration issues that we are attempting to address in the research. Section 3 outlines the types of exploration operations the Exbase system intends to support. Section 4 describes the three view classes that help realize the integration. Section 5 discusses some ramifications of this design. Section 6 concludes.

2 Database-Visualization Integration Considerations

One of our primary goals is to bring the database closer to the user, and the user closer to the database. This is accomplished in Exbase by the management of query results. Bringing the database closer to the user entails offering data selection operations over visualizations of query results. Bringing the user closer to the database requires the mapping of visualization interactions to database and query result manipulations.

The integration requires a unifying data model that bridges the gap between the respective system components, and supports the user-data interactions. The relational data model is based on a formalized tabular representation of simple, atomic data types [Elmasri95], and the primary data manipulation operations are retrievals and updates of persistent data. Visualization data models are primarily data structure models having connectivity and topological specifications [Haber91, Treinish91, Nielson94]. This "impedance mismatch" between the two systems is a classic software design problem, and must be resolved in the database-visualization interface, as shown in Figure 1. Database systems are large and complex software systems that are not easily modifiable. We have greater control over modifying the visualization system and creating an appropriate interface to the database, so we focus on defining these components in our design.

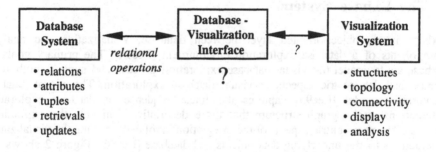

Figure 1. The impedance mismatch between database and visualization.

Knowledge discovery and visual database exploration are highly interactive activities, requiring complex interactions between user, database and analysis tools [Brachman96]. The user generally selects data from the database or data warehouse, and analyzes the selected data using data mining algorithms (clustering, regression, rule extraction, etc.) and visualization. Sometimes queries need to be formulated and issued to the database to retrieve additional data during an analysis. Most interaction scenarios [Keim96] require the user to interact with a visualization of the database and its contents in a graphical manner to construct queries, configure displays, etc. These graphical interactions are then mapped into domain data operations [Lee96]. Further interactions are spawned from analyses and visualizations of queries, as the exploration progresses [Buja96, Lee95, Nicholson84, Owen86, Velleman90, Young91b]. Thus, the connection between the visualization system and database in Figure 1 can contain many types of exploration operations that need to be resolved.

We believe that building around the database data model in the database-visualization interface is required for this integration. Our primary focus is exploring relational data, although much of our development generalizes to other data models. Relational data is widely available, and poses interesting visualization challenges. We must, then:

1. support a relational model of data manipulation,

2. make data selection available to the visualization system, and

3. allow data selection specifications at the visualization display.

Data selection facilities are severely lacking in modern visualization environments, though are a fundamental data exploration operation [Springmeyer92]. Query results can be stored in the database as view specifications, and then referred to in future explorations. Furthermore, as database systems evolve, they will accommodate new data types and possibly analytic operations, making them more supportive of spatial and temporal data prevalent in scientific domains [Wolneiwicz94]. We will have the visualization portion of the interface already in place, and can migrate functionality from the interface to the database, where server-resident processing can be more efficiently implemented over persistent data. We now describe our approach to this integration, the Exbase system.

3 The Exbase System

Exbase is an object-oriented layer between database, visualization and analytic components of a database exploration environment [Lee94]. The primary goals of Exbase are to model the visual database exploration process and support both user-centric and data-centric aspects of visual database exploration. The visual database exploration model [Lee95] captures the linear sequence of database exploration interactions into a graph structure that more descriptively models the exploration process. The user-centric aspects of the integration involve describing the visualization interactions to the underlying data objects and database [Lee96]. Figure 2 shows the primary operations requiring support by the Exbase interface, and the types of objects Exbase manages internally. We are currently focusing efforts on defining the data-centric, database-visualization integration components. Incorporation of data analysis and data mining support will occur at a later date.

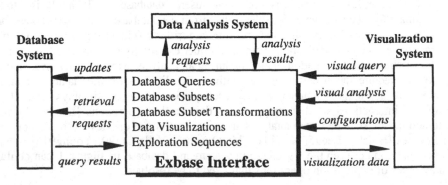

Figure 2. The Exbase Interface, with primary data objects and operations.

4 Exbase View Classes

In arriving at a unifying integration scheme, we have focused our attention on the concept of a *view*. Views are defined in both database and visualization contexts. A database view associates a name with a database query, thereby specifying a mapping from the database to a table. Database views can be queried themselves, because the relational model is closed under relational operations (selections, joins, projections, unions, etc.). Exploiting relational closure by supporting successive querying over extracted data is a very powerful mechanism. A visualization view specifies a mapping of the data elements, expressed as a multidimensional point set of data objects, to a multidimensional point set of display objects [Bergeron89, Hibbard95]. Visualization is critical to the effective presentation of the query result, to show structures graphically rather than textually. Exbase retains in memory multiple database views, along with their associated visualization views. The key issues are how the views are specified and allowed to interact with each other and the user.

The Exbase data model relies on three fundamental view classes: local database views, computed database views and visualization views. Figure 3 shows these classes, and the primary types of data transformations between them in the production of visualizations from database queries.

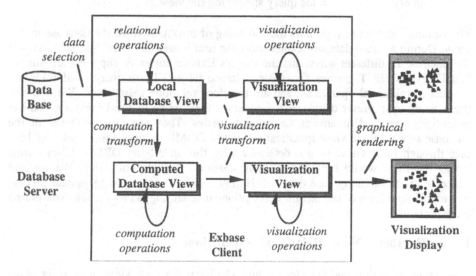

Figure 3. Exbase view structures and primary data output transformations.

In Figure 3, the general procedure is that the user issues data retrieval queries to the DBMS, and proceeds to manipulate the retrieved data further with analytic operations. Queries are data selections, and create local database views. Relational operations, such as data selections, transform local database views into other local database views. The collection of non-relational operations, what we call computations, create computed database views from local database views. Visualization transforms create visualization views from local or computed database views by applying a mapping from data domain structures to display domain structures. Additional visualization operations, such as viewing transformations, can be applied over the visualization view to create other visualization views. Finally, graphical rendering transforms the visualization view into a data visualization, a graphical image of the extracted and/or analyzed data. The remainder of this section describes each of these view structures in detail.

4.1 Local Database Views

A relational database *view* is a named relational expression. It is a temporary or "virtual" relation (a table) that is not stored in the database, but constructed when it is specified in a query. Database queries over the view are transformed to operations over the component base tables via query modification, or over the precomputed view via view materialization. Views are, in general, only in first-normal form, which is a table of atomic data values. A database view is specified by three components:

$$db\_ view \ (name, \ attribute\_list, \ query),$$

where:

name	= the name given to the view,
attribute_list	= the (optional) attribute list of the selection,
query	= the query specifying the view.

The optional attribute list permits the renaming of attributes from the database to the view. During a visual database exploration, the user issues numerous queries to subset the database in different ways, and the queries Exbase currently supports are simple SELECT-PROJECT queries on single database tables. These query results are the product of relational operations, and are therefore relations themselves. We consider them to be *local views* of the base data, since they reside in local memory, and can potentially be used to answer subsequent queries. They can also be stored in the database as a database view specification, if the DBMS permits this. Updating base data through local views is also determined by the underlying DBMS. Client view update facilities would further complicate matters; they do not exist. We are not concerned with updating base data at this time, though we intend to update process metadata in the form of interaction descriptions that are logged to the database during an exploration.

Local Database View Relational Operations

Projection, Selection and Set Operations: The local database view must offer some relational data operations to the visualization system, in order to bring the database closer to the user. The two most important operations are projection and selection. Projection chooses attributes and selection chooses rows from the view, as they do from database tables. They can be also be applied to multiple views that are joined together. There are numerous ways to join tables, and some produce results that might not be meaningful. This is an especially critical fact for visual database exploration, because it is important not to create data that either are not present in the database, or have no meaning in the current context. Furthermore, composing visualizations having unwanted artifacts from incorrect data is unacceptable. It is sufficient to say that local views to be joined must have a common attribute between them, so only valid candidate rows are chosen.

There are two possible types of selection: those that restrict local database views, and those that expand upon them. Restriction is often exemplified by a point query (retrieve rows from a single display location), a range query (retrieve rows based on a range of values of an attribute), or an ad-hoc query that possesses a narrower selection criteria. A selection that expands upon a local database view is still considered a restriction of the entire database. Sometimes queries over local views require additional data to be retrieved from the database. For example, in a financial database application, a point query might need to return company identification information along with the actual attribute values visualized. If the company information is not available in the view, a query must be issued to the database for that data. In this case, a number of rows can be retrieved based on the data driving the current display. Another example would be if a range query is specified that is larger than the range in the view, but partially or fully within the range in the database. An additional query will be required to the database to retrieve that data.

Other meaningful relational operations include set operations (union, intersection and difference) that operate on two local views. As with joining views, there are certain restrictions on performing set operations over local database views. The views in this case must be union-compatible, meaning they must have the same attributes in the same order, to produce a meaningful result. As before, it is important not to create artificial relationships within the retrieved data. Exbase currently supports selection and projection for single local database views. Join and set operation support are future developments of the architecture.

Additional Constructs and Operations: There are several database system constructs and operations supported by the local database view that are not defined in the relational data model: missing values, aggregate functions and query result ordering. Missing values are common in real-world databases, and Exbase missing value handling follows that of the underlying database. They are also accounted for in local database view aggregate functions. When a local database view is created or restricted, the cardinality, number of missing values, and meaningful summary statistics (mean, extents, moments, etc.) are automatically calculated for each attribute, in addition to a sorted index array.

Local Database View Visualization Considerations

The local database view must provide data to be visualized in a consistent and efficiently-processed format. The interactive nature of visual database exploration requires rapid responses to the graphical interactions that reorganize the presentation of the local database view. This requirement influences the data format, data access structures and various support functions.

Visualization requires a numeric data representation for display, and data normalization is a necessary stage in the rendering process. Since many visualizations may be composed for a single local database view, Exbase takes an eager approach to normalization by creating a normalized floating-point representation of all data in the underlying local database view. Each distinct local database view is essentially a "world" unto itself, and the extents of each component attribute constitute the extent of the world coordinate space of the view. Thus, there aren't any other modeling transforms that need to be applied to the data. This is similar to the normalized projection coordinate representation common to graphics and visualization. The actual data retrieved from the database is also available.

The many potential visualizations of a local database view imply the view may be subsetted in memory by projection and selection operations. Restriction is a generalization of the zooming operation, and is a common visualization technique for focusing on an interesting portion of the data. Graphical panning, another visual interaction, translates a subrange through a larger range. Each technique causes a different data subset to be displayed. The local database view configures a *selection vector* that is used as a mask for visualizing only those rows that satisfy a data range selection specification. This vector is created for each data restriction interaction instead of copying data to a new local database view. A query string specifying each restriction is also created, in addition to any new statistical metadata on the attribute distributions.

Local Database View Components

Figure 4 shows the primary components of the local database view. The base data retrieved are stored vertically in arrays on a per-attribute basis, along with metadata such as summary statistics. The normalized floating point representation more closely resembles a table, and has indices that point to entire rows based on attribute values. Missing data values are moved to the end of each index array, and are not used in lookup operations. The base data arrays and index arrays are only manipulated by the local database view. External objects, such as visualization views, use projection and selection vectors to process subsets of the local database view. These vectors, discussed in Section 4.3.2, are configured by the local database view. With each new selection or projection of a local database view, new access vectors and queries specifying them are configured. If we need to go back to the database for any reason (such as a new query), a new local database view must be created.

4.2 Computed Database Views

It is often necessary to manipulate the local database view further with non-relational operations. These include manipulations such as interpolation and registration, statistical functions such as regression and clustering, or application-specific calculations such as particle advection and fluid flow equation solvers. A *computed database view* is the creation of a new data object from a local database view via such an operation. The computed view is not necessarily a relational object itself, because it may contain non-atomic attribute values. Furthermore, its contents may not be present in the database, or its construction might not be specifiable, i.e. by a relational expression, from the database tables.

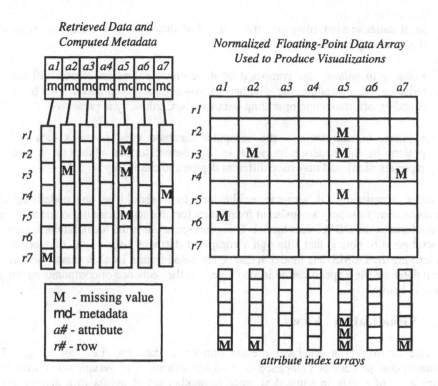

Figure 4. The components of the local database view.

Exbase computed database views are in an early stage of development, and are fundamental to the utility of the integrated environment. Since there are many types of non-relational operations, with application-dependent specifications, it is difficult to define the derived database view in a general fashion. One approach would be to provide an embedded language to specify the derivation. In [Hachem94], the *process* object classes for global change research contain specifications for data derivation, such as the input sets, output set, assertions that constrain the derivation and mappings that contain the functions applied during derivation operations. These are predetermined for each data derivation.

An important notion is that we must be able to specify and reapply the computation, to be able to recreate a data object, or analyze the exploration. It might be important to know how computations alter the data being explored, and incorporate this metadata into the system. We observe that computed database views can differ from local database views in several ways, due to operations that are not expressible in the SQL database manipulation language. Such differences include:

• *reduction of data* - the computed database view loses data through certain operations such as sampling. There are fewer rows in the derived view, but all columns remain the same. All data is present somewhere in the database.

• *expansion of data* - the computed database view gains data through operations such as selective interpolation or replication of data values. The local database view rows are still intact, but there are now additional rows that are not present in the database.

• *change in values* - the computed database views values are altered without reducing or expanding the number of rows through operations such as rounding off, truncating or scaling data values. Cardinality is preserved.

• *change in data format* - the computed database view contains data not present in the database, may be in a different format (such as a tree representation), and may have different degree and cardinality.

In order to maintain a data-centric architecture, there should be one underlying data representation to supply a consistent foundation for all data processing operations, and to conform to the DBMS data model. This representation is the local database view. A crucial point to note is that although a computed database view might not follow the underlying the DBMS data model, it can be recreated from a local database view if the local database view specification is available, and the sequence of computations on the view is known.

4.3 Visualization Views

A visualization is a graphical presentation of a data set, i.e., an image. The visualization process is comprised of two transforms. The *visualization transform* maps a set of points in some data space to another set of points in a display space. These data points often have multiple data values associated with them. The *rendering transform* accomplishes the drawing of the data image to the display, using traditional computer graphics display techniques [Foley90]. Both visualization and rendering are considered data output functions: the visualization transform prepares the data for display and the rendering transform displays the data.

A *visualization view* specifies the visual interface to a local database view. It extends the notion of visualization solely as an output transform by specifying input operations in addition to describing the input data and visualization transform. It permits interaction with the database through the visualization, as described in [Keim96]. We specify a visualization view in the following manner:

> *vview (db_view, dbv_xfms, vis_spec, int_mappings)*

> where:

> *db_view*   = the underlying local database view,
> *dbv_xfms*   = the sequence of data transforms applied to the database view,
> *vis_spec*   = the visualization specification *(vis_rep, mappings, settings):*
>   *vis_rep*   = visualization representation scheme,
>   *mappings* = data-to-visual primitive mappings,
>   *settings*   = visual display settings,
> *int_mappings* = interaction mappings.

We consider the visualization view a surrogate to the local database view, because the user primarily interacts with visualizations. Thus, it requires a reference to the local database view it portrays. It also must specify the sequence of data transformations to link back to the local database view. The visualization specification is the classical method of describing a data visualization. A representation scheme describes the visual output (scatterplot, isosurface, volumetric, etc.), in terms of its display type, display dimensionality and underlying data model. Data-to-visual primitive mappings indicate which attributes (columns) of the database view are represented by the available graphical primitives of the representation scheme. Visual display settings reflect any configurable parameter of the visualization representation and graphical display environment. Finally, the interaction mappings describe the input model over the visualization, and forward graphical articulations to domain data operators [Norman86].

In typical transaction processing database interaction, the visualization, a textual representation, closely matches that of the stored data representation (a relation) and of the mental model the user has of the data (a set of tables). The user often interacts with the database using a textual query language, or through some type of forms interface. In visual database exploration, the visualization offers visual interaction tools to explore the data. We differentiate two types of interactions at the visualization. *Data-independent* interactions are directed towards the visualization display itself, and *data-dependent* interactions are directed at the underlying data [Seetharaman94]. Thus, there is a significant input component to visualization, and this input component brings both the visualization and user closer to the database.

Visualization View Data-Independent Visualization Operations

Data-independent visualization operations do not alter the underlying data, only the transforms applied during rendering. They should be controllable at the visualization user interface to give the user flexibility in fine-tuning a rendering. Some controls effect graphical structures, such as polygonal or iconic component size and color factors [Grinstein92], or the amount of randomness (jitter) applied to icon locations to minimize strong horizontal or vertical artifacts in the display. Other controls effect viewing operations, such as rotating, scaling or translating the data or the display axes. Environment controls effect the general graphics environment variables, such as lighting, camera positioning, and the sequencing through animations.

Using visualization to explore multidimensional data spaces transcends the realistic 3D renderings ubiquitous in the visualization literature. In addition to iconographic displays, graphical methods for exploring multidimensional spaces have been used in the statistics community since the early 1970s (see [Becker88] for an overview). A manual method is to produce several linked (potentially orthogonal) plots of a data space, select data in one display using the cursor, and observe the selected data in a linked display [Andrews81, Buja91]. In this way, multidimensional clusters and other relationships can be determined. Similar, automated processes include rotating between data subspaces [Young91a], plotting linear combinations of data subspaces and scanning arbitrary projections [Asimov85]. In these, the scanning path is often determined algorithmically.

This brings up the general notion that selection and comparison are fundamental exploration operations that should be supported by the visualization, in addition to image generation. Selections are often performed by specifying data subspaces for display or brushing linked displays with the cursor. Visual comparisons between plots and graphs are qualitative in nature. Any data exploration also requires the capability to turn these qualitative visual comparisons into quantitative results, or calls to analysis functions. The ability to annotate visualizations with comments and insights, as well as the ability to manage the entire exploration session is extremely useful. The user often creates numerous visualizations of data, some of which are important, others which are not. Important visualization views need to be saved for future exploration or dissemination, so persistent storage and exploration session navigation mechanisms are required to support visual database explorations.

Visualization View Database Considerations

The data-dependent operations performed at the visualization include selections and projections. These permit the navigation of the multidimensional data space. The visualization view contains a *selection* bit vector that signifies which rows of a local database view are to be rendered. All selections are performed by the local database view object, and require a mapping and rendering to be performed on the new subset. Spatial queries specify some region of display space, and include point queries that isolate a single data object. Brushing plots with the cursor is another type of selection, but does not require a new subset creation from the local database view. It instead merely changes the appearance of the visualization primitives associated with the same data objects in a linked display. Range queries specified through a controller can alter a one or more attribute ranges at a time.

The visualization view also possesses a *projection* vector that contains attribute identifiers signifying the valid (and possibly redundant) attributes, and the visualization primitives each attribute is mapped to. This operation is a permutation of the data already available, and a new data subset does not have to be computed. Thus, the effect of this operation is local - only a mapping and rendering of the previous subset are performed. Associated with this vector is a vector of attribute ranges that reflect the ranges of values of each attribute displayed in the visualization.

The visualization process can apply its own local data derivations to database views, that might further restrict or expand the data to be displayed. The visualization transform already alters the data format. Other transformations include sampling the data, logically combining certain attributes, mapping a subset of the available attributes, graphical clipping and interpolation. Also, if two rows of a local database view possess similar values for two attributes, and these attributes are mapped to the two spatial display axes, then they "collide" in the display space. This means that they occupy the same location on the display, and steps must be taken to handle this eventuality. Options include averaging values, cycling through values, adding a jitter offset or overlaying icons at the collision location. Thus, the data displayed, derived from a local or derived database view, may not show the entire view, or may display more data than contained in the view. This affects any subsequent selection operations. Note that these derivations might be able to be pushed back to the derived database view, to simplify the visualization implementation.

Another consideration is supporting missing data. Missing data is common in real-world databases and telemetry, and commercial databases all have a missing data representation. The visualization system component might handle this by not rendering objects containing such data, interpolating new data, or mapping missing data to some sentinel value for display. This would be application dependent, and should be under user control.

Visualization View Components

Exbase employs an object-oriented hierarchy of visualization views, organized by the type of display produced, as shown in Figure 5. The **VisualizationView** abstract base class contains a link to the underlying local database view, a query specification (which might differ from that of the local database view, based on the subsetting criteria), a textual description, statistical attribute metadata and a selection bit vector signifying which rows of the local database view are visualized. The **Visualization** abstract base class contains graphical user interface (GUI) code common to all concrete subclasses (including data selection control widgets), the set of data-to-visual primitive mappings, and the projection vector that defines the visualization mapping.

Concrete visualization classes are subclassed from the **Visualization** class, and implement their specific functions to map, render, and display coordinate axes, among other functions. Concrete classes also implement their particular type of spatial data selection operations. For example, in Figure 5, subclasses of the **CartesianVis** class have Cartesian projection display spaces, so their visual displays and region definitions differ from the **ParCoordVis** class, which has a parallel projection display space. New visualization techniques need only supply the unique mapping, display and certain input functions that they possess. Our **VisualizationView** class currently supports simple data derivation transforms, such as regular sampling of data values. Interaction mappings are currently supported by methods of the local database view class that alter the selection vector of a visualization object.

We have constructed our visualization hierarchy to suit relational data. Relational database data often does not have any intrinsic spatial structure, topology or connectivity, as typical "scientific" data does. These qualities are imparted to the data during the visualization process. Our visualization techniques are iconographic, and do not utilize any structured data representations such as grids. Note that each concrete visualization class provides its own *Render* function, as opposed to having a single, high-level rendering routine implemented. This is done primarily for performance reasons. Having a high-level rendering routine would still necessitate function calls to lower-level classes to render each icon representing a data point, or use some type of complicated case statement control flow. In this situation, the call overhead, in light of rendering tens or hundreds of thousands of data points, would be unacceptable. Thus, we limit the object-oriented granularity to the visualization technique level and implement efficient, if somewhat redundant, rendering routines.

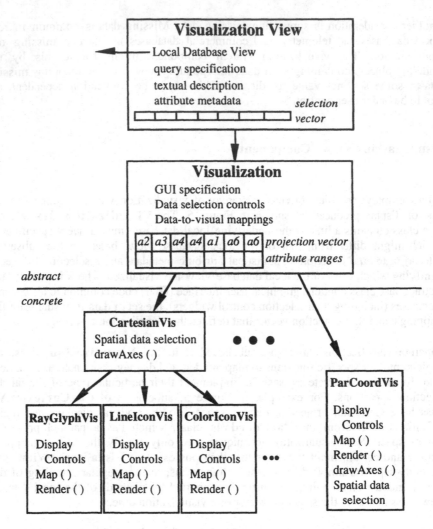

Figure 5. Exbase Visualization View hierarchy.

5 Exbase View Integration Analysis

Though the concept of a view is similar in both systems (a representation of the database), the nature of each system precludes their implementations from being similar. DBMSs are data-centric, emphasizing data selection, and visualization systems are graphics-centric, emphasizing graphics production. This influences the usefulness of each system for data exploration tasks. By combining both systems for data exploration, the appropriate qualities of each can be exploited. Our layered approach to the integration localizes some interaction processing. Visualization display setting interactions only need to re-render data. Visualization mapping configurations (data projections) require a data mapping and rendering. Data selections require computation of a new database view at the local database view or database, a data mapping and a new rendering. Because we have an underlying database system, we can persistently store, manage and retrieve this session metadata that is generated during an exploration, for future analysis and exploitation, as described in [Lee95].

This integration is not without its costs, however. First, the translation between data models requires extra storage and processing for intermediate data representations. This decoupling of visualization impacts overall efficiency, but is necessary for the integration. During visual database exploration, there is a definite tradeoff between interactive response and the need for exploration services. The data selection service is computationally expensive, especially when external media need to be searched. Having some data selection capability in memory will alleviate parts of this problem. We are currently bound to an underlying relational data model, and though our techniques can generalize to other data models having explicit connectivity and topology, their implementation would require much effort in translation and query processing. Our focus on relational data fills a great void in visualization by providing the means to visually explore large databases that are ignored by the visualization community at large.

Exbase currently supplies a single type of local database view, which is modeled on a relational table. This local view is used by a number of different visualization types. To manage all of these views, a visualization manager object is present to provide a listing of all database views and their sub-views (restrictions), and a listing of all the associated visualization views and their sub-views. Each view produces metadata that describes the view contents. A database view shows the query, the attributes and their ranges, and the size of the result. A visualization view shows the representation type, the display settings and the data mappings. It is important to note that the visualization view might not be an exact representation of the database. There are many places during data extraction, transformation and visualization where data can be altered, deleted or created. This is why it is important to retain the data lineage in a sequence of transformations and the query. It is currently an open question as to how fast and large the transform description metadata will grow. This will depend on the application and the user. Testing is required and efficient compression and pruning schemes need to be developed.

6 Conclusion

Visualization entails more activities than viewing images, and when considered as part of a database exploration environment, it takes on new meanings as an input paradigm. Our research into database-visualization integration, based on the view concept, requires the close cooperation of database and visualization entities. Local database views offer data selection to visualizations. Visualization views provide a visual interface to database functions, and supply some database operations over local data as well. Only by defining and implementing such interfaces will we be able to create effective database exploration environments that provide a large number of services to the data analyst and decision maker.

7 Acknowledgments

This research is supported by a grant from the NASA Graduate Students Researchers Program. The author would like to thank Georges Grinstein and John Sieg for their comments and suggestions.

8 References

[Andrews81]   Andrews, D.F., "Statistical Applications of Real-Time Interactive Graphics", in *Interpreting Multivariate Data*, V. Barnett ed., Wiley, 1981, pages 175-185.

[Asimov85]   Asimov. D., "The Grand Tour: A Tool for Viewing Multidimensional Data", *SIAM Journal of Scientific and Statistical Computing*, v6, 1985, pages 128-143.

[Becker88]   Becker, R., W. Cleveland, A. Wilks, "Dynamic Graphics for Data Analysis", in *Dynamic Graphics for Statistics*, W. Cleveland, McGill eds., Wadsworth, Inc., 1988, pages 1-72.

[Brachman96]   Brachman, R., T. Anand, "The Process of Knowledge Discovery in Databases: A Human-Centered Approach", in *Advances in Knowledge Discovery and Data Mining*, U. Fayyad, G. Piatetsky-Shapiro, P. Smyth, and R. Uthurusamy, eds., MIT Press, Cambridge, 1996, pages 37-58.

[Buja91]   Buja, A., J. McDonald, J. Michalak, W. Stuetzle, "Interactive Data Visualization Using Focusing and Linking", *Proceedings of Visualization'91*, 1991, pages 156-163.

[Buja96]   Buja, A., D. Cook, D. Swayne, "Interactive High-Dimensional Data Visualization", *Journal of Computational and Graphical Statistics*, v5, n1, 1996, pages 78-99.

[Chaudhuri95]   Chaudhuri, S, R. Krisnamurthy, S. Potamianos, K. Shim, "Optimizing Queries with Materialized Views", *Proceedings 11th International Conference on Data Engineering*, Taipei, Taiwan, 1995, pages 190-200.

[Elmasri94]   Elmasri, R., S. Navathe, *Fundamentals of Database Systems*, Second Edition, Benjamin Cummings, Redwood City CA, 1994.

[Fayyad96]   Fayyad, U., Piatetsky-Shapiro, G., Smyth, P., "From Data Mining to Knowledge Discovery: An Overwiew", in *Advances in Knowledge Discovery and Data Mining*, Fayyad, U., Piatetsky-Shapiro, G., Smyth, P. and Uthurusamy, R., eds., MIT / AAAI Press, Cambridge MA, 1996, pages 1-36.

[Grinstein92]   Grinstein, G.G., J. Sieg, S. Smith, M. Williams, "Visualization for Knowledge Discovery", *International Journal of Intelligent Systems*, v7, n7, September 1992, pages 637-648.

[Haber91]   Haber, R., B. Lucas and N. Collins, "A Data Model for Scientific Visualization with Provisions for Regular and Irregular Grids", *Proceedings of IEEE Visualization '91*, pp. 298-305, October 1991.

[Keim96]   Keim, D., J.P. Lee, C. Wittenbrink, "Database Issues for Data Visualization Interactions Subgroup Report", in *Database Issues for Data Visualization* (this volume), Springer Verlag, 1996.

[Lee94]   Lee, J.P., "Data Exploration Interactions and the ExBase System", in *Database Issues for Data Visualization*, J.P. Lee and G.G. Grinstein, eds., *Springer-Verlag Lecture Notes in Computer Science*, vol 871, November 1994, pages 118-137.

[Lee95]   Lee, J. P., G.G. Grinstein, "An Architecture for the Retention and Analysis of Visual Explorations of Databases", *Proceedings of Visualization '95*, Atlanta, GA, October 1995, pages 101-109.

[Lee96]   Lee, J.P., G.G. Grinstein, "Describing Visual Interactions to the Database: Closing the Loop Between User and Data", *Proceedings of SPIE: Visual Data Exploration and Analysis III*, vol. 2565, San Jose CA, February 1996, pages 93-103.

[Mamou91]   Mamou, Jean-Claude, C. B. Maderios, "Interactive Manipulation of Object-Oriented Views", *Proceedings 7th International Conference on Data Engineering*, Kobe, Japan, 1991, pages 60-69.

[Nicholson84]   Nicholson, W., D. Carr, P. Crowley, M. Whiting, "The Role of Environments in Managing Data Analysis", *Proceedings of the American Statistics Society, Statistical Computing Section*, 1984, pages 80-84.

[Nielson94]   Nielson, G., P. Brunet, M. Gross, H. Hagen, and S. Klimenko, "Research Issues in Data Modelsing for Scientific Visualization", in *Scientific Visualization: Advances and Challenges*, Academic Press, London, 1994, pages 472-479.

[Norman86]   Norman, D., "Cognitive Engineering", in *User Cenetred System Design*, D. Norman and S. Draper (Eds.), Lawrence Earlbaum Associates, Hillsdale NJ, 1986, pages 31-62.

[Owen86]   Owen, D., "Answers First, Then Questions", *in User Centered System Design*, D. Norman and S. Draper (Eds.), Lawrence Earlbaum Associates, Hillsdale NJ, 1986, pages 361-376.

[Seetharaman94] Seetharaman, K., "A Multisensory Interaction Model for Exploratory Data Visualization", Sc.D. Thesis, University of Massachusetts Lowell, Computer Science Department, August 1994.

[Springmeyer92] Springmeyer, R., M.M. Blattner, N.L. Max, "A Characterization of the Scientific Data Analysis Process", *Proceedings of Visualization'92*, Boston MA, 1992, pages 235-242.

[Treinish91]   Treinish, L. (ed.), "Data Structures and Access Software for Scientific Visualization: A Report of a Workshop at ACM SIGGRAPH'90, *Computer Graphics*, v25, n2, April, 1991.

[Velleman90]   Velleman, P., "Computing and Modern (Exploratory) Data Analysis, *Proceedings of the American Statistics Society, Statistical Computing Section*, 1990, pages 46-54.

[Young91a]   Young, F.W., P. Rheingans, "Visualizing Structure in High-Dimensional Multivariate Data", IBM Journal of Research and Development, v35, n 1/2, 1991, 97-107.

[Young91b]   Young, F.W., J.B. Smith, "Towards a Structured Data Analysis Environment: A Cognition-Based Design", in *Computing and Graphics in Statistics*, A. Buja and P.A. Tukey, eds., Springer Verlag, 1991.

Data Mining and Data Visualization:
Position Paper for the Second IEEE Workshop on
Database Issues for Data Visualization

Dr. Georges Grinstein
Dr. Bhavani Thuraisingham

The MITRE Corporation
202 Burlington Road
Bedford, MA 01730

1 Introduction

The government, corporate, and industrial communities are faced with an ever increasing number of databases. These databases need not only to be managed, but also explored. The first requires secure access to distributed heterogeneous multimedia databases with rich metadata and having to meet timing constraints. The second requires exploratory tools supporting the identification of domain and mission critical elements such as patterns in data access (e.g., security breach determinations), patterns in data (e.g., marketing and clustering), or for patterns in transactions (e.g., data compression), to site a few. Knowledge Discovery in Databases is a relatively new research area that employs a variety of tools to explore and identify structure and patterns in these large databases. Often the data is preprocessed to facilitate such computations (data warehousing). The data is then mined for specific rules that are built incrementally and often steered by users with a specific set of goals in mind.

Data mining is somewhat reminiscent of approaches used in statistical analysis over the last 20 years. Projection pursuit is a technique that strives to identify clusters in n-dimensional data spaces. Projections in increasing dimensional spaces are used to build up to locally optimal clustering of the data. Of late, these techniques are user steered. What has been lacking in the statistical field, and clearly is so in the data mining arena, as well is the involvement of the user in ways other than simply as a primitive input device (select which axis to cluster around and what is the pivot value?). Human beings have rich capabilities in interpreting complex situations still unequaled to any machine. Visualization technologies have recently been used in steering computation, in aiding directed analysis, in query interfaces to complex multimedia databases, and in information presentation and navigation. For example, a user may pose a query to retrieve locations of houses which are priced over 500K in Bedford, Massachusetts. Instead of displaying the results in tabular form, a visualization tool could display in a map with points representing the houses which are priced over 500K.

This paper discusses the integration of data mining and data visualization. In particular, some approaches to this integration are described. One approach is to apply visualization techniques to information that is extracted from the databases through data mining. The second approach is to carry out data visualization first and then apply the data mining tools. The third approach is to use data visualization as a way to complement data mining. The paper is summarized with a discussion of some of the issues and challenges.

2 Approaches

As data mining techniques mature, it will be important to integrate them with visualization techniques. There are three approaches here. One is to use visualization techniques to present the results that are obtained from mining the data in the databases. These results may be in the form of clusters or they could specify correlations between the data in the databases. For example, there may be a correlation between house prices and apartment buildings, such as the neighborhoods which have high priced houses and do not have any apartment buildings. Therefore, when one queries for houses prices in a particular region, the data mining tool could also extract the information about correlations between house prices and apartment building. This information could be displayed in visual form by showing the house prices and graphically displaying the apartment buildings in a map. While techniques for visualizing data in the databases are fairly mature, the issue is whether such techniques may be applied on the results produced by the data mining tools.

In section 1 we gave an example of how data visualization can be used with data mining. As stated earlier, a user may pose a query to retrieve locations of houses which are priced over 500K in Bedford, Massachusetts. Instead of displaying the results in tabular form, a visualization tool could display in a map with points representing the houses which are priced over 500K. This example more or less visualizes the results rather than steering the data mining. Another better example, which uses visualization techniques to steer the mining process, would be to use a multidimensional visualization technique to select attributes (dimensions) that appear "unusual," then mine for sequences among certain dimensions. Example: Looking at some sort of 3-dimensional, multicolor graph showing home prices, interest rate on individual homes, time on market, sale dates, average mortgage interest rates, and connections of homebuyers might show some unusual peaks tied to interest rate and connections. Mining these items might show that certain homeowners who are not well-connected pay higher interest rates, possible evidence of certain practices in lending.

While the first approach applies visualization to data mining, the second approach applies data mining techniques to visualization. The assumption here is that it is easier to apply data mining tools to data in visual form. Therefore, rather than applying the data mining tools to large and complex databases, one captures some of the essential semantics visually, and then applies the data mining tools. There are some issues here. One is that some information might be lost when converting the data in the databases for visual representation. Therefore, the data mining tools may have to be applied on incomplete data. Another issue is developing appropriate data mining tools to be applied on visual data.

The third approach is to use visualization techniques to complement the data mining techniques. For example, one may use data mining techniques to obtain correlations between data or detect patterns. However, visualization techniques may still be needed to obtain a better understanding of the data in the database. The issue here is what data should be mined and what data should be visualized.

3 Summary And Directions

This paper has provided an overview of data mining and data visualization and then discussed some approaches on integrating data mining with data visualization. One approach is to apply visualization techniques to information that is extracted from the databases through data mining. The second approach is to carry out data visualization first and then apply the data mining tools. The third approach is to use data visualization as a way to complement data mining.

There are many issues to be resolved and much research is needed. These include the following: First of all the approaches discussed here need to be investigated further. An architecture for integrating a data mining system with a visualization system needs to be developed. Finally, the data mining algorithms have to be expanded to include the visualization tools. The integration of data mining with data visualization is important for a variety of government, corporate, as well as industrial applications.

Acknowledgments: We thank Dr. Christopher Clifton for comments on this paper.

Requirements and Architecture of an Information Visualization Tool

Sougata Mukherjea[1] and James D. Foley[2]

[1] C & C Research Lab,
NEC USA,
San Jose, CA 95134, USA
[2] Graphics, Visualization & Usability Center,
College of Computing,
Georgia Institute of Technology,
Atlanta, Ga 30332, USA

Abstract. This paper talks about the requirements for an effective information visualization tool. The architecture of Navigational View Builder, a tool to develop visualizations of the information space of hypermedia systems is also described. We then show how the tool satisfies the requirements of an information visualization tool. To conclude the paper we discuss some of the required features of the underlying database for producing effective visualizations.

1 Introduction

Information Visualization is used to convert large amount of information into meaningful and interpretable visual representation. It has been argued that information visualization is particularly important because it allows people to use perceptual reasoning, rather than cognitive reasoning, in carrying out tasks [27]. However, producing effective visualization is not very easy. The visualizations are two or three dimensional projections of generally multidimensional networks representing the information spaces. Finding effective views of such complex network structures that convey all the required information is hard. In particular, this task is impossible without knowledge of the structure and the contents of the information space. Therefore, instead of developing the visualizations automatically, an information visualization tool will be useful. Such a tool will help the designers easily develop effective visualizations of the underlying information space for the end users. It will also help the advanced users perform their data exploration needs.

Over the last two years we have been developing an information visualization tool called the **Navigational View Builder (NVB)**. It can be used to develop visualizations of the information space of hypermedia systems. For example, it has been used to form overview diagrams for a section of the most popular hypermedia system, the *World-Wide Web* [13].

During the course of developing NVB, we identified several requirements for an effective information visualization tool. Section 2 discusses these requirements. Then the architecture of NVB is described in section 3. In section 4 it is shown how NVB fulfills the requirements of an information visualization tool. Section 5 concludes the paper by discussing some of the required features of the underlying database for producing effective visualizations.

2 Requirements of an Information Visualization Tool

We have tired to identify some of the requirements of an effective information visualization tool. These requirements will now be discussed.

- **A complete data exploration tool:**
  Visualization is most useful in the context of a complete data exploration tool. As discussed in [7], three types of tasks need to be performed for data exploration:
  1. *Data manipulation* tasks involve selecting portions of data or transforming data into new simpler forms. These tasks can be used to reduce the complexity of the information space. Since visualizing and comprehending a large, complex information space is difficult, data manipulation modules need to be integrated with data visualization. Examples of data manipulation tasks include transforming a complicated data organization like a graph to a simpler form like a tree, and dynamic queries [30] which allow the selection of only a portion of the data so that less information needs to be visualized.
  2. *Data analysis* tasks involve obtaining statistics on portions of the data. Statistical analysis of the data is very useful since it gives good insights into the underlying information space. Such analysis is useful not only for numeric data but for more abstract information as well. For example, the user may want to find the average value of a numeric attribute or the modal value of an enumerated attribute to get a better understanding of the underlying space.
  3. *Data visualization* tasks involve viewing the data through appropriate visualizations. Besides traditional charts and bar diagrams, visualization methods for different classical data organizations have been developed. For example, *cone tree* [24] and *treemap* [8] are two ways of visualizing hierarchies.
  Therefore, the tool should allow the users to perform various common data manipulation and analysis tasks and allow them to develop different types of visualizations of their information. Besides providing modules for these tasks, the tool should also allow the user to iterate between the tasks.

- **Combine content and structural analysis for data manipulation:**
  The underlying information space has a structure of nodes joined by links. The nodes and links also have content. When the data manipulation modules try to reduce the complexity of the information space they should try

to analyze both the structure and the content of the underlying information space. This will make the modules more powerful. For example, a querying module should not only allow the user to query the contents of the nodes and links but also allow the user to query about the structure; for example, the user should be able to find out all nodes of certain type joined by certain types of links.

In many cases structural or content analysis alone is not very useful. For example, if the underlying information space has a very complicated structure, structural analysis may not be able to extract simpler meaningful structures. On the other hand if the information space does not have useful meta information, content analysis won't be very useful. Therefore, a combination of content and structural analysis is required so that useful data manipulation results can be obtained for most information spaces.

– **Integrate navigation and querying:**
There are two major ways of accessing information: browsing and querying. Browsing, which is accomplished by navigating through the information space, is very appropriate for new and inexperienced users who do not have much understanding of the information space and thus cannot formulate a query. However, if the user knows exactly what information is needed, retrieving the information by browsing will be very time consuming. On the other hand querying will be very appropriate in this case. However, querying suffers from the "all or nothing" phenomenon. Giving a general query retrieves a lot of information. In this case the user should be able to navigate through the information returned by the query. Giving a specialized query returns very little information and the user should be able to browse through other related information. After a better understanding of the information space, a more appropriate query may be given. This method of specifying successively more appropriate queries, known as *querying by successive refinement*, is a very effective strategy. In fact, it has been suggested [28] that the merger of querying and navigation will provide powerful systems of information exploration. Therefore, information visualization tools should allow the user to combine navigation with querying.

– **Give the (experienced) user control over visual bindings:**
To be effective, the visualizations should use visual properties to represent underlying information. This strategy has been used effectively in Scientific and Software Visualization systems like Glyphmaker [23] and Lens [16]. The amount of information in the underlying space is generally much more than the amount of visual properties that can be used. Therefore only the important information should be represented visually. Since the designer may not know the information that will be found to be useful by the user, they should not fix the bindings between the information and the visual properties a-priori. The users should be able to control the bindings dynamically and tailor the visualizations according to their needs.

- **Multiple simultaneous visualizations:**
  Producing an effective visualization of a large, complicated information space that is understandable by the user is difficult. Different visualizations of the same complicated information space, giving different perspectives, may be more useful. Since these views highlight only certain aspects of the space they should be easier to produce and more comprehensible. Neuwirth et al. [18] also observed that the ability to view knowledge from different perspectives is important. Multiple visualizations have been used effectively in several information visualization systems (like IVEE [1] and Harmony [2]).

  User actions in one view should result in changes in the other views as well. For example, if the user selects a node of the information space in one view, the other views should also highlight the selected node. This will allow the user to comprehend the position of any particular node under the different perspectives. For best effects, smooth animation should be used so that the view changes are not abrupt and the user can comprehend the changes easily.

- **Provide detail with context:**
  Generally, the information space that is visualized is too big to fit on a screen. If the size is reduced to fit on the screen, the details becomes too small to be seen. An alternative is to browse the large layout by scrolling and arc traversing. However, this tends to obscure the global structure. The goal should be to display both the details and the context smoothly integrated together in a single space. Providing detail with context has been recognized to be one of the major requirements for effective information visualization. For example, perspective wall [10] and table lens [22] use fish-eye techniques [6] so that the information in the user's focus is shown in detail, smoothly integrated with the context information.

- **Ease-of-use:**
  Like user interface tools [17], one of the main requirements of information visualization tools should be ease-of-use. Depending on the goals of the user and on the information space, different combinations of data exploration operations will be needed. The user should be able to experiment with various options to come up with useful visualizations. Therefore, if it is really difficult or time-consuming to experiment with different data exploration operations the tool will be of limited use. Thus, the ease-of-use of the tool is very important.

- **State Saving:**
  There should be a notion of the *current state* of the system. Data exploration tasks will lead to state changes. It should be possible to save the current state. This will allow the designers to save useful visualizations as well as useful data manipulation and data analysis results for the end users. Moreover, the results of one session may be used in a later session and the users need not start from the beginning in each session.

– **Extensibility:**
It is not possible to predict all the data exploration needs of the user. Therefore, even if several data exploration modules are provided, for some unforeseen task some other modules may be required. For example, a data exploration task may require a new way of visualizing the data or a new data manipulation operation. If the tool cannot be used for these tasks, it will be of limited use. Therefore, the tool should be extensible. It should allow the addition of appropriate code to perform the required functions. Note that one of the major reasons for the popularity of scientific visualization tools like AVS [26] and Iris Explorer [25] is that they allow the addition of new modules besides providing various modules for many common scientific visualization tasks.

– **Generality with respect to type of information:**
A DBMS allows the user to easily build databases for different applications. Similarly, it will be desirable if the tool can be made to work with different information spaces with minimal effort. If it takes a lot of effort to customize the tool for different information spaces, the user will be discouraged to use it for another system and the usefulness of the tool will be reduced.

3 The Architecture

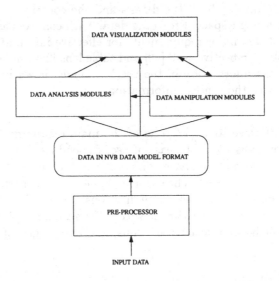

Fig. 1. The architecture of the Navigational View Builder, showing the inter-module information flows.

The Navigational View Builder has various components. Figure 1 shows the architecture and also the flow of information among the various components of the tool. The input information is converted by the pre-processor into the format required by the tool. The data can then flow in various directions depending on the user's request. The data can be directly visualized by a data visualization module. It can also be manipulated to a simpler form before the visualization by a data manipulation module. The user can use various data analysis modules to find statistics of the original data or some form of manipulated data. The user can also manipulate the data using a visualization. For example, the user can select a node in a visualization of a tree and prune all its children. (Visualization and manipulation are the only two modules between which information can flow either way). Note that a number of data manipulation, data analysis and data visualization modules can be used. These different components will now be discussed in detail.

3.1 Pre-processor Module

The input to the Navigational View Builder is a hypermedia information space that is defined with nodes and links. The actual input may be in many different formats and can be derived from different sources. Foreseeing all the different possible formats is not possible. Therefore, the Navigational View Builder assumes that the input information is represented using a fixed interior data model. A pre-processor module is used to convert the input data into the format required by NVB. Obviously, the pre-processor module needs to change for different information spaces.

To demonstrate the potential usefulness of the tool, it has been used to build visualizations of a section of the most popular hypermedia system, the World-Wide Web. This section of the Web describes research activities of the Graphics, Visualization & Usability Center at the Georgia Institute of Technology. Web pages describe the center and its activities, the research projects, the students and faculty and other miscellaneous information.

A pre-processor is used to convert the World-Wide Web information into the format required by the tool. The pre-processor parses the html files to develop the node and link structure. The procedure is explained in [20]. Various information about the nodes and links are also extracted. Information like the author of the page and the file size can be automatically extracted from the files. The access frequency of the nodes is extracted from the log files. However, a problem with the World-Wide Web is the absence of many useful semantic attributes. Therefore, to fully exploit the power of the tool, information like the topic of the page (for example, whether it is a research page or a biographical page) are inserted manually. It should be noted that efforts are underway to incorporate useful meta-data into the World-Wide Web [21]. Hopefully, in the near future all the required information can be extracted automatically by the pre-processor.

3.2 Data Model

The data model underlying the Navigational View Builder is the traditional hypermedia data model [4] described with nodes and links. It is organized as an object-oriented data model. The class hierarchy is as follows: [3]

- There is a root class called *object*. *Node* and *link* are children of class *object*. Links are considered uni-directional.
- Nodes have subclasses for the different media types like *image*, *text*, *audio* and *video* nodes. Links may also be of different types and subclasses are created for each type.
- Depending on the application there will be more subclasses of *nodes* and *links*. For example, for the *World-Wide Web* there will be a subclass of nodes called *file*. A html file will inherit both from *file* and from *text*. Similarly, a gif file will inherit from *file* and *image*.
- All objects have *attributes*. Attributes can be either *schema attributes* which store information about the nodes and links derived from the input data, or *visual attributes* which control the appearance of the objects in the visualizations. For example, *Author* is a schema attribute while *Color* is a visual attribute. Note that unlike visual attributes, many schema attributes will be application dependent.
- Besides the visual attributes and the schema attributes, there are also *interface context attributes*. These attributes depend on the state of the user interface and their values change during the running of the system. Whether a node is the current node of interest or the distance of a node from the current node are examples of interface context attributes.
- The Navigational View Builder assumes that attributes are either *enumerated attributes* or *quantitative attributes*. Attributes of any data type are converted to one of these two types. For example, *Accesses* is a quantitative attribute while *Author* is an enumerated attribute (an integer value is created for each author of the WWW pages). By assuming that there are only these two data types, many of the algorithms and strategies used in NVB are simplified. It also allows the tool to be modified easily for different inputs because provisions need not be made for unforeseen data types. However, since any data type of the underlying database has to be converted to one of these two types, the pre-processor may become complicated.
- The input information space is a graph which has as its attribute a collection of nodes and a list of links. Its class description is:

```
class Graph :public Object
{
    private:
    NodeList* nodes;
    LinkList* links;
    :
    :
};
```

---

[3] This is based on the O_2 DBMS [19].

– The basic model may be expanded to incorporate other classes. For example, a class for trees may be formed if a tree structure is to be visualized. Similarly, a subclass of nodes called *clusters* (a group of related nodes) may be formed.

The overall class hierarchy is summarized in Figure 2. Note that the data model information, both the class hierarchy and the attributes, is available to all the other modules of NVB.

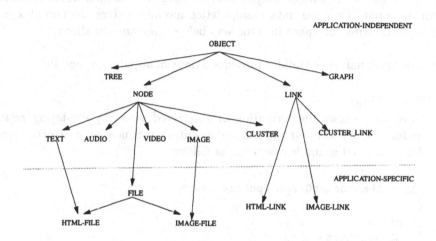

Fig. 2. Figure to summarize the class hierarchy of the Navigational View Builder data model.

3.3 Data Manipulation Modules

The input information space is a large complicated graph. Attractive layout of the graph generally involves many aesthetics like avoiding edge crossings, keeping edge lengths uniform and distributing nodes uniformly. In general, the optimization problems associated with these aesthetics are NP-hard [9]. Extensive research has been done in finding approximate solutions using heuristics and other strategies for graph layout [3]. However, none of these have been very successful in automatically finding a good layout of a large graph in a short time. Other methods of visualizing large graphs (for example SemNet [5]) have also not been very successful.

Therefore, for effective visualizations, the data must be simplified. There are two effective ways of simplifying the input data. Only some portion of the graph may be selected for visualization. Visualization of this smaller graph will be easier. The graph may also be converted to a simpler form and this form may be visualized.

Data manipulation modules are used for these tasks. Data manipulation modules take as input some data organization. These modules select and output only a portion of the input data or output another data organization which is simpler than the input. Thus the data manipulation modules reduce the complexity of the input information space in some way before they are visualized.

The Navigational View Builder provides 3 data manipulation modules:

- **Clustering**:
  Clustering allows the formation of abstracted views by clustering related nodes. It takes as input a graph and as output produces an *abstracted graph*. An abstracted graph is described as follows:

```
class AbstractedGraph :public Graph
{
    private:
    ClusterList* cl;
    :
    :
};
```

  Thus an abstracted graph is a subclass of graph. It has a list of *clusters* which is a collection of related nodes. Thus, abstracted graphs have a smaller number of nodes than the input graph and can be thus visualized more effectively. Clustering is discussed in detail in [14].

- **Filtering**:
  Filtering modules allow the filtering of unwanted information. These modules take as input a graph, select only a portion of the input and output that portion. The selection can be done based on various criteria; for example all nodes whose attribute value is greater than a specified value can be selected. Thus the output is a graph with a smaller number of nodes or links or both.

- **Hierarchization**:
  NVB has an algorithm that allows the formation of hierarchies from complicated hypermedia networks. Thus, the hierarchization module takes a graph as the input and produces a tree as the output. Trees are simpler data structures than graphs and can be visualized more effectively. The hierarchization process is discussed in detail in [15].

3.4 Data Analysis Modules

Data analysis modules calculate statistics for individual nodes or clusters of nodes. These modules take as input any individual node or group of nodes, calculate some statistics for the input and display the result in dialog boxes. For example, the Navigational View Builder allows the calculation of statistics like the average number of accesses for a group of nodes. Thus, the average number of accesses for all WWW pages written by a certain author can be calculated. Similarly, the importance of individual nodes can be calculated as explained in [12]. The importance of the nodes are determined by using two metrics; a connectivity metric indicating how well a node is connected to other nodes in the information space and an access frequency metric indicating how many times the node has been accessed by the user.

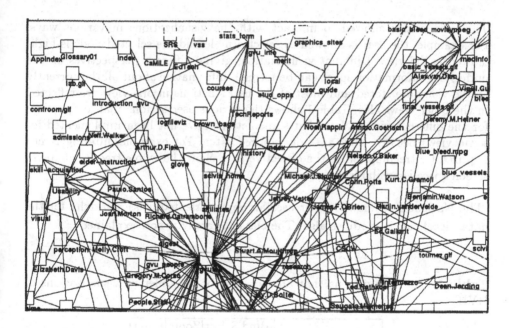

Fig. 3. An initial 2D graph view of the section of the WWW describing research at GVU. The diagram is very complicated.

3.5 Data Visualization Modules

Data visualization modules produce visualizations of different data organizations. Thus, these modules take as input some data organization and produce visualizations of the input.

By default, the Navigational View Builder shows the input as a 2D graph. For example, Figure 3 shows the 2D graph view of the WWW information space that was described in subsection 3.1. This diagram makes it obvious why such diagrams are useless for the user to gain a good understanding of the underlying space. The overall space does not fit on the screen and the complexity of the space makes it impossible for the user to comprehend the data.

Therefore, data manipulation modules may be used to form smaller graphs which can be viewed more effectively as 2D graphs. For abstracted graphs formed by clustering, a 3D graph visualization strategy can also be used in NVB. Moreover, simpler data organizations can be formed from the input graph. For example, a tree can be formed and this tree can be visualized in various ways. NVB allows the visualizations of trees as 2D trees, cone trees, treemaps and as a table of contents of a book. Linear data organizations can also be formed and they can be visualized as perspective walls.

The user is also allowed to interact with the visualizations in various ways. For example, the user is allowed to select a node and the selected node is highlighted in the view. Different visualizations giving different perspectives on the underlying information space can be formed. Information about all the currently active views are stored and most of the user's actions in one view are reflected in the other views also. Table 1 shows the various user actions that are possible for the different views. Note that some actions have not been implemented for some views because they are not required often. For example, filtering is not required for treemaps since the objective is to show the whole tree in whatever screen space is available.

The Navigational View Builder uses an object-oriented class hierarchy for the data visualization modules also. The class hierarchy is now explained.

Table 1. The user actions that are possible for the different visualizations of NVB

	Bind	Select	Zoom	Filter
2D Graph	Yes	Yes	Yes	Yes
3D Graph	Yes	Yes	Yes	Yes
2D Tree	Yes	Yes	Yes	Yes
3D Tree	Yes	Yes	Yes	Yes
Treemap	Yes	Yes	No	No
Table of Contents	Yes	Yes	No	Yes
Perspective Wall	Yes	Yes	Yes	No

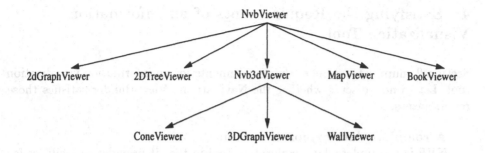

Fig. 4. Figure showing the class hierarchy of the Navigational View Builder visualization modules.

- There is a base class to define various kinds of visualizations. This class is called *NvbViewer*. A popup widget is used for each visualization and this class has a member which specifies the popup widget. The window for the visualization is also a member of this class. The constructor function for the class sets up the toplevel widget. There are 3 important member functions. *RenderFn* is used to render the screen for the visualization. *ExitFn* is used to exit the visualization. (Generally it popdowns the toplevel widget). *Change-Current* is a function that is used to change the visualization to highlight the current node of interest. If the user clicks on a node in one view it becomes the current node and this function is called for all views so that the current node is highlighted in these views as well. In this class these functions specify the default behavior. However, these virtual functions may be overwritten in the subclasses.
- For 3D visualizations a subclass of NvbViewer called *Nvb3dViewer* is used. The Navigational View Builder uses Open Inventor [29] for 3D visualizations. It uses the *Examiner Viewer* of Inventor for the views.
- For each type of visualization a new class is created. For example, for Cone Tree visualization a class called *ConeViewer* is used. As a member it has the tree that is being visualized. Besides providing methods for rendering and selecting a node, some other special methods can also be provided for each class of visualization. For example, for cone trees, methods are provided for pruning and growing different subtrees.

The class hierarchy for the visualization modules is shown in Figure 4.

4 Satisfying the Requirements of an Information Visualization Tool

Section 2 enumerates some of the requirements for an information visualization tool. Let us now discuss whether the Navigational View Builder satisfies those requirements.

- **A complete data exploration tool:**
  NVB is a complete data exploration tool in that it provides capabilities for data manipulation, data analysis and data visualization.

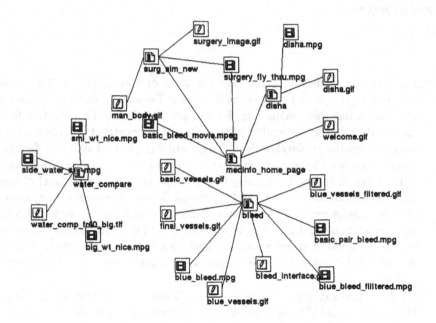

Fig. 5. An example of combining structure-based and content-based filtering: Showing only the html pages linked to both images and movies. Icons represent the media types of the pages.

- **Combine content and structural analysis for data manipulation:**
  The Navigational View Builder has three data manipulation modules: clustering, filtering and hierarchization. Each of these modules use a combination of content and structural analysis. For example, combining structure-based and content-based filtering conditions is allowed. Thus, Figure 5 shows all the html pages that are linked to both images and movies in the GVU information space shown in Figure 3.

70

– **Integrate navigation and querying:**
Various ways of querying (or filtering) are provided in NVB. The various
visualization modules allow the user to navigate through the information
space. For example, the 2D graph allows the user to navigate through scroll
bars. Similarly, the 3D views allow the user to rotate in the X and Y axes,
zoom in and out and also provide various other ways of navigating through
the 3D space. In this way filtering and navigation is integrated in NVB.

– **Give the (experienced) user control over visual bindings:**
NVB allows the binding of visual and schema attributes so that information of the underlying space is represented visually. For example, in Figure 5
icons are used to represent the media types of the pages. The binding can be
changed by the user using an easy-to-use interface. The concept of binding
is explained in [11].

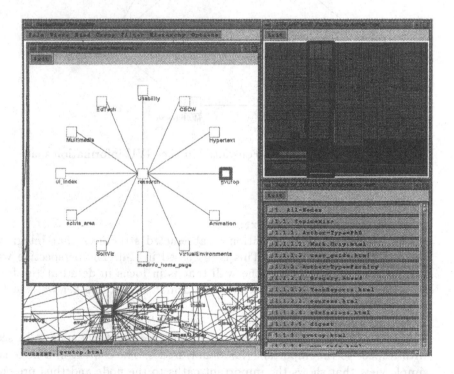

Fig. 6. Multiple visualizations of the information space. The node *gvutop.html*
is the current node.

– **Multiple simultaneous visualizations:**
The input information space can be visualized in various ways. Most of the
user actions in one view are reflected in the other views as well. For example,

selecting a node in one view results in highlighting the node in all the views. Thus, Figure 6 shows multiple simultaneous visualizations for the information space. The node *gvutop.html* is the current node and is highlighted in all views. The user-specified bindings also affect all the views. Smooth animation is used for most state changes.

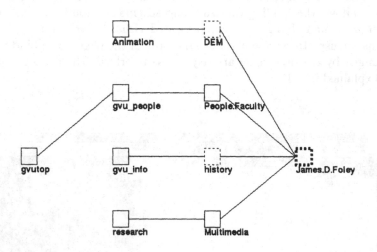

Fig. 7. Context of James.D.Foley.html in the GVU information space.

Provide detail with context:
NVB provides a 3D visualization of abstracted structures that integrates the detail with the context. This is discussed in [14]. The perspective wall visualization of NVB shows the wall that is in focus in detail at the front smoothly integrated with the context information on the other walls at the sides.

Moreover, NVB has a module that allows the context of any node to be seen with respect to the important (*landmark*) nodes. The context of a node is a simple view that shows the important paths to the node and thus presents the position of the node in the overall information space and helps the users if they are lost. This method is described in [12]. Figure 7 shows the context of the home page of the second author of this paper in the information space shown in Figure 3. It shows the paths to the node from landmark nodes. This view gives an idea of the position of Dr. Foley in GVU. It shows that he is a professor in GVU and is interested in various research areas like Multimedia.

– **Ease-of-use:**
The tool is not very difficult to use providing dialog boxes and menu options for the various data exploration tasks. Usability studies were done which showed that the users did not have much trouble doing many of their data exploration tasks. The results of the studies will be discussed in a forthcoming paper.

– **State Saving:**
There is a notion of the current state in NVB. Initially, the current state is the graph that is read as input. Data exploration operations change the current state. For example, filtering may cause the current state to be the portion of the input graph that is selected. Saving the current state of the system is also allowed.

– **Extensibility:**
The underlying object-oriented framework allows the tool to be expanded without much difficulty. For example, suppose an advanced user wants to add a module that clusters nodes based on information retrieval techniques. The required code has to be written and a module has to be created that takes a graph as input and uses the required code to produce an abstracted graph as output. Incorporating the module into the Navigational View Builder and having a menu option for this form of clustering will require little coding. As long as a module takes as inputs and produces as outputs formats that are recognized by the Navigational View Builder, the module can be incorporated into the tool. If the format is not recognized, a class definition for the format needs to be added also. Some pre-defined modules can also be used in the new modules. For example, since the hierarchization algorithm is based on clustering, the hierarchization module uses the clustering module.

Creating new visualizations is also moderately easy for a graphics programmer. For each new visualization, a class has to be defined as a child of the base classes for the visualizations, NvbViewer or Nvb3dViewer. The required methods (like the rendering method) have to be written if the default behaviors for the methods that are specified in the base classes are not applicable. If some other methods are required they can be also included.

– **Generality with respect to type of information:**
Tailoring the tool for a different information space requires as much work as is required to tailor an object-oriented DBMS for a new application. First, the application-dependent class hierarchy has to be modified. For example, for an automobile database, classes should be defined to describe cars. The class called *file* that is used for the WWW must be replaced by a class called *car*. Subclasses need to be created for this class for the different media types. Different schema attributes need to be defined also. Attributes like the topic of a WWW page needs to be replaced by attributes like the price of a car.

Moreover, a pre-processor is required to read in the actual data into the format of the object-oriented model used in NVB. The pre-processor will depend on the actual format of the input data. If the data already resides in a database, a simple program will be able to convert it to the format required by NVB.

Note that the tool can be used for any section of the World-Wide Web. The pre-processor module should be used to extract the structure of that section of the Web. Of course, the meta-information may not be available, making some of the strategies of NVB less effective.

5 Conclusion

We have discussed the requirements of an information visualization tool. To be really effective, the underlying database should also have certain desirable features to help the visualization process. Let us conclude the paper by discussing two important features:

- For content analysis the underlying information space should have many useful semantic attributes defined. However, a problem with the World-Wide Web is the absence of significant meta-information. Therefore, to fully exploit the power of the tool information like the topic of the page (for example, whether it is a research page or a biographical page) were inserted manually. For the success of such tools, the underlying space should provide lots of meaningful semantic attributes to help the content analysis of the space.
- As we discussed before, a pre-processor is required to make the tool to work with different information spaces. Depending on the underlying information space, the pre-processor will be of varying levels of complexity. There needs to be a great deal of communication between the database community and the visualization community so that the interface between the visualization tools and the underlying database is standardized. The standardization will enable information visualization tools to work with different information spaces with minimal effort.

Hopefully, in the near future all the commercially available Data Base Management Systems will have a visualization component which will allow the users to easily develop effective visualizations of their data.

Acknowledgement

We will like to thank John Stasko for his useful comments.

References

1. C. Ahlberg and E. Wistrand. IVEE: An Information Visualization and Exploration Environment. In *Proceedings of the 1995 Information Visualization Symposium*, pages 66–73, Atlanta, Ga, 1995.

74

74

74

74

2. K. Andrews, F. Kappe, and H. Maurer. Serving Information to the Web with Hyper-G. *Computer Networks and ISDN Systems. Special Issue on the Third International World-Wide Web Conference, Darmstadt, Germany*, 27(6):919–926, April 1995.

3. G. Battista, P. Eades, R. Tamassia, and I. Tollis. Algorithms for Drawing Graphs: an Annotated Bibliography. Technical report, Brown University, June 1993.

4. J. Conklin. Hypertext: An Introduction and Survey. *IEEE Computer*, 20(9):17–41, 1987.

5. K. Fairchild, S. Poltrok, and G. Furnas. Semnet: Three-dimensional Graphic Representations of Large Knowledge Bases. In R. Guindon, editor, *Cognitive Science and its Applications for Human-Computer Interaction.* Lawrence Erlbaum, 1988.

6. G. Furnas. Generalized Fisheye Views. In *Proceedings of the ACM SIGCHI '86 Conference on Human Factors in Computing Systems*, pages 16–23, Boston, Ma, April 1986.

7. J. Goldstein and S. Roth. Using Aggregation and Dynamic Queries for Exploring Large Data Sets. In *Proceedings of the ACM SIGCHI '94 Conference on Human Factors in Computing Systems*, pages 23–29, Boston, Ma, April 1994.

8. B. Johnson and B. Shneiderman. Treemaps: A Space-filling Approach to the Visualization of Hierarchical Information. In *Proceedings of IEEE Visualization '91 Conference*, pages 284–291, San Diego, Ca, October 1991.

9. D. Johnson. The NP-Completeness Column: an Ongoing Guide. *Journal of Algorithms*, 5(2):147–160, 1984.

10. J. D. Mackinlay, S. Card, and G. Robertson. Perspective Wall: Detail and Context Smoothly Integrated. In *Proceedings of the ACM SIGCHI '91 Conference on Human Factors in Computing Systems*, pages 173–179, New Orleans, La, April 1991.

11. S. Mukherjea and J. Foley. Navigational View Builder: A Tool for Building Navigational Views of Information Spaces. In *ACM SIGCHI '94 Conference Companion*, pages 289–290, Boston, Ma, April 1994.

12. S. Mukherjea and J. Foley. Showing the Context of Nodes in the World-Wide Web. In *ACM SIGCHI '95 Conference Companion*, pages 326–327, Denver, Colorado, May 1995.

13. S. Mukherjea and J. Foley. Visualizing the World-Wide Web with the Navigational View Builder. *Computer Networks and ISDN Systems. Special Issue on the Third International World-Wide Web Conference, Darmstadt, Germany*, 27(6):1075–1087, April 1995.

14. S. Mukherjea, J. Foley, and S. Hudson. Interactive Clustering for Navigating in Hypermedia Systems. In *Proceedings of the ACM European Conference of Hypermedia Technology*, pages 136–144, Edinburgh, Scotland, September 1994.

15. S. Mukherjea, J. Foley, and S. Hudson. Visualizing Complex Hypermedia Networks through Multiple Hierarchical Views. In *Proceedings of the ACM SIGCHI '95 Conference on Human Factors in Computing Systems*, pages 331–337, Denver, Co, May 1995.

16. S. Mukherjea and J. Stasko. Towards Visual Debugging: Integrating Algorithm Animation Capabilities within a Source Level Debugger. *ACM Transaction on Computer-Human Interaction*, 1(3):215–244, September 1994.

17. B. Myers. User Interface Tools: Introduction and Survey. *IEEE Software*, 1(15):15–23, January 1989.

18. C. Neuwirth, D. Kauffer, R. Chimera, and G. Terilyn. The Notes Program: A Hypertext Application for Writing from Source Texts. In *Proceedings of Hypertext '87 Conference*, pages 121–135, Chapel Hill, NC, November 1987.

19. O2 Technology, 78035 Versailles Cedex, France. *The O₂ User Manual Version 4.0*, 1992.

20. J. Pitkow and K. Bharat. WEBVIZ: A Tool for World-Wide Web Access Log Visualization. In *Proceedings of the First International World-Wide Web Conference*, Geneva, Switzerland, May 1994.

21. J. Pitkow and R. Jones. Towards an Intelligent Publisihing Environment. *Computer Networks and ISDN Systems. Special Issue on the Third International World-Wide Web Conference, Darmstadt, Germany*, 27(6):729–737, April 1995.

22. R. Rao and S. Card. The Table Lens: Merging Graphical and Symbolic Representations in an Interactive Focus+Context Visualization for Tabular Information. In *Proceedings of the ACM SIGCHI '94 Conference on Human Factors in Computing Systems*, pages 318–322, Boston, Ma, April 1994.

23. W. Ribarsky, E. Ayers, J. Elbe, and S. Mukherjea. Glyphmaker: Creating Customized Visualizations of Complex Data. *IEEE Computer*, 27(7):57–64, July 1994.

24. G. G. Robertson, J. D. Mackinlay, and S. Card. Cone Trees: Animated 3D Visualizations of Hierarchical Information. In *Proceedings of the ACM SIGCHI '91 Conference on Human Factors in Computing Systems*, pages 189–194, New Orleans, La, April 1991.

25. Silicon Graphics, Mountain View, California. *IRIS Explorer User's Guide*, 1992.

26. C. Upson, T. Faulhaber, D. Kaminis, D. Laidlaw, D. Schlegel, J. Vroom, R. Gurwitz, and A. Van Dam. The Application Visualization System: A Computational Environment for Scientific Visualization. *IEEE Computer Graphics and Applications*, 9(4):30–42, 1989.

27. K. Vicente and J. Rasmussen. The Ecology of Human Machine Systems: II. Mediating "direct perception" in Complex Domain. *Ecological Psychology*, 2:207–249, 1990.

28. J. Waterworth and M. Chignell. A Model for Information Exploration. *Hypermedia*, 3(1):33–58, 1991.

29. J. Wernecke. *The Inventor Mentor: Programming Object-Oriented 3D Graphics with Open Inventor*. Addison-Wesley Publishing Company, 1994.

30. C. Williamson and B. Shneiderman. The Dynamic HomeFinder: Evaluating Dynamic Queries in a Real-Estate Information Exploration System. In *Proceedings of the ACM SIGIR '92 Conference on Research and Development in Information Retrieval*, pages 338–346, Copenhagen, Denmark, June 1992.

Mathematical Structures of Data and Their Implications for Visualization

William Hibbard
Space Science and Engineering Center
University of Wisconsin-Madison
whibbard@macc.wisc.edu

1 Introduction

There has been considerable interest in the systematic study of the data that are the input to visualization, reflected in workshops at the Siggraph '90 conference [Treinish, 1991] and the Visualization '93 conference [Lee and Grinstein, 1994]. There have been at least two efforts to define mathematical structures for data in the context of visualization. The first is the *field data model* [Haber, Lucas and Collins, 1991] (also sometimes called the fiber bundle data model), based on the idea that the input data for scientific visualization are often functions over differentiable manifolds, sampled at regular or irregular grids. The second is the *lattice data model* [Hibbard, Dyer and Paul, 1994], based on the idea that scientific data objects are usually approximations to mathematical objects, and that data objects can be ordered according to the precision of that approximation.

In this paper we discuss the prospects for extending the mathematical study of data to a mathematical study of visualization mappings. We let U denote a set of data objects, let V denote a set of displays, and let $D : U \rightarrow V$ denote a visualization mapping that transforms data objects into displays. Since the mapping D is implemented as an automated computational process it has been primarily studied in terms of algorithms and programming techniques. However, the study of mathematical structures on U (i.e., the study of visualization data models) can be extended to study the mapping D. First note that a randomly chosen function of the form $D : U \rightarrow V$ will produce displays $D(u)$ that are poor depictions of data objects $u \in U$. Thus our study centers around the questions:

What subset E of all functions $D : U \rightarrow V$ produce acceptable depictions of data? We call this set E a *visualization repertoire*.

What conditions should we impose on $D : U \rightarrow V$ to define a repertoire E? Conditions on D will be stated in terms of mathematical structures on U and V.

Scientific data objects are typically representations of functions. Mathematics supplies us with many examples of how to define structures on sets whose members are functions [Dunford and Schwartz, 1957]. These *function spaces* are studied in terms of their algebraic structures (e.g., they may be *linear vector spaces* over the field $\mathbf{R}$ of real numbers), their metric structures (e.g., the distance between two bounded continuous functions $f, g : S \rightarrow \mathbf{R}$ may be defined as: $|f - g| =$

$sup\{|f(s) - g(s)| \mid s \in S\})$, and their topologies (often derived from their metric structures).

Mathematics also supplies us with examples of conditions on mappings (often called *operators*) between function spaces. If U and V are linear vector spaces then the operator $D : U \to V$ is *linear* if it satisfies the following conditions:

(1) $\forall u, u' \in U.\ D(u + u') = D(u) + D(u')$
(2) $\forall r \in \mathbf{R}.\ \forall u \in U.\ D(r \times u) = r \times D(u)$

The derivative is an example of a linear operator on the space of infinitely-differentiable continuous functions. If U and V are metric spaces then the operator $D : U \to V$ is *isometric* if it satisfies the following conditions:

(3) $\forall u, u' \in U.\ |u - u'| = |D(u) - D(u')|$

The Fourier transform is an example of an isometric (and linear) operator on the function space $L_2(\mathbf{R})$ (see [Dunford and Schwartz, 1957] for a definition of $L_2(\mathbf{R})$ - this is a set of real-valued functions with essentially an infinite-dimensional Cartesian metric).

2 The Field Data Model

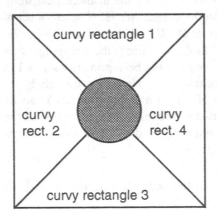

Here's a Cartesian 2-D square with a hole in it. We have divided the square into four curvy rectangles. Each curvy rectangle has the simple topology of the original square. Together they make the complex topology of the square-with-a-hole-in-it.

Figure 1. Topologically rectangular patches sewed together to make a function domain with irregular topology.

The field data model describes functions whose domains have complex topologies, such as those used to describe fluid flows around objects with complex shapes (e.g., turbine blades or aircraft). It models a field F as a union of field elements F_i. Figure 1 shows how the topologically irregular domain of the field F is pieced together from topologically rectangular domains of the field elements F_i. The field element F_i is essentially a function from a *base* Ω_i (a subset of a *base-*

coordinate space B_i) to a *dependent variable space Y*. The base Ω_i is the range of a function from a *manifold domain* ω_i (typically an n-dimensional rectangle) into B_i. Figure 2 illustrates these functions on a single field element. The field F includes information about how boundaries of the various bases Ω_i are connected together (note that this stitched together union of bases may have a very complex topology). Finally, field data objects are actually sets of samples of field values on finite grids. See [Haber, Lucas and Collins, 1991] for a more detailed discussion of the field data model.

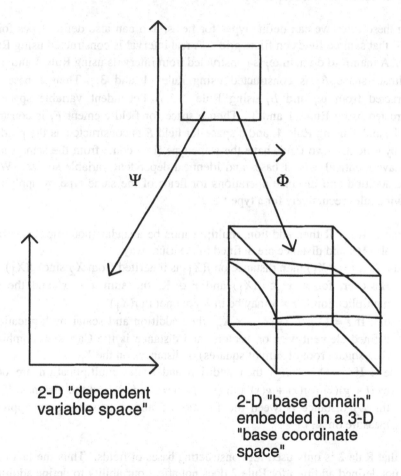

2-D "manifold domain" embedded in a 2-D "manifold coordinate space"

Ψ

Φ

2-D "dependent variable space"

2-D "base domain" embedded in a 3-D "base coordinate space"

Figure 2. Defining function values on one topologically rectangular patch.

It is difficult to define mathematical structures on the space of all field data objects, since different fields may have bases and dependent variable spaces with different dimensionalities. However, we can define such structures on sets of fields of the same type. Define a set T of types by the following type construction rules (note that each type is identified with a set):

Rule 1. $\mathbf{R} \in T$. That is, the real numbers are a type (and of course this type is identified with the set of real numbers).

Rule 2. If $X_1, X_2 \in T$ and $f : X_1 \to X_2$ is continuous then $f(X_1) \in T$. This type is identified with the set $\{f(x) \mid x \in X_1\}$.

Rule 3. If $X_1, X_2, ..., X_n \in T$ then $(X_1 \times X_2 \times ... \times X_n) \in T$. This type is identified with the set of vectors of members of $X_1, X_2, ..., X_n$.

Rule 4. If $X_1, X_2 \in T$ then $(X_1 \to X_2) \in T$. This type is identified with the set of all functions from X_1 to X_2.

Using these rules we can define types for fields, and can also define types for data objects that sample fields on finite grids. A real interval is constructed using Rules 1 and 2. A manifold domain ω_i is constructed from intervals using Rule 3 and a base-coordinate space B_i is constructed using Rules 1 and 3. Then a base Ω_i is constructed from ω_i and B_i using Rule 2. A dependent variable space Y is constructed using Rules 1 and 3. Then a space for field element F_i is constructed from Ω_i and Y using Rule 4, and a space for field F is constructed as the product of these by Rule 3. Two fields have the same type (i.e., come from the same space) if they have identical sets of bases and identical dependent variable spaces. We can define addition and distance operations for fields of the same type by applying the following rules recursively for a type $t \in T$:

Rule 1: If $t = \mathbf{R}$ then addition, multiplication be a scalar (note the scalar field is also $\mathbf{R}$), and distance are defined in the usual way.

Rule 2: If $t = f(X_1)$ then distance on $f(X_1)$ is inherited from X_2 since $f(X_1) \subseteq X_2$. However, for $x, x' \in f(X_1)$ and $r \in \mathbf{R}$, the sum $x + x'$ and the scalar multiplication $r \times x$ may be in X_2 but not in $f(X_1)$.

Rule 3: If $t = (X_1 \times X_2 \times ... \times X_n)$ then addition and scalar multiplication are defined element-wise on vectors, and distance is the Cartesian combination (i.e., square root of sum of squares) of distances on the X_i.

Rule 4: If $t = (X_1 \to X_2)$ then addition and scalar multiplication are defined by $(f + g)(x) = f(x) + g(x)$ and $(r \times f)(x) = r \times f(x)$, and the distance $|f - g|$ is the L_2 distance between the functions f and g (assuming an appropriate measure on X_1).

Note that Rule 2 is only used for constructing bases of fields. Thus the fact that we have not defined addition for Rule 2 does not affect our ability to define addition for fields of the same type. Note also that, given a willingness to resample and interpolate grid values, we can define addition and distance operations for field data objects that have fields of the same type, even when they have different sets of grid points.

Thus sets of fields of the same type are linear vector spaces with metrics. Furthermore, as noted in [Haber, Lucas and Collins, 1991] and in [Lucas, Abrams, Collins, Epstein, Gresh and McAuliffe, 1992], fields can represent displays as well as scientific data objects, so if we may assume that both U and V are sets of fields. If we further assume U is a set of fields of one type, and similarly for V, then U and V have algebraic and metric structures. This makes it possible to impose linearity and isometry as conditions on the definition of a visualization repertoire E. Are these useful conditions?

Displays in V that are 2-D or 3-D color fields (i.e., 2-D images or 3-D volume renderings) can be represented as fields with type $(\mathbf{R}^2 \to \mathbf{R}^3)$ (this type consists of colored 2-D images) or $(\mathbf{R}^3 \to \mathbf{R}^3)$ (this type consists of colored 3-D volume images). It is possible to measure distances between typical human perceptions of color and to use these to define a metric on a three-dimensional color space [CIE, 1968; Robertson, 1988; Robertson and O'Callaghan, 1988]. It is similarly possible to define metrics on texture perception [Li and Robertson, 1995]. We can apply this to the definition of a display space V (with type $(\mathbf{R}^2 \to \mathbf{R}^3)$ or $(\mathbf{R}^3 \to \mathbf{R}^3)$)). If a visualization mapping $D : U \to V$ satisfies the isometric condition then the perceived distances between displays represent actual information about data objects. Thus isometry is a useful condition.

Linearity is more questionable. Assuming again that displays in V are 2-D or 3-D color fields, linearity implies that (at least in the displays of some data objects) color values range over all real values, including negative values. However, if actual data objects are restricted to positive values (for example, radiances observed by satellites can only be positive) then linearity may be a reasonable condition.

3 The Lattice Data Model

The lattice data model is based on the approximate nature of most scientific data objects. Data objects must be represented by finite strings over finite alphabets so there are at most a countable number of data objects, whereas there are an uncountable number of mathematical objects. Since each mathematical object must be represented by some data object, in general each data object $u \in U$ must represent a set $math(u)$ of mathematical objects. We can define an order relation on U by:

(4) $u \le u' \Leftrightarrow math(u') \subseteq math(u)$

This order relation is based on precision: u' is more precise than u because it represents a more restricted set of mathematical objects. There are several ways that this order relation is explicit in scientific data. First, the use of *missing data indicators* to denote sensor failures or arithmetical faults (e.g., division by zero). A missing value can represent any mathematical value and thus by Eq. (4) is $\le$ any other data value. Second, the use of error bars to indicate an interval of possible values. A containing interval represents a larger set of values than a smaller interval and thus by Eq. (4) is ≤ the smaller interval. Third, functions are usually represented by finite sets of samples of their values (for example, a satellite image is a finite sampling of a continuous radiance field). A lower resolution sampling is consistent with many different high resolution samplings and thus by Eq. (4) is ≤ those high resolution samplings. Note that the order relation in Eq. (4) can also be applied to V, since displays are finite data objects with finite pixel or voxel resolutions, finite numbers of colors, and discrete animation steps.

There are natural ways to unify data objects of many different data types in a kind of ordered set called a *complete lattice* [Davey and Priestly, 1990; Hibbard, Dyer and Paul, 1994; Hibbard, 1995; Schmidt, 1986; Scott, 1971; Scott, 1976]. Thus we assume that U and V are complete lattices.

In order to define conditions on the visualization repertoire in terms of lattice structures, we use *expressiveness conditions* originally defined in [Mackinlay, 1986]. These conditions say that displays should express all the facts about data objects, and only those facts. We interpret facts about data objects as monotone predicates of the form $P : U \rightarrow \{undefined, true\}$. [To say that P is *monotone* means that $u \leq u' \Rightarrow P(u) \leq P(u')$. Furthermore, we assume that *undefined* < *true*. This interpretation is based on the assumption that facts about data objects represent facts about mathematical objects.] Then we can interpret the expressiveness conditions by Requirements 1 and 2, as follows:

Requirement 1. For every monotone predicate $P: U \rightarrow \{undefined, true\}$, there is a monotone predicate $Q: V \rightarrow \{undefined, true\}$ such that $P(u) = Q(D(u))$ for each $u \in U$.

Requirement 2. For every monotone predicate $Q : D(U) \rightarrow \{undefined, true\}$, there is a monotone predicate $P : U \rightarrow \{undefined, true\}$ such that $Q(v) = P(D^{-1}(v))$ for each $v \in D(U)$. [Here we use $D(U)$ in place of V so we don't assume that D is onto.]

A visualization mapping $D : U \rightarrow V$ satisfies these requirements if and only if it is a *lattice isomorphism* [Hibbard, 1995]. This means that, for all $u, u', u'' \in U$:

(5) $D(u \vee u') = D(u) \vee D(u')$
(6) $D(u \wedge u') = D(u) \wedge D(u')$
(7) D is a bijection (i.e., one-to-one and onto)

This result applies generally to any data and display models U and V that are complete lattices.

As described in the section of this paper on field data models, data objects are constructed as complex aggregates of primitive values, and data objects are partitioned into many different data types. The notions of missing data, error bound intervals, and finite samplings of arrays can be applied to develop lattice-structured data models appropriate for field data. In [Hibbard, 1995] we showed that given such data and display models U and V, the result that visualization mappings $D : U \rightarrow V$ are lattice isomorphisms implies that:

Mappings from data aggregates to display aggregates can be factored into mappings from data primitives to display primitives.

This statement is made more precisely in [Hibbard, 1995] and is illustrated in Figure 3. Intuitively, it just says that to display a time series of temperatures, for example, we need to map time to one graphical primitive (say the X axis of the display screen) and map temperature to another graphical primitive (say the Y axis of the display screen). While this has generally been accepted as standard procedure, it is interesting that it is a consequence of the expressiveness conditions. Interpreted in the context of lattice-structured data and display models, we conclude that the expressiveness conditions are useful.

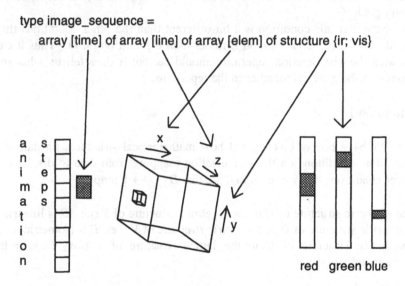

Figure 3. A mapping from a data aggregate to a display aggregate is decomposed into mappings from data primitives to display primitives.

4 Symmetry

In the section on the field data model we saw that an isometry condition could express a useful property of human perception. Here we note another property of perception that is so familiar that we may take it for granted. Namely, that perception is invariant to certain symmetries of displays. There are no absolute references for time and location, so our perception must be invariant to translations of displays in time or in location.

In order to express these symmetries of displays, assume that the display space V has the type $(\mathbf{R}^4 \rightarrow \mathbf{R}^3)$, where the $\mathbf{R}^4$ base includes one time dimension for animation and three spatial dimensions for voxel location (and the $\mathbf{R}^3$ dependent variable space represents color). Then translations of displays in time and location are arbitrary translations in $\mathbf{R}^4$. Such symmetries form a group, which we denote by G. Each $g \in G$ is a mapping $g : \mathbf{R}^4 \to \mathbf{R}^4$. The statement that perception is invariant to the symmetries in G can be precisely formulated as a condition on the visualization repertoire E, as follows:

(8) $\qquad \forall g \in G. \ \forall D \in E. \ (\lambda u \in U. \ D(u) \circ g) \in E$

This needs a little explanation. $D(u) \in V = (\mathbf{R}^4 \to \mathbf{R}^3)$ so $D(u)$ is a function from $\mathbf{R}^4$ to $\mathbf{R}^3$. Since g is a function from $\mathbf{R}^4$ to $\mathbf{R}^4$ the functional composition $D(u) \circ g$ is a function from $\mathbf{R}^4$ to $\mathbf{R}^3$ and hence a member of V. Then $(\lambda u \in U. \ D(u) \circ g)$ is a function from U to V, and our condition just says that this must be a member of the repertoire E when D is a member of the repertoire E and when g is a member of the symmetry group G.

Note that this condition is a bit different than the other conditions that we discussed, since it is a condition on E rather than a condition on D. Thus it cannot tell us what the visualization repertoire should be, but it does tell us what sets of functions must be grouped together in the repertoire.

5 Conclusion

We have briefly investigated how mathematical structures on data can be used to define conditions on the visualization mapping from data to displays. The first three conditions that we discussed are that $D : U \to V$ map:

The algebraic structure of U to the algebraic structure of V (i.e., D is linear).
The metric structure of U to the metric structure of V (i.e., D is isometric).
The lattice structure of U to the lattice structure of V (i.e., D is a lattice isomorphism).

Thus for each of three kinds of mathematical structures on the data and display models U and V, the conditions state that D should define a correspondence between the structure of U and the structure of V. This is an interesting similarity of form between these three conditions. The fourth condition is a bit different, relating the structure of the repertoire E to the structure of a symmetry group G on the display model V.

While these ideas are certainly not fully developed, they define an interesting approach to visualization. They suggest the possibility of expressing properties of human perception and visualization requirements in terms of mathematical structures, and deriving visualization mappings by mathematical analysis. We note that the problems of symbolic integration and theorem proving were once solved heuristically (i.e., solved by applying expert "rules of thumb"), and

84

are now solved systematically. It may be possible to solve the problem of designing visualizations in a similarly systematic way.

References

CIE, 1978; CIE recommendations on uniform color spaces - color difference equations, psychometric color terms. CIE Publication No. 15(E-13.1) 1971/(TC-1.3) 1978, Supplement No. 2, 9-12, Bureau Central de la CIE, Paris.

Davey, B. A., and H. A. Priestly, 1990; Introduction to Lattices and Order. Cambridge University Press.

Dunford, N., and J. T. Schwartz, 1957; Linear Operators. Interscience Publishers.

Haber, R. B., B. Lucas and N. Collins, 1991; A data model for scientific visualization with provisions for regular and irregular grids. Proc. Visualization 91. IEEE. 298-305.

Hibbard, W. L., C. R. Dyer, and B. E. Paul, 1994; A lattice model for data display. Proc. IEEE Visualization '94, 310-317.

Hibbard, W. L., 1995; Visualizing ScientificComputations: A System Based on Lattice-Structured Data and Display Models. PhD Thesis. Univ. of Wisc. Comp. Sci. Dept. Tech. Report #1226. Also available as compressed postscript files from ftp://iris.ssec.wisc.edi/pub/lattice/.

Lee, J. P., and G. G. Grinstein, 1994; Database Issues for Data Visualization. Proc. of IEEE Visualization '93 Workshop. Springer-Verlag.

Lucas, B., G. D. Abrams, N. S. Collins, D. A. Epstein, D. L. Gresh, and K. P. McAuliffe, 1992; An architecture for a scientific visualization system. Proc. IEEE Visualization '92, 107-114.

Mackinlay, J., 1986; Automating the design of graphical presentations of relational information. ACM Transactions on Graphics, 5(2), 110-141.

Robertson, P.K., 1988; Visualizing color gamuts: a user interface for the effective use of perceptual color spaces in data analysis. IEEE Computer Graphics and Applications 8(5), 50-64.

Robertson, P.K., and J.F. O'Callaghan, 1988; The application of perceptual color spaces to the display of remotely sensed imagery. IEEE Transactions on Geoscience and Remote Sensing 26(1), 49-59.

Li, R., and P. K. Robertson, 1995; Towards perceptual control of Markov random field textures. In Perceptual Issues in Visualization, G. Grinstein and H. Levkowitz, ed. Springer-Verlag, 83-94.

Schmidt, D. A., 1986; Denotational Semantics. Wm.C.Brown.

Scott, D. S., 1971; The lattice of flow diagrams. In Symposium on Semantics of Algorithmic Languages, E. Engler. ed. Springer-Verlag, 311-366.

Scott, D. S., 1976; Data types as lattices. Siam J. Comput., 5(3), 522-587.

Treinish, L. A., 1991; SIGGRAPH '90 workshop report: data structure and access software for scientific visualization. Computer Graphics 25(2), 104-118.

Semantics and Mathematics of Scientific Data Sampling

David T. Kao[1], R. Daniel Bergeron[1], Michael J. Cullinane[2], Ted M. Sparr[1]

[1] Department of Computer Science***, University of New Hampshire, U.S.A.
[2] Department of Mathematics, University of New Hampshire, U.S.A.

Abstract. Data sampling is the first step in the process of scientific data analysis. This paper focuses on some mathematical aspects of data sampling. From this perspective, *data* are viewed as mathematical functions instead of just values. We show that *continuity* is the single most important quality of data (viewed as functions) which makes scientific data analysis and visualization meaningful and/or possible. By separating issues related to data functions from those related to the domains of data functions, we are able to define *continuous* data in two distinct contexts. This paper also provides a framework and the necessary mathematical language for the modeling and description of data.

1 Introduction

Interrelationships in scientific data are fundamentally more implicit and difficult to capture than relationships in most other database applications. In other areas, relationships are known (or assumed) in advance and expressed directly as metadata before data are acquired. In contrast, a scientific database system must manage data before its semantic structure is well understood [SBM93].

Many attempts have been made to define a comprehensive data model for representing complex scientific data [BCH$^+$94]. Most of them are of only limited success [FJP90]. Notable work includes the *lattice model* by Bergeron and Grinstein [BG89, KBS94], the *AVS model* by Gelberg et al. [GKPS90], the *fiber bundle model* by Haber, Lucas and Collins [HLC91], and the *computational grid model* by Speray and Kennon [SK91]. This paper studies some important issues of the first step in the process of scientific data analysis – *data sampling*. Better understanding in both the semantics and mathematics of the sampling process will bring insights to the modeling and analysis of the sampled data.

Since most of the *physical objects* under study are inherently infinite, to complete the analysis in a finite amount of time, we have to deal with finite data samples. In our context, a physical object to be sampled can come from a wide range of domains, such as a volume of the atmosphere, a magnetic energy field, a piece of land, a mass of soil, or a specific biological population. Data sampling results in a set of *data values*, called a *data set*. Depending on the nature of

---

*** This research was supported in part by the National Science Foundation under Grant IRI-9117153.

the physical phenomena to be observed and the sampling techniques employed to collect the data, a data set is an *approximation* of the physical object at a specific time or over a particular time period.

The goal of scientific data analysis is to derive *theories* or *models* which explain real world phenomena and behavior. Through the analysis process, we ultimately want to understand the real world (in other words, the physical object in question) better. To achieve this purpose, we have to know the relationship between a particular data set and the physical object it approximates. As we mentioned earlier, this relationship is determined by the following two factors:

1. the nature of the physical object, and
2. the sampling methodology.

This paper is focused on the first factor. We approach the issue by studying the semantics and mathematics of the data sampling process. From this perspective, we treat data as a mathematical function instead of a set of values. Thus, the data sampling process can be modeled mathematically and studied precisely.

Section §2 introduces the idea of data as functions and the two kinds of semantics associated with data sampling. It also establishes the relationship between the *continuous semantic* and *continuity*. Then the idea of continuity is generalized through the use of *distance functions* in Section §3. Section §4 further generalizes continuity to *topological spaces*. Section §5 separates the issues of data functions from data domains. This allows us to define *continuous* versus *discontinuous* data from the data function perspective, and *continuous* versus *discrete* data from the data domain perspective. Section §6 contains concluding remarks and directions for future research.

Due to space constraints, all propositions in the paper are given without proofs. Interested readers can either derive the proofs on their own or find the proofs in [KBCS95].

2 Data as Functions

Mathematically, *data* can be considered as a function (or mapping) from a certain *domain space* to a *value space* (i.e., the space of data values). The domain space is the mathematical representation of the real world where the physical object of interest exists. It is a set of possible points where the phenomena or behavior to be observed takes place. Each element in the domain space is called a *data point*. The mathematical representation of a data point can have any form. Most likely it consists of the spatial and/or temporal index of the physical object.

In the broadest sense, the value space is just a set of finite-length vectors. Given such a vector $(a_1, a_2, \ldots, a_n)$, the a_i's are called *attributes*. Based on different subsets of those attributes, the value space can have many different orders – or no order at all. In traditional data analysis terminology, *categorical data* is used to represent a value space which is not ordered. Note that even though the value space is usually an infinite set, for all computational purposes, only finitely many different data values can be represented and distinguished.

2.1 Semantics of Data Sampling

The *sampling of data* is the process of observing the data values at a finite subset of points over the domain space. Those points – where data values are observed – are called *sample points*. Two kinds of semantics are possible for this kind of sampling:

discontinuous semantic: The data value at a sample point is considered valid only at that specific point.

continuous semantic: The data value at a sample point is considered to be a valid approximation for some neighborhood of the point.

Note that we use the term "neighborhood" loosely to represent "nearby" data points. The precise definition of *neighborhood* is given later.

Which of the two semantics should be applied is determined by the nature of the data at hand but not the sampling methodology employed. Clearly, data interpreted with the discontinuous semantic precludes common data analysis practices such as *interpolation* or *resampling*. In the next subsection, we study a mathematical characteristic of data which validates the continuous semantic.

2.2 Continuous Semantic and Continuity

As soon as we treat data as a mathematical function, data can be studied and classified based upon the mathematical properties it possesses. It is not hard to see that in order to validate the continuous sampling semantic, the data (considered as a function) has to be *continuous*.

Let $\mathbb{R}$ be the set of real numbers and let $f : A \to \mathbb{R}$, where $A \subseteq \mathbb{R}$. Recall what it means for f to be *continuous* at a point $p \in A$.

Definition 1. [CONTINUITY] Let $f : A \to \mathbb{R}$, $A \subseteq \mathbb{R}$, and $p \in A$. f is *continuous* at p provided that $lim_{x \to p} f(x)$ exists and $lim_{x \to p} = f(p)$.

Intuitively, saying that $lim_{x \to p} f(x) = f(p)$ means that by choosing the members of the domain of f "sufficiently close" to p, the corresponding functional values can be made to stay within any pre-assigned distance $\varepsilon > 0$ of $f(p)$. Thus, we may state the following proposition.

Proposition 2. [CONTINUITY] *Let $f : A \to \mathbb{R}$, $A \subseteq \mathbb{R}$, and $p \in A$. The following are equivalent:*

1. *f is continuous at p.*
2. *$\forall \varepsilon > 0, \exists \delta > 0$ such that $\forall q \in A, q \in (p-\delta, p+\delta) \implies f(q) \in (f(p)-\varepsilon, f(p)+\varepsilon)$.*

The positive real number δ which corresponds to the given ε precisely describes what we mean by "sufficiently close" to p. If our function f represents data, Proposition 2 promotes continuity as a mathematical characteristic of the data which validates the continuous sampling semantic. The interval $(f(p)-\varepsilon, f(p)+\varepsilon)$

89

describes exactly which numbers (data values) $f(p)$ can "validly approximate", while the interval $(p - \delta, p + \delta)$ describes exactly what data points are to be considered "near" p (in the sense that the data values at these points can be "validly approximated" by $f(p)$).

2.3 Data Sampling and Visualization

Let f be a data function (i.e., physical phenomena) from domain space D to value space V. The results of data sampling on f is a data set $f' \subseteq D' \times V'$, where $D' \subseteq D$ and $V' \subseteq V$. Let g be the transformation (i.e., continuous function) which maps the values in value space V to display information in the ideal display space W, which has infinite resolution and range. Let g' be the transformation from V' to W', where W' is a finite practical display space. g' is an approximation of g, and under some circumstances, $g' = g|_{V'}$, where $g|_{V'}$ represents the function g restricted to the domain V'.

Ideally, scientific data visualization/analysis is the process of deriving a theory or model of f from $g \cdot f$. However, since we have f' instead of f, actual scientific visualization/analysis is the process of deriving a theory or model of f from $g' \cdot f'$. The continuity of f implies the continuity of $g \cdot f$. In this case, $g' \cdot f'$ is a valid approximation of $g \cdot f$. Figure 1 illustrates the relationship between data sampling and the visualization process.

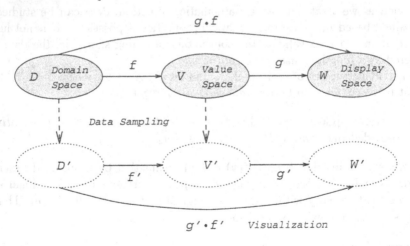

Figure 1

3 Distance Functions and Continuity

In describing what we mean by a continuous function $f : A \to \mathbb{R}$, where $A \subseteq \mathbb{R}$, we have made implicit use of the usual distance between real numbers on the real line. It seems reasonable that an appropriate generalization of continuous functions should be obtainable when there exist some notions of distances among the points in the domains and ranges of the functions we wish to consider.

Definition 3. A *distance function* for a nonempty set X is a function $d : X \times X \to [0, \infty)$ such that

1. $\forall p \in X, d(p, p) = 0$;
2. $\forall p, q, r \in X, d(p, q) \leq d(p, r) + d(r, q)$.

The notation $d(p, q)$ is read as *the distance from p to q*.

The distance functions defined in Definition 3 are usually known in mathematics as *quasimetrics*. Note that (1) requires that the distance from a point to itself be 0, while (2) effectively tells us that when we wish to "move" from one point p to another point q, there is no advantage (from the point of view of minimizing distance) in "visiting" some other point of X along the way. Condition (2) is commonly known as the *triangle inequality*.

Example 1. Let $d_n : \mathbb{R}^n \times \mathbb{R}^n \to [0, \infty), n \in \mathbf{N}$, be defined by

$$d_n((p_1, \ldots, p_n), (q_1, \ldots, q_n)) = \sqrt{\sum_{i=1}^n (p_i - q_i)^2} \ .$$

This distance function is called the *usual distance function* for $\mathbb{R}^n$. □

Example 2. Let X be a nonempty set and define $d : X \times X \to [0, \infty)$ by

$$d(p, q) = \begin{cases} 0, \text{ if } p = q; \\ 1, \text{ otherwise.} \end{cases}$$

Clearly, d is a distance function for X. □

Example 3. Let $X = \{p, q\}$ and define $d : X \times X \to [0, \infty)$ by

$$d(p, p) = d(q, q) = d(q, p) = 0 \ ,$$
$$d(p, q) = 1 \ .$$

Clearly, d is a distance function for X. □

Example 3 calls to our attention that:

1. Even when $p \neq q$, it may be true that $d(p, q) = 0$.
2. For distinct p, q, it is possible that $d(p, q) \neq d(q, p)$.

Distance functions which are subject to more or fewer axioms are commonly utilized and studied in various fields of mathematics. Observe that if d is the usual distance function for $\mathbb{R}$, we can re-express Proposition 2 as follows:

f is continuous at p if and only if for each $\varepsilon > 0$ there exists $\delta > 0$ such that $\forall q \in A, d(p, q) < \delta \Longrightarrow d(f(p), f(q)) < \varepsilon$.

Our next definition simply generalizes the notion of continuity to a function whose domain and range both have distance functions defined on them.

Definition 4. [CONTINUITY] Let X, Y be nonempty sets and let d_X, d_Y be distance functions for X and Y, respectively. A function $f : X \to Y$ is *continuous* at a point $p \in X$ if for each $\varepsilon > 0$ there exists $\delta > 0$ such that $\forall q \in X, d_X(p, q) < \delta \implies d_Y(f(p), f(q)) < \varepsilon$.

We want to keep in mind how this definition can be interpreted in light of the continuous semantic regarding the sampling of data. If our data is represented by a function $f : X \to Y$, where X, Y have distance functions d_X, d_Y defined on them, then continuity of f at a point $p \in X$ is a mathematically precise way of guaranteeing that $f(p)$, the data value at the sampled point p, is a valid approximation of the data values at unsampled points which are sufficiently close to p.

Definition 5. Let d be a distance function for a set X. Given $p \in X$ and $\varepsilon > 0$ we define

$$S_d(p, \varepsilon) = \{q \in X | d(p, q) < \varepsilon\}$$

as the *sphere centered at p of radius ε*.

Example 4. If d_1 is the usual distance function for $\mathbb{R}$, then $S_{d_1}(p, \varepsilon)$, where $p \in \mathbb{R}$ and $\varepsilon > 0$, is the open interval $(p - \varepsilon, p + \varepsilon)$ consisting of all real numbers strictly between $p - \varepsilon$ and $p + \varepsilon$.

If d_2 is the usual distance function for $\mathbb{R}^2$, then $S_{d_2}(p, \varepsilon)$, where $p \in \mathbb{R}^2$ and $\varepsilon > 0$, consists of all points in the interior of the circle centered at p of radius ε.

If d_3 is the usual distance function for $\mathbb{R}^3$, then $S_{d_3}(p, \varepsilon)$, where $p \in \mathbb{R}^3$ and $\varepsilon > 0$, consists of all points in the interior of the sphere (here we are using the word sphere in the context of three-dimensional Euclidean geometry) centered at p of radius ε. □

Example 5. Let X and d be as defined in Example 2. Then for each $p \in X$,

$$S_d(p, \varepsilon) = \begin{cases} \{p\}, \text{ if } 0 < \varepsilon \leq 1; \\ X, \quad \text{if } \varepsilon > 1. \end{cases}$$

□

Example 6. Let X and d be as defined in Example 3. We have

$$S_d(p, \varepsilon) = \begin{cases} \{p\}, \quad \text{if } 0 < \varepsilon \leq 1; \\ \{p, q\}, \text{if } \varepsilon > 1. \end{cases}$$

$$S_d(q, \varepsilon) = \{p, q\} \text{ for every } \varepsilon > 0.$$

□

It is possible to utilize the notion of sphere to re-express the definition of continuity given in Definition 4.

Proposition 6. [CONTINUITY] *Let X, Y be nonempty sets, and d_X, d_Y be distance functions for X and Y, respectively. For $f : X \to Y$ and $p \in X$, the following are equivalent:*

1. f is continuous at p.

2. $\forall \varepsilon > 0, \exists \delta > 0$ such that $f[S_{d_X}(p, \delta)] \subseteq S_{d_Y}(f(p), \varepsilon)$.

Again, we wish to emphasize that the sphere centered at p of radius $\varepsilon > 0$ consists of exactly those points which are less than ε units away from p. Thus, intuitively, a sphere consists of certain points which are close to (as measured by the sphere's radius) the sphere's center. It seems intuitively reasonable to regard any sphere centered at a point p as a "neighborhood" of the point p. In some contexts, it is desirable to allow supersets of neighborhoods to be neighborhoods. We therefore state the following definition.

Definition 7. Let d be a distance function for the set X and $p \in X$. A *neighborhood* (abbreviated *nbhd*) of p is any superset of a sphere centered at p. In particular, note that any sphere centered at p will be a nbhd of p.

It is now possible to characterize continuity of a function whose domain and range both have distance functions defined on them in terms of the notion of nbhd of a point.

Proposition 8. [CONTINUITY] *Let* X, Y *be nonempty sets and* d_X, d_Y *be distance functions for* X *and* Y, *respectively. For* $f : X \to Y$ *and* $p \in X$, *the following are equivalent:*

1. *f is continuous at p.*
2. *For each nbhd N of $f(p)$, there exists a nbhd M of p such that $f[M] \subseteq N$.*

What we have just seen is that the concept of *continuity* of a function $f : X \to Y$ can be defined in any setting where suitable notions of neighborhoods of points exist on the sets X and Y. In the next section of this paper we discuss such settings.

4 Topology and Continuity

During the early part of this century, mathematicians developed the notions of *topology* and *topological space* in order to provide a general setting for the study of continuous functions. We believe that this setting can provide an effective basis for understanding and modeling scientific data.

Definition 9. Let X be a nonempty set. A *topology* on X is a collection $\mathcal{T}$ of subsets of X which satisfies the following axioms:

1. $\emptyset, X \in \mathcal{T}$.
2. If $A_i \in \mathcal{T}, \forall i \in I$, then $\bigcup_{i \in I} A_i \in \mathcal{T}$ (i.e., $\mathcal{T}$ is closed under arbitrary unions).
3. If $A_1, \ldots, A_n \in \mathcal{T}$ for some positive integer n, then $\bigcap_{i=1}^{n} A_i \in \mathcal{T}$ (i.e., $\mathcal{T}$ is closed under finite intersections).

When X is a set and $\mathcal{T}$ is a topology on X, the ordered pair $(X, \mathcal{T})$ is then called a *topological space*. The members of the topology $\mathcal{T}$ are called *open sets*.

Definition 10. Let $(X, \mathcal{T})$ be a topological space. A *base* of $\mathcal{T}$ is a subset $\mathcal{B}$ of $\mathcal{T}$ such that every open set is a union of elements of $\mathcal{B}$. Those open sets in $\mathcal{B}$ are called *basic opens*. Let $\mathcal{P}(X)$ denote the power set of X. If $\mathcal{A} \subseteq \mathcal{P}(X)$ s.t. $\bigcup \mathcal{A} = X$ (i.e., $\mathcal{A}$ is a *cover* of X) and $\mathcal{T}$ is the *least topology* (ordered by set-inclusion) containing $\mathcal{A}$, we say that $\mathcal{A}$ is a *subbase* of $\mathcal{T}$.

Every base of a topology $\mathcal{T}$ is also a subbase of $\mathcal{T}$. $\mathcal{A}$ is a subbase of $\mathcal{T}$ iff the collection of finite intersections of elements of $\mathcal{A}$ is a base of $\mathcal{T}$.

Example 7. Let d be a distance function for the set X. We can define a topology $\mathcal{T}_d$ on X using the distance function d. A set $A \subseteq X$ is open if, for each $p \in A$, there exists a sphere $S_d(p, \varepsilon), \varepsilon > 0$, which is a subset of A. That is

$$\mathcal{T}_d = \{A \subseteq X | \forall p \in A, \exists \varepsilon > 0 \text{ such that } S_d(p, \varepsilon) \subseteq A\}$$

It is easily verified that $\mathcal{T}_d$ is a topology on X. In fact, if d is the usual distance function for $\mathbb{R}^n$, then $\mathcal{T}_d$ is called the *usual topology* on $\mathbb{R}^n$. □

Example 8. Let X and d be as in Example 3. Every subset of X is open except $\{q\}$, since there is no sphere centered at q which does not also include p as a member. Hence, in this case, $\mathcal{T}_d = \{\emptyset, \{p, q\}, \{p\}\}$. □

Example 9. For any nonempty set X, the power set of X, denoted $\mathcal{P}(X)$, is a topology on X. This topology is usually called the *discrete topology* on X. □

An interesting question to raise at this point is the following:

> Given a topology $\mathcal{T}$ on a set X, is there a distance function d for X such that $\mathcal{T} = \mathcal{T}_d$?

For example, for the distance function d of Example 2, $\mathcal{T}_d$ is the discrete topology on X. However, in general, the answer to the above question is no. On the other hand, Kopperman shows that all topologies on any given set can be obtained through the use of "suitably generalized" distance functions [Kop88]. These distance functions are allowed to take their values in a more general structure which he calls a *value semigroup* (a value semigroup behaves somewhat like $[0, \infty)$ in an algebraic and order-theoretic way).

If $\mathcal{T}$ is a topology on a set X and $p \in X$, we can use the topology to introduce neighborhoods of p in the following way.

Definition 11. Let $(X, \mathcal{T})$ be a topological space and $p \in X$. A *neighborhood* (abbreviated *nbhd*) of p is any superset of an open set containing p (i.e., $N \subseteq X$ is a nbhd of p if $\exists G \in \mathcal{T}$ such that $p \in G \subseteq N$). Thus, an open set is a nbhd of each of its points.

When one first encounters the notions of topology and open set, the concepts can often appear intimidating and abstract. However, the notion of nbhd of a point is much more intuitive and visually appealing. The next proposition is helpful in gaining a better understanding of what open sets (i.e., the members of a topology) really are.

Proposition 12. *Let $(X, \mathcal{T})$ be a topological space and $A \subseteq X$. The following are equivalent:*

1. *$A \in \mathcal{T}$ (i.e., A is an open set).*
2. *A contains a nbhd of each of its points.*

Note the parallel between "nbhd of p" in the context of a topological space and "nbhd of p" in the context of a set equipped with a distance function. The notion of sphere was used in defining what is meant by a nbhd in the latter context; since spheres may not be available in the broader context of topological spaces, it is not possible to use them to define the notion of nbhd in an arbitrary topological space. The replacement of "sphere" by open set works nicely because, as the following proposition states, the two notions of nbhd we have introduced agree in the case that the topological space under consideration arises from a distance function.

Proposition 13. *Let d be a distance function for X, $p \in X$, and $N \subseteq X$. The following are equivalent:*

1. *N is a nbhd of p (in the context of the set X equipped with the distance function d).*
2. *N is a nbhd of p (in the context of the topological space $(X, \mathcal{T}_d)$).*

We are now ready to define what we mean by continuity of a function between topological spaces. Proposition 13 and Proposition 8 make it clear that this notion of continuity of a function between topological spaces, when the topological spaces are generated from distance functions, is equivalent to the notion of continuity studied in Section 3.

Definition 14. [CONTINUITY] Let $(X, \mathcal{T}_X)$, $(Y, \mathcal{T}_Y)$ be topological spaces, $f : X \to Y$, and $p \in X$. f is *continuous* at p if for each nbhd N of $f(p)$ there exists a nbhd M of p such that $f[M] \subseteq N$.

We now want to introduce a topological concept which makes precise the idea of a point $p \in X$ being "close to" a set $A \subseteq X$, assuming X has some topology $\mathcal{T}$ defined on it.

Definition 15. Let $(X, \mathcal{T})$ be a topological space, $p \in X$, and $A \subseteq X$. p is a *limit point* of A provided that for each nbhd N of p, $(N - \{p\}) \cap A \neq \emptyset$. The collection of all limit points of A is denoted by $\mathrm{Lim}_{\mathcal{T}}(A)$.

Thus, p is a limit point of A if every nbhd of p contains a point of A other than p. Intuitively, we can view limit points of a set $A \subseteq X$ as those points which, while not necessarily members of A, are "close to" the set A (in a sense described more precisely by the topology $\mathcal{T}$ imposed on X).

Example 10. Let $\mathcal{T}$ be the usual topology for $\mathbb{R}$ and let $A = (0, 1)$ and $B = (0, 1) \cup \{2\}$. Then $\mathrm{Lim}_{\mathcal{T}}(A) = [0, 1]$ and $\mathrm{Lim}_{\mathcal{T}}(B) = [0, 1]$. Note that $(1.5, 2.5)$ is a nbhd of 2 which does not contain a point of B other than 2, so $2 \notin \mathrm{Lim}_{\mathcal{T}}(B)$.

□

Of course, in an intuitive sense, if a point is a member of a set, it seems reasonable that it should be considered "close to" the set. The previous example, though, shows that not all members of a set are necessarily limit points of the set. Hence, we introduce one final topological concept.

Definition 16. Let $(X, \mathcal{T})$ be a topological space and let $A \subseteq X$. The *closure* of A, denoted $\mathrm{Cl}_{\mathcal{T}}(A)$, is the set $A \cup \mathrm{Lim}_{\mathcal{T}}(A)$.

Intuitively, the closure of a set represents all of the points which the topology recognizes as being "close to" the set. In Example 10, $\mathrm{Cl}_{\mathcal{T}}(A) = [0, 1]$ and $\mathrm{Cl}_{\mathcal{T}}(B) = [0, 1] \cup \{2\}$.

We are now ready to characterize continuity of functions between topological spaces in a way that is mathematically precise, extremely general, and intuitively appealing (when the closure of a set is thought of as the collection of points "close to" the set).

Proposition 17. [CONTINUITY] *Let* $(X, \mathcal{T}_X), (Y, \mathcal{T}_Y)$ *be topological spaces,* $f : X \to Y$, *and* $p \in X$. *The following are equivalent:*

1. f *is continuous at* p.
2. $\forall A \subseteq X$, *if* $p \in \mathrm{Cl}_{\mathcal{T}_X}(A)$, *then* $f(p) \in \mathrm{Cl}_{\mathcal{T}_Y}(f[A])$.

Readers interested in general topology are encouraged to read [Mun75, Cai94]. For those who want to study topology from a computer science perspective, [Smy92] provides a good starting point.

5 Data Functions and Domain Spaces

In the previous section, we extended the definition of continuous function from the context of distance functions to the context of topological spaces. Treating data as functions, we can classify data into two categories based on their mathematical characteristics.

Definition 18. Data is *continuous* if the function which represents it is continuous; otherwise, it is *discontinuous*.

Proposition 19. *Let* $(X, \mathcal{T}_X), (Y, \mathcal{T}_Y)$ *be topological spaces and* $f : X \to Y$. f *is continuous if* $\mathcal{T}_X$ *is the discrete topology.*

This means as long as $\mathcal{T}_X$ is the discrete topology, an arbitrary function $f : X \to Y$ is guaranteed to be continuous. This kind of data is *vacuously continuous*. This situation corresponds exactly to the discontinuous semantic, as we are not able to use the data values at sampled points to approximate the data values at unsampled points. It is easy to see that the continuous semantic can only be applied to continuous data if the data is not vacuously continuous.

Similar to the way we categorize data according to the characteristics of the functions which represent them (in this case, continuity), we can also categorize domain spaces of data based on the mathematical structures (either order or topology) imposed on them.

Definition 20. Let $(P, \leq)$ be a linearly ordered set (i.e., totally ordered set). $(P, \leq)$ is *dense*, if $\forall p, q \in P, p \leq q$ and $p \neq q \implies \exists r \in P, r \neq p$ and $r \neq q$ such that $p \leq r \leq q$.

Definition 21. A domain space is *continuous* if and only if it is dense; otherwise, it is *discrete*.

Note that a domain space has to be linearly ordered to be dense. Clearly, a discrete domain space may be different from a domain space with the discrete topology. In fact, a discrete domain space might not have any order at all.

Now it becomes clear that data can be classified either by the function which represents it (continuous or discontinuous) or the domain of that function (continuous or discrete). As the following examples demonstrate, Definition 21 matches our original intuition about the structure of data, while Definition 18 matches the semantics of data sampling.

Example 11. Let us take all the listed residential phone numbers in the U.S.A. as the domain space, $\mathcal{D}$. Treating each phone number as a 10-digit integer, there is a natural total order on $\mathcal{D}$. Then, what does it mean when we say one phone number is greater or less than another? Clearly, the natural order which comes with the domain space is not an informative one. Since $\mathcal{D}$ is finite (there are at most 10^{10} possible 10-digit listed phone numbers), no matter what kind of order we impose on $\mathcal{D}$, it is not dense. Thus, the domain space is discrete.

Even though the natural order on $\mathcal{D}$ is meaningless, there exists some mathematical structure on $\mathcal{D}$ based upon the multilevel switching hierarchy of the telephone system. Each telephone has wires which go directly to the telephone company's nearest *end office*. In the United States there are more than 20,000 end offices. The concatenation of the 3-digit area code and the first three digits of the telephone number uniquely specify an end office. Then all the end offices sharing the same area code are connected to one or several *regional offices*.

The mathematical structure on $\mathcal{D}$ can be naturally modeled by a topology $\mathcal{T}_{\mathcal{D}}$ which has one of its *subbases* consisting of (1) sets of phone numbers sharing the same end office, and (2) sets of phone numbers sharing the same area code[†]. A meaningful metric can be easily derived from $\mathcal{D}$.

Given $n_1, n_2 \in \mathcal{D}$, let us define a distance function d on $\mathcal{D}$ as follows:

$$d(n_1, n_2) = \begin{cases} 0, \text{ if } n_1, n_2 \text{ share the same end office;} \\ 1, \text{ if } n_1, n_2 \text{ share the same area code but not the same end office;} \\ 2, \text{ otherwise.} \end{cases}$$

Clearly $\mathcal{T}_d = \mathcal{T}_{\mathcal{D}}$ (see Example 7). Assuming there is exactly one person associated with each listed phone number, we can define the following three kinds of data:

[†] In fact, $\mathcal{T}_{\mathcal{D}}$ has a *base* consisting of only the sets of phone numbers sharing the same end office.

1. $f_1 : \mathcal{D} \to \mathbf{R} \times \mathbf{R}$

   Given $n \in \mathcal{D}$, then $f_1(n) = (x, y)$, where x and y are the longitude and latitude of the corresponding resident's home. Given two positions $p = (x_p, y_p)$ and $q = (x_q, y_q)$, let $d_G(p, q)$ be the geographical (i.e., physical) distance between p and q.

2. $f_2 : \mathcal{D} \to \mathbf{R}$

   Given $n \in \mathcal{D}$, then $f_2(n) = r$, where r is the blood lead level (in PPM) of the person having telephone number n.

3. $f_3 : \mathcal{D} \to \mathbf{N}$

   Given $n \in \mathcal{D}$, then $f_3(n) = i$, where i is the person's current age.

Based on d defined on $\mathcal{D}$ (or $\mathcal{T}_\mathcal{D}$, from the topological point of view), f_1 seems to be continuous, since phone numbers which are close in $\mathcal{D}$ stay close geographically. However, a quick check with Proposition 8 shows that f_1 is actually discontinuous. For instance, given a sufficiently small nbhd N of $f_1(603\text{-}659\text{-}2737)$, N might not properly contain $f_1[\mathcal{D}_{603\text{-}659\text{-}2737}]$, where $\mathcal{D}_{603\text{-}659\text{-}2737}$ represents the set of all telephone numbers having the end office of 603-659-2737. Note that $\mathcal{D}_{603\text{-}659\text{-}2737}$ is the smallest nbhd which contains 603-659-2737 in $\mathcal{D}$. In fact, we can make N so small that only the image of 603-659-2737 (and probably other phone numbers in the same household) is inside N.

Nonetheless, the domain metric d is valid (even though f_1 is discontinuous), because the location of a particular phone number can be approximated by locations of other phone numbers sharing the same end office. The continuity of the function f_1 can be achieved by replacing d_G with a new distance function d_V defined by

$$d_V(p, q) \equiv \max(d_G(p, q) - \mu, 0)$$

where μ is the maximum distance between any two telephone numbers sharing the same end office. Now for an arbitrary phone number n, every nbhd of $f_1(n)$ will contain $f_1[\mathcal{D}_n]$, since the geographical distance between two arbitrary phone numbers in $\mathcal{D}_n$ would be less than or equal to μ. Thus, f_1 is indeed continuous with d_V defined on its range.

Clearly, f_2 is also discontinuous, although the continuous semantic seems to apply. Assuming most people drink tap water instead of bottled water, one person's blood lead level could be a good estimate of those of other people whose phone numbers are close in $\mathcal{D}$. On the other hand, f_3 is not only discontinuous, but also can only be interpreted using the discontinuous semantic. $\square$

Example 11 demonstrates the important notion that continuity of a data function is a sufficient but not necessary condition for the application of the continuous semantic.

Example 12. [Social Security Numbers] Let us take all the assigned social security numbers as the domain space, $\mathfrak{S}$. Since $\mathfrak{S}$ is finite (there are at most 10^9 distinct SS#), $\mathfrak{S}$ is discrete. Unlike the telephone numbers example, there is no natural distance function which can be defined on $\mathfrak{S}$. Without loss of generality, a trivial distance function d can be given as follows:

$$d(s_1, s_2) = \begin{cases} 0, \text{ if } s_1 = s_2; \\ 1, \text{ otherwise.} \end{cases}$$

As in Example 7, a topology $\mathcal{T}_d$ can be defined on $\mathfrak{S}$ based upon d. Clearly, $\mathcal{T}_d$ is the discrete topology, and any data function defined on $(\mathfrak{S}, \mathcal{T}_d)$ is vacuously continuous – not a very interesting data domain for scientific data analysis. Only the discontinuous semantic can be applied here. □

Example 13. [Time Series Data] Suppose we have a ground-based device to measure the Gamma ray intensity from the sun, and the device gives measurements at one second intervals. However, due to sudden cloud movements which might block the sunlight, there might be short time periods when we get inaccurately low measurements. Since the time-measurement data function is continuous by nature, for relatively short periods of time, the data can be recovered from "nearby" accurate measurements. □

From the above examples, we see the functional independence between a data function and its domain space. However, it is also obvious that the mathematical structure on the domain space has implicit influence on the data functions depending on it.

6 Conclusion and Future Research

The main point we are trying to promote is that, once data has been represented as a function $f : D \to V$, meaningful analysis or interpolation of the data can be done only when one considers the "additional mathematical structure" which is naturally imposed on the sets D and V.

In general, the natural mathematical structure of the value space V is obvious. For the domain space D, the mathematical structure may be imposed implicitly rather than explicitly, so it can often be challenging to determine exactly what we have "in front of us", especially when the additional structure is a topology, since many researchers outside mathematics are unfamiliar with the notions of topology and topological space. There are situations in which the mathematical structure on D is unknown, and thus it is not possible to determine whether f is continuous or not. Clearly, a different approach has to be employed.

Let us assume that f is indeed continuous, and the visualization process illustrated in Figure 1 can thus be applied. Under this assumption, $g' \cdot f'$ is a valid approximation of $g \cdot f$. Suppose there is a known function $h : D \to V$ with known mathematical structure on D. If there is similarity between the visualization of $g' \cdot f'$ and $g' \cdot h'$, chances are that f and h have the same mathematical structure imposed on D (see Figure 2). By comparing $g' \cdot f'$ with $g' \cdot h', h \in \mathcal{H}$, where $\mathcal{H}$ is a set of well known functions from D to V, we might be able to find the implicit mathematical structure imposed on D and thus understand f better. In fact, the procedure just described is the objective of *exploratory data analysis* which is to discover, quantify and validate the interrelationship among data [Tuk77].

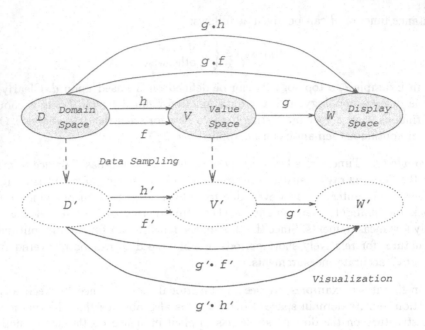

Figure 2

The approach taken in this paper allows us to separate the issues of domain spaces from those of data functions. It provides a coherent framework to deal with both continuous and discrete data sets. We have at our disposal an array of mathematical tools to model precisely the relationship among points in data domain spaces. This facilitates the data analysis process by putting the focus on the data functions themselves.

When a data set has several mathematical structures naturally associated with it (a partial order and a topology, for instance), it is very important to consider the interplay which exists among these structures. Understanding the mathematical structures of the domain spaces and data viewed as functions may provide a solid foundation for formalizing the data analysis paradigm and bringing insights into data visualization and data representation.

In the process of formulating the ideas presented in this paper, we also realize that under many circumstances, useful and mathematically precise continuous data functions do not exist. In order to deal with those situations, it seems desirable to have a more comprehensive (relaxed in semantics but mathematically precise) definition for continuous function.

ACKNOWLEDGMENT

Thanks are due to Samuel D. Shore; his insights and research in the field of general topology have had a major influence in shaping the authors' understanding of and approach to the mathematical worlds of topology and distance.

References

[BCH+94] R. D. Bergeron, W. Cody, W. Hibbard, D. T. Kao, K. D. Miceli, L. A. Treinish, and S. Walther. Database Issues for Data Visualization: Developing a Data Model. In J. P. Lee and G. G. Grinstein, editors, *Database Issues for Data Visualization*, number 871 in Lecture Notes in Computer Science, pages 3–15. Springer-Verlag, 1994.

[BG89] R. D. Bergeron and G. G. Grinstein. A Reference Model for the Visualization of Multi-dimensional Data. In *Proceedings of Eurographics '89*, Hamburg, F. R. G., September 1989. North Holland Publishing Company.

[Cai94] G. L. Cain. *Introduction to General Topology*. Addison-Wesley Publishing Company, Reading, Massachusetts, 1994.

[FJP90] J. C. French, A. K. Jones, and J. L. Pfaltz. A Summary of the NSF Scientific Database Workshop. In *Proceedings of the 5th International Conference on Statistical and Scientific Database Management*, Charlotte, North Carolina, April 1990.

[GKPS90] L. Gelberg, D. Kamins, D. Parker, and J. Sacks. Visualization Techniques for Structured and Unstructured Scientific Data. In *Proceedings of ACM SIGGRAPH '90*, 1990.

[HLC91] R. B. Haber, B. Lucas, and N. Collins. A Data Model for Scientific Visualization with Provisions for Regular and Irregular Grids. In *Proceedings of IEEE Visualization '91*, San Diego, California, October 1991.

[KBCS95] D. T. Kao, R. D. Bergeron, M. J. Cullinane, and T. M. Sparr. Semantics and Mathematics of Scientific Data Sampling. Technical Report 95-14, Department of Computer Science, University of New Hampshire, October 1995.

[KBS94] D. T. Kao, R. D. Bergeron, and T. M. Sparr. An Extended Schema Model for Scientific Data. In J. P. Lee and G. G. Grinstein, editors, *Database Issues for Data Visualization*, number 871 in Lecture Notes in Computer Science, pages 69–82. Springer-Verlag, 1994.

[Kop88] R. Kopperman. All Topologies Come from Generalized Metrics. *American Mathematical Monthly*, 95(2):89–97, February 1988.

[Mun75] J. Munkres. *Topology: A First Course*. Prentice-Hall, Inc., Englewood Cliffs, New Jersey, 1975.

[SBM93] T. M. Sparr, R. D. Bergeron, and L. D. Meeker. A Visualization-Based Model for a Scientific Database System. In *Focus on Scientific Visualization*. Springer-Verlag, 1993.

[SK91] D. Speray and S. Kennon. Volume Probes: Interactive Data Exploration on Arbitrary Grids. *Computer Graphics*, 24(5), November 1991.

[Smy92] M. B. Smyth. Topology. In S. Abramsky, D. M. Gabbay, and T. S. E. Maibaum, editors, *Handbook of Logic in Computer Science, Volume 1, Background: Mathematical Structures*, Oxford Science Publication. Clarendon Press, Oxford, England, 1992.

[Tuk77] J. D. Tukey. *Exploratory Data Analysis*. Addison-Wesley Publishing Company, Reading, Massachusetts, 1977.

Enhancing the Visual Clustering of Query-Dependent Database Visualization Techniques Using Screen-Filling Curves

Daniel A. Keim

Institute for Computer Science, University of Munich
Leopoldstr. 11B, D-80802 Munich, Germany
keim@informatik.uni-muenchen.de

Abstract. An important goal of visualization technology is to support the exploration and analysis of very large databases. Visualization techniques may help in database exploration by providing a comprehensive overview of the database. Pixel-oriented visualization techniques have been developed to visualize as many data items as possible on the display at one point of time. The basic idea of pixel-oriented techniques is to map each data value to a colored pixel and present the data values belonging to different dimensions (attributes) in separate subwindows. In case of the query-dependent techniques, the pixels are arranged and colored according to the relevance for the query, providing a visual impression of the query result and of its relevance with respect to the query. One problem of the current query-dependent pixel-oriented visualization techniques is that their local clustering properties are insufficient. In this paper, we therefore generalize the original pixel-oriented techniques and propose new variants which retain the overall arrangement but enhance the clustering properties by using screen-filling curves locally. Different screen-filling curves (Snake, Peano-Hilbert, Morton) with different sizes (2, 4, 8, 16) may be used. We evaluate the possible variants and compare the resulting visualizations. The visualizations show that screen-filling curves clearly enhance the visual clustering of query-dependent pixel-oriented visualization techniques, but it also becomes clear that there is no significant difference between the different screen-filling curves.

Keywords: Visualizing Large Data Sets, Visualizing Multidimensional Multivariate Data, Database Exploration, Visual Query Systems

1   Introduction

An important goal of visualization technology is to support the exploration and analysis of very large amounts of data which are usually stored in databases. Since the number and size of the databases are growing rapidly, there is a need for novel visualization techniques which allow a visualization of larger amounts of data.

Most of today's databases store typical transaction-generated multi-attribute data which does not have any inherent two- or three-dimensional semantics and therefore does not lend itself to some two- or three-dimensional visualization. In general, databases can be seen as multidimensional data sets with the attributes of the database corresponding to the dimensions of the multidimensional data set. There are a variety of well-known techniques for visualizing arbitrary multidimensional data sets: scatterplot matrices and coplots [And 72, Cle 93], geometric projection techniques (e.g., [Hub 85, ID 90]), iconic display techniques (e.g., [Che 73, SGB 91]), pixel-oriented techniques (e.g., [Kei 94, KKS 93, KKA 95]), hierarchical techniques (e.g., [BF 90, Shn 92]), dynamic techniques (e.g., [BMMS 91, AWS 92, Eic 94, ADLP 95]), and combinations hereof (e.g., [Asi 85, AS 94]). Most techniques, however, are only suitable for rather small data sets consisting of at most a few thousand data items. Only dynamic and pixel-oriented techniques are able to handle larger data sets with hundreds of thousands of data items. Dynamic techniques reveal interesting properties of the data by generating series of visualizations. In general, however, only a limited portion of the data can be visualized at one point of time. In contrast, pixel-oriented techniques are able to visualize very large amounts of data at a certain point of time. On current displays, they allow a visualization of up-to 1,000,000 data values.

2 Pixel-oriented Visualization Techniques

The basic idea of pixel-oriented techniques is to map each data value to a colored pixel and present the data values belonging to different dimensions (attributes) in separate subwindows. Pixel-oriented visualization techniques can be divided into query-independent techniques which directly visualize the data (or a certain portion of it) and query-dependent techniques which visualize the data in the context of a specific query. Examples for the class of query-independent techniques are the screen-filling curve and recursive pattern techniques. The screen-filling curve techniques are based on the well-known Morton and Peano-Hilbert curve algorithms [Pea 90, Hil 91, Mor 66], and the

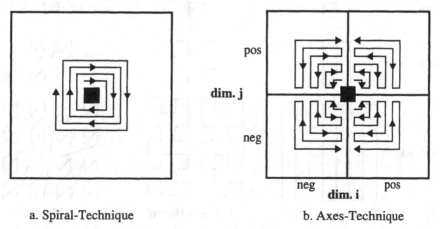

a. Spiral-Technique   b. Axes-Technique

Figure 1: Primary Arrangement

recursive pattern technique is based on a generic recursive scheme which generalizes a wide range of pixel-oriented arrangements for displaying large data sets [KKA 95]. Examples for the class of query-dependent techniques are the Spiral- and Axes-techniques [KKS 93, KK 94], which visualize the distances with respect to a database query. The arrangement of Spiral- and Axes-techniques centers the most relevant data items (data items fulfilling the query) in the middle of the window, and less relevant data items (data items approximately fulfilling the query) are arranged in a rectangular spiral-shape to the outside of the window (cf. Figure 1a). In case of the Axes-technique, the data set is partitioned into four subsets according to the direction of the distance for two dimensions: for one dimension negative distances are arranged to the left, positive ones to the right and for the other dimension negative distances are arranged to the bottom, positive ones to the top (cf. Figure 1b).

3 Generalization of the Query-dependent Visualization Techniques

A problem of the Spiral- and Axes-visualization techniques is that the local clustering properties of the spiral arrangement are rather weak. Since the spiral is only one pixel wide, it is perceptually impossible to detect small clusters. The reason for this problem is that the mapping from the ordered sequence of data items to the position of the pixels on the two-dimensional display does not preserve locality. More specific, the probability that two pixels which are close together on the screen are also close together in the one-dimensional ordered sequence of data items is rather low. Arrangements which do provide a maximum of locality preservation are wave- or snake-like arrangements such as those used in the recursive pattern technique and screen-filling curves (Peano-Hilbert and Morton curve). A problem of those techniques, however, is that the most relevant

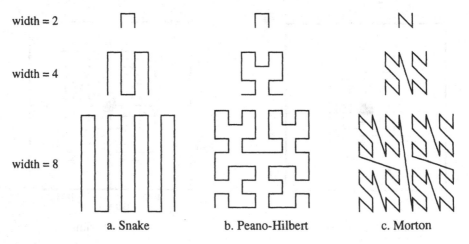

width = 2

width = 4

width = 8

a. Snake   b. Peano-Hilbert   c. Morton

Figure 2: Secondary Arragement

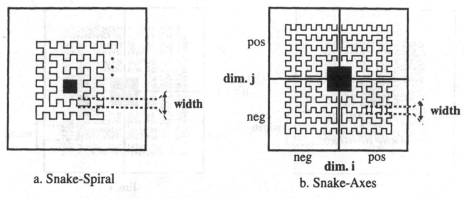

a. Snake-Spiral   b. Snake-Axes

Figure 3: Snake Variants (width = 2)

data items are placed in one corner of the visualization and that the ordering of data items does not become clear in the visualization.

Our new techniques aim at combining the advantages of both, the query-dependent techniques and the screen-filling curves, while at the same time avoiding their disadvantages. Our new generalized Spiral- and Axes-techniques retain the overall arrangement of the original Spiral- and Axes-technique, centering the most relevant data items in the middle of the screen, but enhance the clustering properties of the arrangement by using screen-filling curves locally. This means in case of the generalized Spiral-technique that the primary arrangement remains a rectangular spiral shape (cf. Figure 1a). In contrast to the original technique, however, the spiral is composed of small Snake-, Peano-Hilbert-, or Morton-like curves, which make up the secondary arrangement (cf. Figure 2). The width of the spiral is determined by the size of the 'small' curves. In case of the Snake variants, the width can be varied arbitrarily. The structure of the Peano-Hilbert and Morton curve does not allow arbitrary widths since the width is determined by the order of the Peano-Hilbert and Morton curves. For curves with order

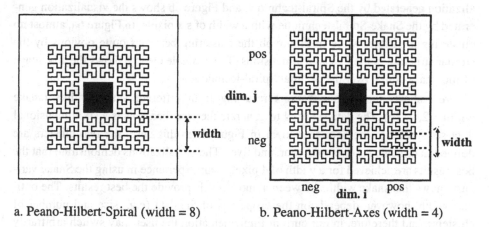

a. Peano-Hilbert-Spiral (width = 8)   b. Peano-Hilbert-Axes (width = 4)

Figure 4: Peano-Hilbert Variants

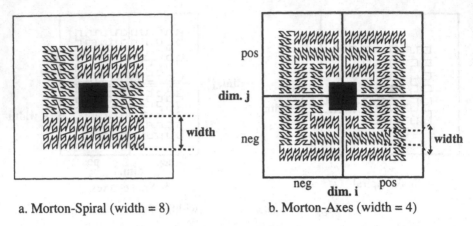

a. Morton-Spiral (width = 8)   b. Morton-Axes (width = 4)

Figure 5: Morton Variants

one the resulting width is $2^1 = 2$, for curves with order two the width is $2^2 = 4$, for curves with order three the width is $2^3 = 8$, and for curves with order four the width is $2^4 = 16$ (cf. Figure 2). In Figures 3-5, the Snake, Peano-Hilbert, and Morton variants of the Spiral- and Axes-techniques are presented. The variants can be seen as generalization of the original Spiral- and Axes-techniques which now become the special case of the Snake, Peano-Hilbert, and Morton variants with width one.

In the following, we show the advantage of improving the local clustering of query-dependent visualization techniques by screen-filling curves. In Figure 6, we provide an example visualization showing the effect of using the Snake variant of the Spiral-technique. The data set used consists of about 24,000 test data items with eight dimensions. Most of the data set (20,000 data items) is randomly generated in the range [-100, 100]. The remaining 4000 data items split up into two clusters which are only defined on the first five dimensions and are inserted at specific locations of the eight-dimensional space. The query used is [-20, 20] for each of the dimensions. Figure 6a shows the visualization generated by the Spiral-technique and Figure 6b shows the visualization generated by the Snake-Spiral-technique with a width of six pixels. In Figure 6a, almost no clustering is visible, while in Figure 6b the clustering becomes quite obvious by the similar structure in the first five dimensions. The example clearly shows the advantage of the Snake-Spiral over the original Spiral-technique.

Figure 7 shows three visualizations resulting from different snake widths (snake width = 2, 4, 16). The data set used to generate the visualizations is a six-dimensional data set similar to the data set shown in Figure 6 (in this case, the two clusters are defined in dimensions one, two, four, and five). The visualizations demonstrate that the best results are achieved for a width of 4 pixels. Our experience in using the Snake variants shows that snake widths between 4 and 8 pixels provide the best results. The optimal width, however, depends on the properties of the data (e.g., size and number of clusters), and therefore, in our current implementation the user may switch arbitrarily between different widths.

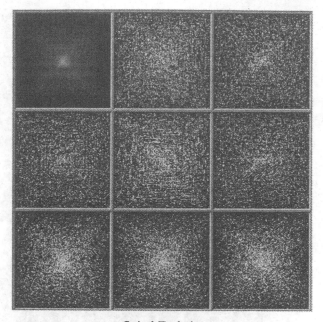

a. Spiral-Technique

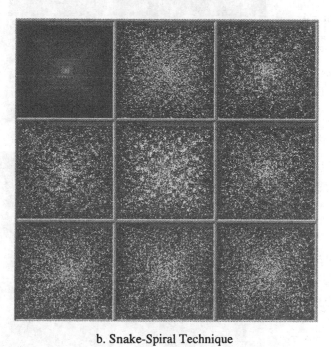

b. Snake-Spiral Technique

Figure 6: Comparison of the original Spiral and the Snake-Spiral Technique

Snake-Width = 2

Snake-Width = 4

Snake-Width = 16

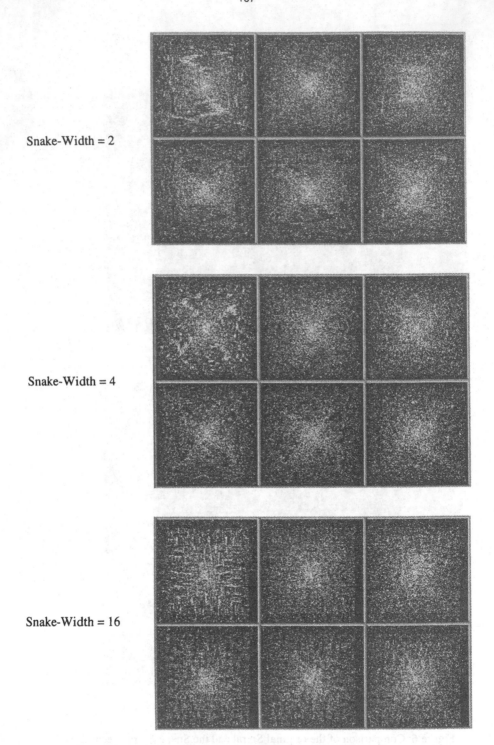

Figure 7: Comparison of Different Widths (Snake-Spiral Technique)

Snake-Axes

Peano-Hilbert-Axes

Morton-Axes

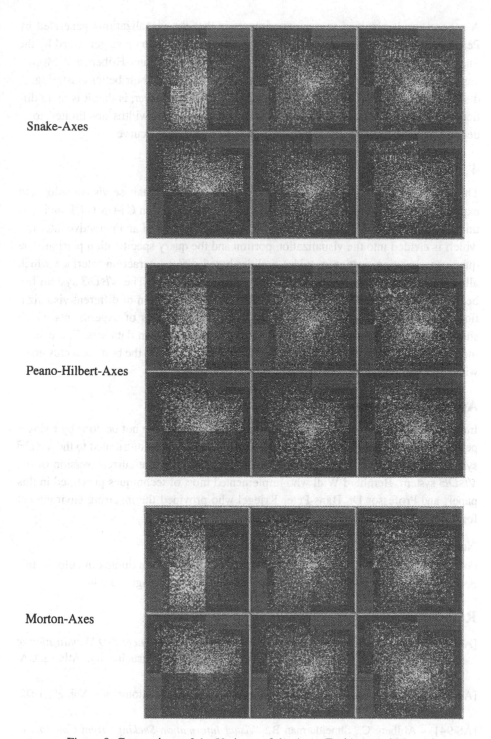

Figure 8: Comparison of the Variants of the Axes-Techique (width = 16)

A second result obtained in our experiments is that the visualizations generated by Peano-Hilbert and the Morton variants are in general similar to those generated by the Snake variants (cf. Figure 8). Only for larger widths, the Peano-Hilbert and Morton variants provide better results than the Snake variants due to their better clustering. A disadvantage of the Peano-Hilbert and Morton variants, however, is that it is more difficult to follow the local curve and that the possible spiral widths are limited to 2^i depending on the order i of the local Peano-Hilbert or Morton curve.

4 Conclusions

The described techniques are all integrated into the *VisDB* database visualization and exploration environment. The *VisDB* system is implemented in C++/MOTIF and runs under X-Windows on HP 7xx machines. The system consists of an interactive interface which is divided into the visualization portion and the query specification portion. The query specification portion provides a slider-based direct-interaction interface which allows an intuitive specification of queries [Kei 94, KK 94]. The *VisDB* system has been specially designed to support the analysis and comparison of different visualization techniques. The goal of future work is to perform series of experiments which show the advantage of our new techniques on a wide range on data sets. The experiments are also important to determine the widths which provide the best local clustering without deteriorating the global arrangement.

Acknowledgments

Implementing a complex system such as the *VisDB* system can not be done by a single person. My thank goes to all my colleagues and students who contributed to the *VisDB* system, especially Juraj Porada who implemented most of the current version of the *VisDB* system, Bernhard Widl who implemented most of techniques presented in this paper, and Professor Dr. Hans-Peter Kriegel who provided the inspiring environment for doing the research reported in this paper.

Note

For technical reasons, it was not possible to publish the screen dumps in color in this book. If you are interested, we will gladly forward the color pages to you.

References

[ADLP 95] Anupam V., Dar S., Leibfried T., Petajan E.: *'DataSpace: 3-D Visualization of Large Databases'*, Proc. Int. Symp. on Information Visualization, Atlanta, GA, 1995, pp. 82-88.

[And 72] Andrews D. F.: *'Plots of High-Dimensional Data'*, Biometrics, Vol. 29, 1972, pp. 125-136.

[AS 94] Ahlberg C., Shneiderman B.: *'Visual Information Seeking: Tight Coupling of Dynamic Query Filters with Starfield Displays'*, Proc. ACM CHI Int. Conf. on Human Factors in Computing (CHI'94), Boston, MA, 1994, pp. 313-317.

[Asi 85]   Asimov D.: *'The Grand Tour: A Tool For Viewing Multidimensional Data'*, SIAM Journal of Science & Stat. Comp., Vol. 6, 1985, pp. 128-143.

[AWS 92]   Ahlberg C., Williamson C., Shneiderman B.: *'Dynamic Queries for Information Exploration: An Implementation and Evaluation'*, Proc. ACM CHI Int. Conf. on Human Factors in Computing (CHI'92), Monterey, CA, 1992, pp. 619-626.

[BF 90]   Beshers C., Feiner S.: *'Visualizing n-Dimensional Virtual Worlds with n-Vision'*, Computer Graphics, Vol. 24, No. 2, 1990, pp. 37-38.

[BMMS 91]Buja A., McDonald J. A., Michalak J., Stuetzle W.: *'Interactive Data Visualization Using Focusing and Linking'*, Visualization '91, San Diego, CA, 1991, pp. 156-163.

[Che 73]   Chernoff H.: *'The Use of Faces to Represent Points in k-Dimensional Space Graphically'*, Journal Amer. Statistical Association, Vol. 68, pp 361-368.

[Cle 93]   Cleveland W. S.: *'Visualizing Data'*, AT&T Bell Laboratories, Murray Hill, NJ, Hobart Press, Summit NJ, 1993.

[Eic 94]   Eick S.: *'Data Visualization Sliders'*, Proc. ACM UIST'94, 1994, pp. 119-120.

[Hil 91]   Hilbert D.: *'Über stetige Abbildung einer Line auf ein Flächenstück'*, Math. Annalen, Vol. 38, 1891, pp. 459-460.

[Hub 85]   Huber P. J.: *'Projection Pursuit'*, The Annals of Statistics, Vol. 13, No. 2, 1985, pp. 435-474.

[ID 90]   Inselberg A., Dimsdale B.: *'Parallel Coordinates: A Tool for Visualizing Multi-Dimensional Geometry'*, Visualization '90, San Francisco, CA, 1990, pp. 361-370.

[Kei 94]   Keim D. A.: *'Visual Support for Query Specification and Data Mining'*, Ph.D. Dissertation, University of Munich, July 1994, Shaker-Publishing Company, Aachen, Germany, 1995, ISBN 3-8265-0594-8.

[KK 94]   Keim D. A., Kriegel H.-P.: *'VisDB: Database Exploration using Multidimensional Visualization'*, Computer Graphics & Applications, Sept. 1994, pp. 40-49.

[KKA 95]   Keim D. A., Kriegel H.-P., Ankerst M.: *'Recursive Pattern: A Technique for Visualizing Very Large Amounts of Data'*, Proc. Visualization '95, Atlanta, GA, 1995, pp. 279-286.

[KKS 94]   Keim D. A., Kriegel H.-P., Seidl T.: *'Supporting Data Mining of Large Databases by Visual Feedback Queries'*, Proc. 10th Int. Conf. on Data Engineering, Houston, TX, 1994, pp. 302-313.

[Mor 66]   Morton G. M.: *'A Computer Oriented Geodetic Data Base and a New Technique in File Sequencing'*, IBM Ltd. Ottawa, Canada, 1966.

[Pea 90]   Peano G.: *'Sur une courbe qui remplit toute une aire plaine'*, Math. Annalen, Vol. 36, 1890, pp. 157-160.

[SGB 91]   Smith S., Grinstein G., Bergeron R. D.: *'Interactive Data Exploration with a Supercomputer'*, Visualization '91, San Diego, CA, 1991, pp. 248-254.

[Shn 92]   Shneiderman B.: *'Tree Visualization with Treemaps: A 2-D Space-filling Approach'*, ACM Trans. on Graphics, Vol. 11, No. 1, 1992, pp. 92-99.

Realtime Database Support for Environmental Visualization*

Craig M. Wittenbrink, Eric Rosen, Alex Pang,
Suresh K. Lodha, and Patrick Mantey

Baskin Center for Computer Engineering & Information Sciences University of
California, Santa Cruz Santa Cruz, CA 95064

Abstract. Much research has been done on interfacing databases to
visualization applications, and there are many varied approaches. We
describe the lessons learned during the design and development of the
REINAS software (Real-time Environmental Information Network and
Analysis System). We have developed visualization applications that
have been in public use for several years and that visualize data from relational database engines. Our most popular tools are World Wide Web
access tools. Our most sophisticated tools have novel user interfaces–
Spray and CSpray. In this paper we present the interface and API (application programming interface) issues, as well as the development of the
required middleware. The REINAS system is a complete data management system whose requirements and construction were driven primarily
by the visualization needs, and therefore presents a unique view of how
to utilize commercial relational database technologies for environmental
visualization.

1 Overview

The REINAS–Real–time Environmental Information Network and Analysis system–
is an information management system, including a relational database and middleware, intended to marry data and visualization for environmental science. The
project is an Office of Naval Research university research initiative for bringing
environmental science into a more intimate relationship with state of the art
visualization and information technology. Figure 1 shows a high-level view of
the system. Lines indicate physical or wireless network connections. Lines are
bi-directional unless indicated otherwise. Data flows generally from left to right,
and feedback and control generally flow from right to left.

As the most visible part of our project we have numerous applications that
interface to relational database technology. Much of the behind the scenes work
has been in developing the system middleware and database schema [9], but
the interface has also held numerous challenges. We have satisfied several of
the challenges, and face in the near term some additional large challenges. To
demonstrate our contribution, we first describe our project, solutions to date,
and the trade-offs in different interface approaches.

* This project is supported by ONR grant N00014-92-J-1807

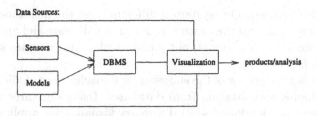

Fig. 1. Major REINAS components.

This paper focuses on the interface between the REINAS database component and the visualization component. In particular, we discuss how the challenges of supporting real–time data ingest and visualization have driven the design and the staged implementation of these components. The project goals are: our focus on regional real–time environmental science; our charter for a relocatable system; our requirement to support both real–time and retrospective data; and our requirement to support three classes of users with various needs: (a) scientists (meteorologists and oceanographers) who want the flexibility of accessing and combining various data sources for visualization and analyses; (b) operational users (e.g. forecasters) who want standard products; and (c) instrumentation and remote sensing users who need to validate and monitor an instrument centric view of the data.

We have three data sources to satisfy our users that work in parallel each with different tradeoffs, advantages, and disadvantages:

1. A long term data management relational database schema, designed for holding metadata, and guided by research in visualization.
2. A short term data management relational database schema, designed for minimal setup time but not attempting to hold metadata important for long term data management.
3. Environmental files for exchange, stand alone use, and legacy support. We currently support file formats specific to the project, and some more general formats such as HDF.

Related Work. There are similar systems to REINAS, and there is similar work in combining visualization to databases. We briefly review some of the relevant related work. A large multi-year development project, which focuses on global environmental science is the Sequoia 2000 project [16]. Stonebreaker et al. have also developed custom visualization tools, one which they call Tioga [17]. Another Sequoia 2000 prototype effort, developed interfaces to existing visualization programs [7]. Gershon et al. [4] overview the fundamental problems in large data managment and visualization. There are real-time systems that use less sophisticated database systems [3, 6, 15], and others that run at much less than the seconds timing of REINAS [5, 11]. The work most similar to ours, using a middleware and an API approach to create the interface, is in the GIS literature [1, 2]. In addition, see [8] for recent research articles in interfacing visualization to database. Our system is different than the mentioned literature, in that it does real-time to the second, provides middleware and apis for custom applications, works on a regional, not global, scale, and provides sophisticated 3D visualization.

This paper is an overview of the successes, approaches, and challenges we have faced in developing visualization from databases. Using our three data sources listed above we have developed several primary visualization applications: Xmet, Spray, CSpray, and www-Met. All of these applications interface to the second source mentioned above. Spray interacts with both relational database schema approaches and legacy files. Xmet and www-Met interact with only the simpler schema, but will be converted to use the full featured schema as it becomes more fully operational. The interfacing of the applications to the schema has been done primarily through custom API's supported by middleware crafted to handle environmental data.

2 Visualization Applications

2.1 Spray Rendering

We now present brief overviews of our visualization applications in an outside in or top to bottom description of REINAS. There are four major visualization applications: Spray, CSpray, Xmet, and World Wide Web Clients. In the following section, we describe the interfaces used to bring data into these applications.

The visualization component of Spray is organized into three different modes of operation targeted towards three different classes of users. These are the monitor mode for instrumentation engineers and recreational users to monitor the current state of instruments as well as the environment; the forecast mode for operational users who are interested in generating standard forecast products; and the analysis mode for scientists to perform retrospective analysis on their data. We now look at the each mode in more detail and how each interface with the database.

Monitor Mode. In monitor mode, users have a bird's eye view of the region of interest. See Figure 2. Environmental sensors are represented by simple icons. By selecting one or more of these sensors using a point and click interface or through a pulldown menu, users can view interpolated fields of a physical parameter (e.g. humidity, wind vector, etc.) or query individual sensors for time plots of the parameters they measure. The list of sensors currently supported include: fixed and portable meteorological stations, NOAA buoys, CODARS, wind profilers, seal tracks [12], and ADCP.

Currently, not all the data from these sensors are coming off the database. For example, some of them have to be retrieved from the sensor logs once every hour and stored in a local file. On the other hand, realtime data from Met stations are available through the Met server and can be used to interpolate the environmental field or generate time plots as the data arrives. The seal tracks and the mobile land and water based Met platforms are also of interest as GPS readings provide their current locations and can be used to aid the visual display.

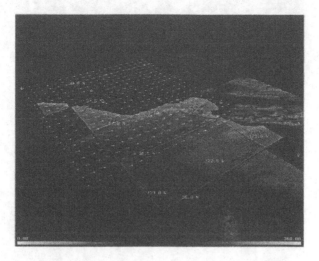

Fig. 2. View of the Monterey Bay showing location of some sensors and an interpolated wind field from a subset of these sensors.

Forecast Mode. Operational forecasters are interested in generating standard products from forecast models and satellite observations. These products may include animated GOES satellite images, as well as maps that show contours of 500mb pressure field at 60m spacing of geopotential height against vorticity, 850mb pressure field at 30m spacing of geopotential height against relative humidity (shaded above 90%), and others. Aside from standard products, users can also generate customized products e.g. different projections, different contour spacing, and heights. One can also register and overlay observation data with products e.g. wind barbs and animated GOES images. Figure 3 shows a typical forecast product.

Currently, satellite images are periodically and automatically retrieved via the Naval Postgraduate School. The images are stored locally in files and will be stored as blobs in the database.

Analysis Mode. This mode allows the scientific users to perform retrospective analysis on synoptic data. It allows users to explore large data sets interactively using different visualization techniques. It is also extensible and can easily grow with users' needs. The underlying mechanism that provides the visualization capability in analysis mode is based on spray rendering [13]. Spray rendering provides the users with the metaphor of spray painting their data sets as a means of visualizing them. In its simplest form, data are painted or rendered visible by

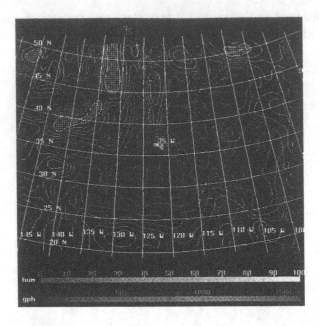

Fig. 3. Sample standard forecast product where regions of relative humidity above 90% are cross-hatched.

the color of the paint particles. By using different types of paint particles, data can be visualized in different ways. The key component of spray rendering is how the paint particles are defined. They are essentially smart particles (or sparts) which are sent into the data space to seek out features of interest and highlight them. Among the advantages of this visualization framework are: grid independence (sparts operate in a local subset of the data space and do not care whether data is regularly or irregularly gridded), ability to handle large data sets (sparts can be "large" and provide a lower resolution view of the data set or they can be "small" and provide a detailed view of an area of interest), extensible (it is easy to design new sparts). Sparts can also travel through time-dependent data sets. Figure 4 shows the interfaces available in analysis mode as well as illustrates some of the possible visualization methods.

Spray is an evolving research system. Currently, it works with rectilinear grids only. Entire data sets are read in from files and do not take advantage of the particle nature of the sparts. We envision that once the data is ingested into the database, the sparts can make the equivalent of SQL calls to travel through the data space by requesting for the appropriate subset of the data from the database. Some caching and coherency measures need to be taken to ensure that the current database technology does not get bogged down with too many small requests. Finally, one can also exploit the inherent parallelism in the independence among sparts to operate on local subsets of the data.

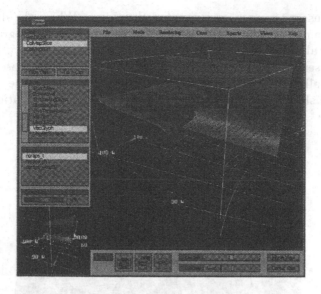

Fig. 4. Sample visualization in analysis mode using spray rendering.

2.2 Collaborative Spray

To facilitate the sharing of data and collaboration among science colleagues, we have also added a collaborative feature to the REINAS visualization system, enabling geographically distributed researchers to work within a shared virtual workspace and create visualization products [14]. There are several components that are needed to make this feasible: session manager, sharing data/cans, floor control, multiple window, audio/video support, and different collaboration/compression levels. Figure 5 shows some of these.

Users can collaborate at different levels. Sharing can occur at the image (visualization product), spray can (abstract visualization objects – AVOs), or data stream (raw data) level. At the image level, participants can see what the other participants see and may perhaps be able to change view points. At the can level, participants have access to a list of public spray cans put up by other participants. These public cans will generate AVOs from the remote hosts and distribute them to other participants. Users may also give permission to other participants to have direct access to data streams and replicate those on local machines for faster response times. The different levels of collaboration also imply different requirements for compression. Tradeoffs will have to be made between graphics workstation capabilities, network bandwidth and compression levels. Objects that need to be transmitted can either be images, AVOs (together with can parameters and other transformation matrices), or raw data.

This is an excellent opportunity where database technology can help the visualization. With a collaborative system, the data does not have to reside in one central database. In fact, the data could be distributed around several heterogeneous databases. The visualization application acts as a common front end for the users to query and visualize their data. Where the data actually resides can be made transparent to them. The current CSpray program performs this task by allowing you to visualize another participant's data. Because the requests are sent to the participant with the data, remote database queries can be made by all of the participants without sharing the data. The visualization products are shared, because each participant acts as a visualization server for everyone else.

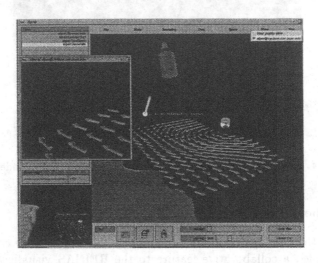

Fig. 5. Collaborative visualization. The large graphics window shows the viewpoint of the local user. The smaller window shows what the collaborator is looking at. The "eye-con" shows the location of the other participant.

2.3 Xmet

Xmet was initially designed to be a system debugging tool that included some primitive visualization capability. However, along with the Xmet API server, and related software that populates a simple database, **Xmet** became the prototypical REINAS client application.

As a network application, **Xmet** was designed using the client-server model. Multiple instantiations of the **Xmet** client interact with a single "**XmetServer**". Although facilities exist for running multiple servers should performance degrade, this has rarely proven necessary. Communication between client and server is abstracted using the Xmet API (discussed later) and accomplished using Internet socket streams.

As a visualization application, **Xmet** was designed with very modest goals in mind, namely the display of concurrent time-series data. It was later expanded to also allow the display of two-dimensional CODAR ocean surface current radial and vector data, including CODAR animations. Figure 6 shows a screen

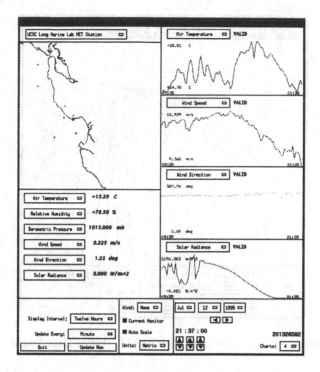

Fig. 6. Xmet: The Prototypical REINAS Client Application

shot from a typical **Xmet** session. The map window in the upper-left shows the Monterey Bay coastline and surrounding region, with glyphs indicating the position of real-time meteorological stations whose data is available through the server. The current site is emphasized, indicating that conditions from the Long Marine Lab meteorological station are being displayed. Below the map, current conditions for various sensors are given; to the right, graphs of sensor stream values over the previous twelve hours show how temperature, wind, and solar irradiance vary from mid-morning to early evening. Individual pop-up menus allow the strip-chart graphs to be user configured. Additional controls at the bottom allow the user to navigate through time, display wind-barb glyphs, fix the strip-chart display interval, and control the frequency at which the displayed current conditions and strip-charts are updated.

In alternate modes, the user may decide to configure **Xmet** with zero strip-charts and zoom in on the view of Monterey Bay as shown in Figure 7. In this case, CODAR ocean surface current radial data is under investigation, with meteorological conditions from the various stations overlaid using wind-barb glyphs.

From a visualization standpoint, **Xmet** lags far behind the modern, GL-based Spray and CSpray; however, its compactness, portability, and relative ease of use have made it fairly popular among REINAS users. Binaries for Sun/4, DEC ULTRIX, RS/6000, HP/UX, SGI, A/UX, and BSD/OS platforms have been built and continue to be widely distributed.

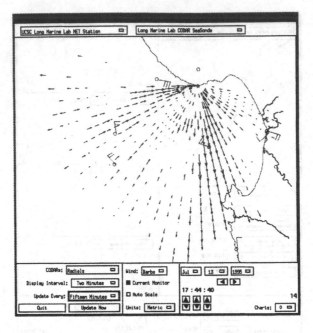

Fig. 7. Xmet: Configured for CODAR Radial Data Display

2.4   World Wide Web Clients

The growing popularity of the World Wide Web (WWW), and our desire to provide real-time demonstrations to users who were not previously aware of REINAS, led to the development of HTML aware applications, which when used in conjunction with the National Center for Supercomputing Application's httpd server, provide a WWW interface to the Xmet API.

The www-Met application is integrated into a virtual tour of the Monterey Bay region, highlighting sites where the project has deployed or connected instrumentation (interested readers are invited to visit:
http://sapphire.cse.ucsc.edu/reinas-instrument-tour/. Web visitors are first presented with a map of the region (Figure 8) allowing them to select a site to visit. Pages describing each site, and the instrumentation accessible through REINAS at that site, can be reached in this way. Where meteorological instrumentation is present, users can choose to query for current and recent weather conditions; Figure 10 shows a sample query with its results.

Although far more primitive than either Xmet or the Spray and CSpray applications detailed previously, the instrument site web tour currently receives approximately 4800 interactions generating over 1500 separate requests for data from the database in a given month. Despite its simple interface and relatively primitive visualization options, www-Met's usage statistics dwarf that of Xmet and Spray.

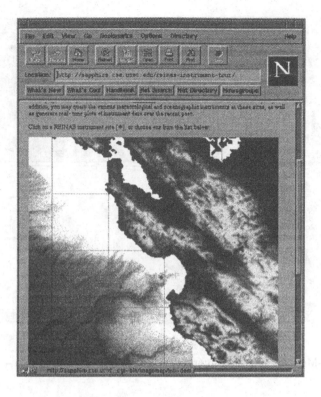

Fig. 8. www-Met: Opening Screen

A similar web oriented application is **www-CODAR**, which displays a real-time ocean surface current vector map, via the Xmet API (see Figure 11). **www-CODAR** received over 570 visitors in June, 1995, the first full month it was publicly accessible. Each vector map typically requires about 400 database queries to produce under the Xmet API; hence, these 570 visitors symbolize over a quarter-million Xmet API transactions alone.

3   Application Programming Interfaces

The primary interface of our distributed applications to the database engines and to files is through several application programming interfaces (APIs). There are three primary APIs now in use. The **Xmet** API currently provides a generic interface to the simpler schema; the RSObject (for R(EINA)S) API provides an interface to the full featured schema at a higher level; and the REINAS low level API provides a mechanism to simply passes SQL queries directly to the database engine, as well as handling ferrying data back and forth. The RSObject API is written on top of the REINAS low level API, and also has facilities to access data from the Xmet server using the Xmet API, and to files accessing them directly. In this section we quickly describe them, and the issues and design trade-offs that were used.

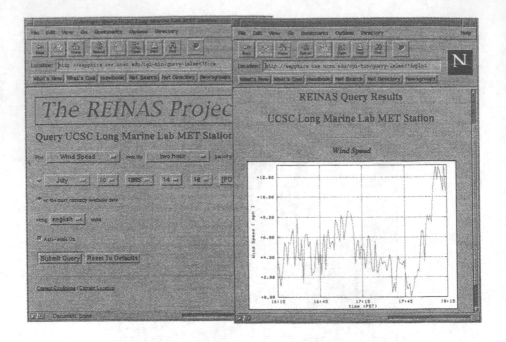

Fig. 9. www-Met: A Sample Query Form

Fig. 10. A Sample Query Result

3.1 Xmet API

The Xmet API is opcode based, with most opcodes occurring in request/reply pairs. A list of Xmet opcodes is given in Figure 12. All Xmet API requests conform to a standard type, detailed in Figure 13; the opcode and parameter values determine the precise meaning of the request. Replies are similarly formatted in a standard type, detailed in Figure 14. For example, to request the most current weather conditions from meteorlogical site #2, a request structure with the **opcode** field set to *mo-getcurrent* and **iop1** set to 2 is forwarded to the server through a library routine. The server replies with a reply structure identified containing a *mo-retcurrent* opcode and **iop1** set to 2. The weather conditions are encoded in the **data** field, with extracted with other library calls. The **tstamp** field identifies the time for which the data is valid. The remaining fields are unused in this transaction.

Although admittedly primitive, this simple API has demonstrated remarkable utility, and has been used by such diverse applications as high-end visualization systems such as Spray and CSpray, various X/Motif toolkit applications,

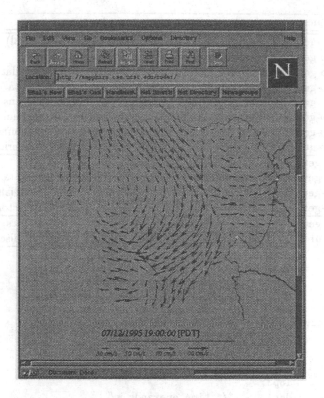

Fig. 11. Ocean Surface Currents on the World Wide Web

world-wide-web server glue code, and simple text-oriented client programs, on a variety of architectures. Functionality can and has been extended simply by defining new opcodes and updating the server (most of the queries and all CO-DAR support was added in this way). Inline compression, handled by the library routines which send and receive requests and replies, addresses basic concerns about network transport efficiency.

Although the application programmer is limited in the types of requests that can be made to the server when using this API, the ease with which common requests can be made has helped make this interface the most popular (in terms of number of applications developed and transactions handled) among REINAS project client applications to date.

3.2 RSObject API

The RSObject API was designed for the handling of environmental data. In the design of this API, there were goals in object oriented design of the entire API and to satisfy several goals fundamental to language design. The design issues are numerous and involve tradeoffs in 1) type checking, 2) security principle 3) efficiency 3) maintainability 4) readability 5) flexibility [10]. Others have delved

request	reply	function
mo-getinit	mo-retinit	initialization (meteorological)
mo-getinfo	mo-retinfo	return site metadata
mo-getcurrent	mo-retcurrent	most current meteorological data
mo-getall	mo-retall	arbitrary meteorlogical data
mo-getavg-all	mo-retavg-all	arbitrary meteorlogical means
mo-getmax-all	mo-retmax-all	arbitrary meteorlogical maximums
mo-getmin-all	mo-retmin-all	arbitrary meteorlogical minimums
mo-getseries	mo-retseries	arbitrary meteorlogical timeseries
co-getinit	co-retinit	initialization (CODAR)
co-getinfo	co-retinfo	return CODAR site metadata
co-getradials	co-retradials	return arbitrary CODAR radials
co-getvector	co-retvector	return arbitrary CODAR vector
so-getrecent	so-retrecent	return server usage statistics
none	so-retdie	inform client of server's demise

Fig. 12. Xmet API Opcodes

```
typedef struct {
    long        opcode;     /* request opcode */
    long        iop1,       /* integer operands (32-bit) */
                iop2,
                iop3;
    TimeType    dop1,       /* time operands */
                dop2;
} XmetRequestType;
```

Fig. 13. Xmet API Request Structure

into object oriented API designs such as Bernath [1], Berrill et al. [2], and Lee et al. [8].

In designing the RSObject API we considered numerous alternatives, and settled upon one which was best in terms of the metrics given. The RSObject API uses separate types, but passes objects around using pointers for efficiency and generic calls. We do dynamic type checking on the object type. What follows is a list of the metrics that we used to evaluate various API choices:

1. Type checking: compile(static) No
2. Type checking: runtime (dynamic) Yes
3. developing supporting: easy, fewer routines to support
4. efficiency: must do run-time checks
5. API use: simple to understand, simple to use
6. multiple get's use multiple typed variables, and checking will be done for you RSGet(. . . temp,) RSGet(. . uncertainty . .)

```
typedef struct {
    long        opcode;     /* reply opcode */
    long        iop1,       /* integer operands */
                iop2;
    long        mask1,      /* logical operands */
                mask2;
    TimeType    tstamp;     /* time operand */
    long        *data;      /* variable length opcode specific data */
} XmetReplyType;
```

Fig. 14. Xmet API Reply Structure

7. Abstraction: Yes. abstraction in definition and implementation
8. Automation: Yes
9. Defense in Depth: Yes (mostly)
10. Information Hiding: Yes. Only the known scientific types are visible. enumeration constants are hidden.
11. Labeling: NA
12. Localized Cost: No, dynamic object checking is cost for all accesses
13. Manifest Interface: Yes
14. Orthogonality: Yes
15. Portability: Yes
16. Preservation of Information: Yes
17. Security: Yes
18. Simplicity: Yes (and No harder to implement)
19. Structure: yes
20. Syntactic Consistency: Yes
21. Zero-One-Infinity: NA

The API we designed yields a score of 15 versus 8 and 13 for two other likely alternatives, where each feature is given one point. This proposed solution uses separate types, passes objects using pointers to amortize method cost, allows dynamic type checking more in line with an object oriented programming style, and allows extension to use X resource type constants. Here is an example query of the API:

```
status = RSGet(object, objectType, &returnObject)
```

The object which is to be queried has multiple settings, such as locality, time, and other qualifiers, which can be set on the object such as RSSet() calls. This provides for arbitrary manipulation of the object's characteristics as well as the ability to enhance objects, not use visible constants (magic numbers), and do dynamic default behavior of objects upon creation. The type of data to be queried is a variable found in the return type itself. The objects may be queried often with queries that don't change the object itself, simply the return values.

We also use a multiple class hierarchy using C type definition design. Some objects can be created while other base class objects are static declarable, providing a reasonable mix for efficiency ease of use and type checking. As examples, there are types, elements, and aggregations. Environmental parameter units are specified as part of the container in which they are retrieved from. The field descriptor gives the actual units. Units are described within the RSField descriptor. If a user wishes to change the units, an RSSet operation is performed, and the corresponding field will reflect the change. For example, for a fully generic temperature object, the filled in values may be the result of the query, or may have been set by the user, so they are more like commands.

The return values from the data base engine are in character format. The REINAS low level API passes these and the internals of the RSObjects convert these to binary (int, float, double), and then populate the structures that are visible to the user program. The major class type is statically defined, such as RSParameter, and then the minor class is dynamically by the result of the query. The programmer must have knowledge of the basic scientific types. They must be aware of how to manipulate and operate on those types. An example struct follows:

```
typedef struct rsparameter{
int type;
float latitude;
float longitude;
float z;
float time;
float fval;
}RSParameter;
```

The application programmer uses the parameter, description lists, series, and localities, to manipulate and interact with both the real time vacuum, accessing data before they are loaded, and the data base. Localities define the bouding box in space and/or time that allows culling of the environmental queries. The descriptor list is an array of RSField's that are used to encode the data types. Numerous methods are supported and objects, such as getting one measurement, getting an entire time series, and getting a large field of scattered data. We have also developed some convenience functions for object duplication, and querying the size of data that can come back.

4 Underlying Issues

The applications and APIs simply show our results to date. We now discuss several underlying issues that are important in the development of the REINAS system.

4.1 Granularity of Data Access

The underlying issues in interfacing the visualization programs really lie with their intended usage. With Spray visualization we have been able, and were required, to experiment with the granularity of requests made to the database. Because of the particle nature of Spray, each spart operates independently on its local data subset. Two immediate consequences are that the size of the local space may be varied, and that each local subset, whether overlapping with another region or not, can be operated on independently. These two are important considerations if sparts are to separately make queries to the database. If the granularity is set too fine, the overhead of setting up the calls will overwhelm the database server. On the other extreme, if the granularity is too coarse, the advantages of working on small blocks of data are lost. At any rate, some caching and coherency measures need to be taken to ensure that the current database technology does not get bogged down with too many small requests. In general, sparts travel in more or less the same direction, hence spatial and temporal coherency is high. However, optimistic caching of anticipated trajectories may not always be practical. Take for instance the case of sparts that trace out ribbons in flow fields. If the flow is highly divergent or turbulent, the sparts may request widely different regions of the data space to integrate its next position. Similarly, some preprocessing of the data may be necessary to help optimize database queries. For instance, when dealing with or querying scattered data sets, it may make sense to bin the data into different sub-regions or arrange them in a hierarchical structure.

Even when optimizing for simplicity, as was done with the simple Xmet API, questions about the appropriate level of granularity arose. In particular, the best way to formulate the result of a request for ocean surface current vectors was not immediately obvious. The difficulty stems from the nature of the data, and not the characteristics of the visualization; in this case, a snapshot of the ocean surface current includes an arbitrary and varying number of vectors. A reply might group all possible vectors together, a convenient but inefficient approach in this case. Or, a formulation requiring each vector to be returned independently adopted, a more flexible but also inefficient approach (in terms of number of transactions). The later approach was adopted, and appears to be working well.

4.2 Simple, Safe Code

In practice, the Xmet API is easier to use than either of the API's which access the richer schema. The Xmet API was developed first, with a fairly primitive understanding of the types of queries that would be useful, and the quickly became the conduit for a large share of REINAS visualization clients. This occurred because of the ease of use and speed at which the API could be extended when new environmental data or new types of queries were introduced. The Xmet API is simple enough for fast maintenance, and many changes may be made in hours or days. The Xmet API is also simple enough so that it can be quickly understood, and application transactions require only a few lines of code. As a result, it is used by a variety of REINAS client programs.

In addition, the Xmet API could be and was extended without affecting (usually) the functionality of previously written clients. Functionality was extended by adding opcodes; the request and reply structures were never changed. As a result, clients only needed to be updated if they specifically needed to take advantage of the queries available through the new opcodes. This desirable feature has been carried through to the RSObjects API, as it was written with the advantages and shortcomings of Xmet in mind. Although the Xmet API limits the type of queries that can be made to the enumerated commands, it is extensible enough that, in practice, this is not a significant drawback. The command approach does break clients, when the enumeration of command types, or the result flags must be or are inadvertantly modified, but errors were quickly tracked down.

The REINAS low level API, and RSObjects API, are more powerful, and require more effort to understand as they include sophisticated features like SQL support, blocking and nonblocking reads, multiple handles, and must support the full featured schema that has hundreds more data types. There of course, remains much work for improving query performance that is not completely the responsibility of the database. For example, some Xmet queries result in a large number of transactions between client and server. In this phase of the project, these performance issues have not become too important, even with hundreds of users a week. Often, disk space has become a more considerable problem for project management, and application support. Currently, older data are archived off-line in anticipation of using a tertiary storage solution. These API trade-offs show how different small and large software projects are in terms of their extensibility and development cycles. The difficulties in developing a large software system have not dissappeared, but in attempting to solve a large part of the data management problem we have at least used an incremental approach and completed the prototype of a much more sophisticated system. We hope to soon complete newer visualization applications which fully exploit the RSObject API and the features of the REINAS System.

4.3   User Interface

The separation of functionality into three modes to meet the needs of the three user classes creates an obstacle after extended use. Users need to switch from one mode to another mode because the functionality is not directly available under that mode. Another drawback to modes is that certain data are unavailable in each mode. For example, monitor mode has access to sensor measured data but not to model data, as in analysis mode. This prevents users from in comparing the numerical forecasts versus the actual measurements. We have since redesigned the interface to take these limitations into account. The current, ongoing visualization development effort is now tool based instead of mode based. That is, users will activate one or more tools to do data transformations and/or visualizations. Each tool will have a set of input ports that can be associated with different data streams either from files or from the database. Output from each tool can be routed to a graphics window for rendering, or back to the database or file for saving. Tools accomplish the functionality provided previously in the different modes e.g. field interpolation, contour lines, isosurfaces, etc. They are actually made up of simpler elements that work on a chunk of data at a time, the results of which are passed to other elements within the tool. That is, requests are continually made to retrieve a subset of the data for the tool to work on. Within the tool, elements process the data in a dataflow fashion, and may also send feedback to request neighboring data. In this fashion, we have married the dataflow approach with the active agent approach. The underlying execution model is transparent to the user as they are simply interacting with different tools.

5 Challenges and Lessons Learned

In the environmental sciences it has been traditional to place environmental data into proprietary file formats. The visualizations made from these formats have been custom developed, but the difficulty in using other researcher's data has been not only the conversion of the formats, but the understanding of the lineage of the data. The REINAS project has been focused on trying to aid in the development and experimentation of systems that would solve the long term data management problem. While this is a fundamental difficulty, it is not the only aspect of our research. We have also looked in depth into the marriage of our visualization applications to this experimental information system. In so doing, we have developed a range of solutions that have interesting trade-offs.

By simply using a relational database, and putting the environmental data into tables, we were able to provide a large jump in functionality over using files alone. A centralized server accessing the database, and handling distributed network requests through a primitive but extensible API has been very success-ful in serving a wide range of visualization applications. The Xmet, www-Met, www-codar, and Spray applications demonstrate the succeful integration of a relatively simple schema (less than 500 lines of SQL), with a server, and a net-work client/server-based API. In addition, new sources and queries can be added to the system fairly quickly because of the overall simplicity of the system. But, despite its success, this system does not solve the long term data management problem.

A schema designed primarily by our collaborator, Bruce Gritton, of MBARI holds promise for helping to solve the long term data management problem. The added cost for capturing and using the additional meta-data, and relations among the data, is the complexity. The current schema is over 7000 lines of SQL. To maintain, insert, and verify instrument data that is loaded requires a full time database administrator. There has been a considerable amount of work put into simplifying the process of adding new instruments, but it still requires about the complexity of developing and debugging a Unix device driver. To capitalize on the features available in this full featured schema, we have developed a pass through low level API, and a higher level object oriented API for environmental data. This allows the in memory representation to match the database, while not forcing the application programmer to use SQL directly. Our research goals were to have Spray rendering use smart particles to drive the queries, but the level of support by the database and the Unix OS for networked programming are such that this was impractical. We have therefore implemented a blocking query approach that may be improved to use a caching scheme for effective performance. The visualizations that may be done are similar to those done with files, but there is more flexibility in developing time series visualizations, and in selecting and deselecting sources.

Our near-future research involves the enhancement of the information system to hold more data, such as AVHRR, Ocean Models, etc. and to do a closer integration of measurement and model data. This is where our science users are driving us as they need to compare the effectiveness of their models in capturing real world phenomena. They may also use the visualization to experiment with different ways to interpolate the measurement data, which is necessary to kickstart the models. Further into the future are the video applications on which experimentation is just beginning, both from the technology side and from the science side. It may be that relational database technology will not support the multimedia performance necessary for a video database, and the numerous vendor extensions do not clearly solve these either. In the end we can only hope to develop the appropriate interface so that our visualization applications become wired to the latest valid scientific data sources, while still supporting the legacy sources.

Acknowledgments

We would like to acknowledge the efforts of some of the students who have been active in REINAS, including: Bruce Montague, Carles Pi-Sunyer, Bryan Mealy, David Kulp, Skip Macy, Tom Goodman, Jeff Edgett, and Jim Spring. We would also like to thank the many colleagues involved in this collaborative effort, especially our science colleagues Professor Wendell Nuss, Bruce Gritton, Kang Tao, Dr. Francesco Chavez, Dr. Dan Fernandez, and Professor Jeff Paduan. The REINAS systems group has been instrumental in providing the foundation from which to develop a real application test bed – led by Professor Darrell Long and Chair Pat Mantey and supported by Andrew Muir. The REINAS visualization team, Tom Goodman, Naim Alper, Jonathan Gibbs, Jeff Furman, Elijah Saxon, and Michael Clifton, have provided much of the coding, and development for the Spray and CSpray applications. In addition, John Wiederhold, Catherine Tornabene, and Ted Dunn helped develop the network of Monterey Bay area instrumentation that attracts most of our users.

References

1. Tracey Bernath. Distributed GIS visualization system. In *GIS/LIS Proceedings, Vol. 1*, pages 51–58. American Society for Photogrammetry and Remote Sensing, November 1992.

2. Arthur Berrill and George Moon. An object oriented approach to an integrated GIS system. In *Proceedings of GIS/LIS*, pages 59–63, San Jose, CA, November 1992. American Society for Photogrammetry and Remote Sensing.

3. Randall S. Cerveny et al. Development of a real-time interactive storm-monitoring program in Phonenix, Arizona. *Bulletin of the American Meteorological Society*, 73(6):773–779, June 1992.

4. Nahum D. Gershon and C. Grant Miller. Dealing with the data deluge. Special report: Environment, part 2. *IEEE Spectrum*, 30(7):28–32, July 1993.

5. S. Howes. Use of satellite and radar images in operational precipitation nowcasting. *Journal of the British Interplanetary Society*, 41(10):455–460, October 1988.

6. J.M. Intriery, C.G. Little, W.J. Shaw, R.M. Banta, P.A. Durkee, and R.M. Hardesty. The land/sea breeze experiment (LASBEX). *Bulletin of the American Meteorological Society*, 71(5):656, May 1990.

7. Peter Kochevar et al. Bridging the gap between visualization and data management: A simple visualization management system. In *Proceedings of Visualization 93*, pages 94–101, San Jose, CA, October 1993. IEEE.

8. John P. Lee and Georges G. Grinstein, editors. *Database Issues for Data Visualization, IEEE Visualization '93 Workshop.* Springer–Verlag, 1994.

9. D.D.E. Long, P.E. Mantey, C. M. Wittenbrink, T.R. Haining, and B.R. Montague. REINAS the real-time environmental information network and analysis system. In *Proceedings of COMPCON*, pages 482–487, San Francisco, CA, March 1995. IEEE.

10. Bruce J. MacLennan. *Principles of Programming Languages: Design, Evaluation, and Implementation.* Holt, Rinehart, and Winston, New York, second edition, 1987.

11. M.D. Milnes. Interpretation of remotely sensed images using historic data. *Journal of the British Interplanetary Society*, 41(10):451–454, October 1988.

12. Guy W. Oliver. Visualizing the tracking and diving behavior of marine mammals. In *Proc. Visualization*, page in press, Atlanta, GA, October 1995. IEEE.

13. Alex Pang. Spray rendering. *IEEE Computer Graphics and Applications*, 14(5):57 – 63, 1994.

14. Alex Pang, Craig M. Wittenbrink, and Tom Goodman. CSpray: A collaborative scientific visualization application. In *Proceedings SPIE IS &T's Conference Proceedings on Electronic Imaging: Multimedia Computing and Networking*, volume 2417, pages 317–326, February 1995.

15. D.J. Schwab and K.W. Bedford. Initial implementation of the great lakes forecasting system: A real-time system for predicting lake circulation and thermal structure. *Water Poll. Res. J.*, 29(2/3):203–220, 1994.

16. Michael Stonebraker. Sequoia 2000: A reflection on the first three years. *IEEE Computational Science and Engineering*, 1(4):63–72, Winter 1994.

17. Michael Stonebraker et al. Tioga: A database-oriented visualization tool. In *Proceedings of Visualization 93*, pages 86–93, San Jose, CA, October 1993. IEEE.

Metalevel Database Programming and Visualization with POETView

Matthias Neugebauer

matthias_neugebauer@poet.de

POET Software Hamburg

Abstract. The separation of data model and presentation has been shown to be highly useful for the visualization of data. The Model-View-Controller (MVC) paradigm used by Smalltalk has been accepted as the de facto standard in this area. Over the past two years, a new software architecture has been developed based on the MVC approach. This architecture takes into account the special requirements of the C++ language, object databases (such as POET) and C++ class libraries for GUI development. It is used in commercial products, however it is not available in itself as a separate product. POETView is intended for use in internal tool production and in external project development.

The development of POETView was motivated by the need for reusable user interface and data model components. As significantly more effort is generally required to develop the graphical interface of an application than the algorithms used in the model, we have tried to allow the reuse of existing components whenever possible in different contexts.

However, components are not found only at the user interface level. The data model also contains reusable components. We consider reusability to be most effective when the components can be reused in binary form. These objects must therefore be able to communicate with each other at run-time which data are to be displayed. This protocol is at the heart of the POETView architecture. It allows a presentation component to obtain data from the associated data model components and to display them as desired. The protocol also manages any necessary meta-data. In this way, components can be combined at run-time, since the static or compile-time definition of possible aggregations is not necessary.

1 Introduction

This paper presents a framework for the visualization and manipulation of data in object-oriented databases. It essentially concerns ideas and concepts; the presentation of concrete implementations details is avoided.

POETView is not available as a product, but is used rather for the production of database tools. These include database inspectors (on the class and instance level) as well as tools for the administration of databases (user management, workspaces, reorganization) and servers (monitoring, shutdown).

Unlike applications which are based on a concrete class model, universal database tools are developed independently from the application-specific data model.

For this reason, meta-information (class descriptions, inheritance structure, attributes, methods) are the basis of the visualization. The visualization framework must be able to access this meta-information as simply, reliably and efficiently as possible. All components must therefore hook into this meta-information. Visualization components which are used to represent specific classes such "Person" are not sufficient. Components which are able to work with any arbitrary class model are far more useful.

For this purpose a framework has been developed which serves as an intermediate layer between the database and the user interface. Based on the Smalltalk Model-View-Controller (MVC) architecture, POETView is made up of *subjects* and *views*. A subject makes data available to the views for visualization.

Data distribution and update are assured by an update mechanism. This mechanism is used by the view to display the data which it has obtained from the subject. Modifications undertaken by the user on the screen are distributed using the subject's update notification mechanism, which in turn passes along the modifications to the corresponding data source, normally the database.

Once the modifications have been taken into account, the subject informs all dependent views of the change in question so that the latter can update the corresponding display.

Data exchange between subject and view is based on a universally comprehensible protocol. In order for this to function, the data meta-information must be generated at run-time, since the database must first be opened before the schema can be known. Only in this way can truly generic visualization components be obtained.

2 Goals and Non-Goals

The following requirements were taken into account in the design of POETView.

- Concurrency Control
  Normally, concurrency is controlled in databases through the use of locks and transactions. A given application accesses the database as if it were the only one using it. POETView must also react to events sent by the database. Deletion, modification and locking are examples of such asynchronous events. Unlike user interface events, they come from "below" and cause changes to the user interface.
- Handling of Large Data Volumes
  In handling large volumes of data, it is essential to assure that only truly essential data are kept in memory, since the database capacity is almost certainly greater than the main memory capacity. Network access must be reduced to a minimum, since they have a significant negative effect on system response time.
- Support for the POET Object Model
  The Subject-View protocol must support the entire POET object model, so that every object structure may be freely exchanged between and understood

by subject and views. The POET object model is based on the C++ model and on a specification published by the Object Database Management Group (ODMG). [1]. Specifically, the following elements are supported:

- atomic or base types (integer, float, date, time, BLOBs, strings, ...)
- complex objects, compound data types
- polymorphic object references
- containers
- relations, 1:1, 1:m, m:n relations
- inheritance/polymorphism
- methods (not yet implemented)

This object model goes much further than that supported by relational systems, in which only atomic data types can normally be used as table attributes.

- Reusability of Components and Design

The highest possible level of reusability should be attained. Reusability is supported on various levels:

- Design

Standard scenarios should be realisable using ready-made, standard designs.

- Components

Visualization components and data sources should be reusable in binary form in all possible contexts. It should be possible for all components (subject, views, ...) to be combined arbitrarily (Plug & Play)

- Localization

The framework should be localisable. In addition to the translation of interface text, all locale-specific formatting issues must be taken into account (for example, both European and American norms for the formatting of dates should be available).

- Portability

Design and implementation must be free of platform-specific concepts and practices. The goal is to be able to port the user interface onto any given platform.

POETView does not include a portable GUI class library. The programming interface (API) accesses the POETView class interface through the use of mix-in classes. Although this reduces the portability to other class libraries, it enables the elimination of an additional functional layer and the code that this would necessitate.

---

[1] POET Software is a voting member of the ODMG and is the chair of its C++ working group

3 Architecture

3.1 Separation of Data and Visualization

The separation of internal data representation and the associated visualization has been shown to be a useful paradigm. The loading and display of data are demanding tasks which must be managed by specialised objects. An object which displays itself using polymorphic methods exists only as an example in object-oriented literature. Why should all the ways in which an object can be visualised be integrated directly into the object itself? An additional type of visualization can then only be obtained by modifying the object (and possibly its interface). It is much better to leave the tasks related to the display of data to objects which are specialized for this purpose. Such an approach requires, however, that the instances involved be able to provide information about the data which is to be displayed. The language used in POETView for this purpose is

The Subject/View Protocol The Subject/View protocol is at the heart of the POETView architecture. It enables communication between subject and view, acting as a common language. As such, it must

- support the complete Object Model
- preserve the separation of data and behavior.
  The protocol must not therefore restrict itself to data, but must also make an object's methods accessible to the view so that they can be activated by the user. Operations on the object can, for example, be made accessible to the user through the use of a contextual menu or buttons in the view.
- moderate run-time overhead
  The usual rule against run-time overhead is not entirely respected here. Because a meta-data protocol is used to interpret the data, the performance cannot be identical to a statically coded implementation. The performance of the framework has an important, although not primary, importance. Several optimizations have been undertaken, inasmuch as they do not reduce the universality of the approach and actually simplify its utilization. For example, the aspects of a subject are transfered together rather than separately, and when possible the values are not copied, but rather transfered as references. Optimizations have not been undertaken if they would reduce the universality of the architecture, since development times are a very critical factor and would be adversely affected.

Data are primarily transfered in aspects which have been assembled into aspect set containers. An aspect contains

- value
- name or identifier
- type
- status (validated, modified, read-only, ...). Only status information which does not relate to the user interface is relevant here, as the subject does not concern itself with the display of data.

Mapping onto the POET Object Model

– Atomic values

The following atomic types must be supported: Integer, short, unsigned short, long, unsigned long, float, double, enumerations, byte, PtString[2], d_String[3], PtDate[4], d_Date[5], PtTime[6], d_Time[7], PtDateTime[8], d_Timestamp[9], d_Interval[10], PtObjId[11], PtClassId[12], PtRef[13], PtBlob[14]

Values must be transfered in their native format (date, time, ...) and must not be converted/formatted into a character string, since this conversion is only necessary in order to display the data. A subject does not know, however, how a date (e.g. 12/24/95) should be displayed in a given context, so it leaves this job to the GUI class library.

– complex objects, references

Complex objects are composed of attributes belonging to one of the afore-mentioned categories (atomic types, complex objects, references, containers, relations). They are broken down recursively into atomic data types.

We have chosen the subject as the medium for the encapsulation of complex data types, since it already possesses the necessary functionality. A subject is a container for attributes which can be accessed using the Subject-View protocol. The attributes are assembled into so-called aspect sets. Each aspect can also be a subject in its own right, allowing the creation of complex objects. For this reason, the recursivity of the data model must also be taken into account.

– container, relation

A container is a set [15] of separate objects, which can in turn be atomic, complex, references, containers, ... The individual elements can be identified by index or by surrogate. A subject is also used for this purpose.

– methods

Methods are defined by the additional *verb* parameter. They are not transfered into the aspect set.

---

[2] POET string type
[3] ODMG-93 string type
[4] POET date type
[5] ODMG-93 date type
[6] POET time type
[7] ODMG-93 time type
[8] POET type for time and date
[9] ODMG-93 type for time and date
[10] ODMG-93 type for time interval
[11] POET surrogate/object id
[12] POET class description identifier
[13] POET object reference, contains a PtObjId, a PtClassId and a database identifier for cross database references
[14] POET Binary Large Object
[15] The mathematically meaning is not intended in this case.

Dialogs and Views *Views* are the atomic unit of visualization for POETView. No classes for *controls* (such as buttons or listboxes) are provided, since they are considered to be the responsibility of the GUI class library. A given concrete implementation of a view provides the functionality necessary to use these controls.

In order to attain the highest possible level of reusability — for example, to be able to use *views* in different contexts, — the idea of *dialogs* is introduced. A dialog is a window (modal, modeless, floating palette, ...) which contains an arbitrary number of views.

The view uses the dialog's abstract interface and is therefore independent of the specific appearance and properties of the dialog.

A range of dialogs are available for use without modification, as they do not contain any visualization-specific code. Specialization is generally not required, since the actual display of data is performed by the view and not by the dialog.

The class dialog interface has the following form: [16]

```
interface Dialog {
    void addView (in View view2add);
    void removeView (in View view2remove);
    void deleteDependentViews ();
    ViewArrangement setArrangement (in ViewArrangement arrangement2set);
    ViewArrangement getArrangement ();
};

interface ModalDialog : Dialog, ModalWindow {
    ...
};

interface ModelessDialog : Dialog, ModelessWindow {
    ...
};

interface FloatingDialog : Dialog, FloatingWindow {
    ...
};

...
```

Dialog::addView() and Dialog::removeView() are used to attach a view to the dialog and to detach it when it is no longer needed. When a dialog is closed, Dialog::deleteDependentViews() is called in order to remove the remaining views.

The Dialog::setArrangement() and Dialog::getArrangement() methods are used for automatic geometry management (see below).

```
interface View {

    void update (in AspectSet values,
```

---

[16] all class definitions are written in OMG-IDL, see [6]

```
        in Surrogate objectPos,
        in Verb verb)
    raises (...);

void show (in Dialog parent);
    raises (...);

void hide (in Dialog parent);
    raises (...);

void getPosAndSize ( out short &x,
                     out short &y,
                     out short &width,
                     out short &height);
    raises (...);

void resize (in Dialog parent,
             in short x,
             in short y,
             in short width,
             in short height);
    raises (...);
};
```

View::update() is called by the subject when the data it contains has been modified. This can be caused either by changes in the associated view(s) or by actions[17] undertaken in the database.

View::show(), View::hide() are used to display a view or to remove it from the screen.

View::getPosAndSize() returns the current position and size of the view. This information is also used for automatic geometry management. A new layout is generated using the data received from the views. View::resize() informs the view of its new position and size.

Subjects Subjects are an encapsulation of the data management logic. They control the connection to the database or other data sources. The view sees only the subject interface and knows nothing about the actual data sources.

Subjects contain a set of similar objects. The individual objects are accessed using their position, which can be either an index or an object ID.

Data are available in a container which contains all necessary attributes. The aspect set is typically created by the subject, since only the subject knows which data are present.

```
interface Subject {
    void validate( inout AspectSet values,
```

---

[17] asychronous events such as saving, deleting, ... which may have been performed by other applications in other address spaces or on other machines.

```
                in Surrogate objectPos,
                in Verb verb )
        raises ( ValidationError, ...);

    void update (inout AspectSet values,
                in Surrogate objectPos,
                in Verb verb)
        raises (ValidationError, ...);

    void getValue (inout AspectSet values,
                in Surrogate objectPos)
        raises (ObjectNotFound, ...);

    AspectSet gimmeYourAspects ();
            raises (NoAspectSetAvailable, ...);

    AspectId getSurrogateAspectId ();
            raises (...);

    long getObjectsCount ();
        raises (...);

    int isContainer (); raises (...);
    int isReference (); raises (...);
    int isCompound (); raises (...);
    int isRelation (); raises (...);

    void addDependent (in View dependentView);
        raises (...);
    void removeDependent (in PvView dependentView);
        raises (...);

    Verbs gimmeYourVerbs (in Surrogate objectPos);
        raises (...);
};
```

With Subject::gimmeYourAspects(), the view can find out which information the subject contains.

An aspect set is returned containing all aspects. The values are not set or are represented by dummy values. The actual data can be obtained using Subject::getValue(). A subject can represent individual objects or sets of objects. Individual objects in a set are identified by their position. Which attribute is used as an identifier can be found out by using Subject::getSurrogateAspectId().

If data are modified, they must then be validated with Subject::validate(). If the data are not valid, the corresponding aspect in the aspect set will be flagged with the status *notValid*. In this way, the view can inform the user where the error occurred. Subject::update() writes the modified data to the database after validation is complete. The status information is also used here to identify

---

139

modified attributes, so that only new values need be transfered and stored.
   The subjects enable

- *views* to operate on any arbitrary data source
- optimizations of the data link to be encapsulated. This makes possible an advantageous division of labor during software development. Database specialists can take care of the development of the subject, whereas the user interface group is responsible for the views.
- the reuse of exising subjects and views during the implementation phase. [18].

3.2 Automatic View Layouting: View Arrangements

View arrangements are objects which handle the automatic layouting of the views in a dialog. They can be combined arbitrarily at run-time with any dialogs and views. If a dialog window is to be managed by a given view arrangement, the arrangement in question is made known to the dialog, and from this moment on the view arrangement is informed of any new views added to the dialog. The view arrangement then queries the new view as to its dimensions and position and generates the desired layout. Each view is then informed of the position and size which it is to use.
   For this purpose , the view has a certain number of special methods:

```
interface View {

...

// determine the screen dimensions of the view.
   // Used for dynamic view arrangements
   void getPosAndSize ( out short &x,
                        out short &y,
                        out short &width,
                        out short &height);
      raises (...);

   // The view is informed of the position and size it is to use
   void resize (in Dialog parent,
                in short x,
                in short y,
                in short width,
                in short height);
      raises (...);
};

interface ViewArrangement {
```

---

[18] This idea is not simply a pie-in-the-sky proposition, but was actually used for the development of our database tools. The development of the graphical interface for our OQL tool required approximately three days.

```
    // attaches a new view
    void addView (View view2add);

    // detaches a view
    void removeView (View view2remove);

    // the size of the dialog has been changed
    void resize ();

    // change the layout of the views
    void rearrange ();
};
```

A library exists containing flexible algorithms for the generation of arbitrary display layouts.

3.3 Nesting Presentations: Compound Views

The structure discussed above allows only the aggregation of views inside a dialog. It does not permit the nesting of view hierarchies.

A view can only be displayed in a dialog. It receives a parent window from the dialog and its layout may be controlled by a view arrangement. A dialog can only contain views and a view arrangement can only manage views.

Arbitrary nested structures can be built up through the use of a view which is also a dialog. The compound view is added to the dialog as a view and is managed by the arrangement attached to the dialog in question. At the same time, this view acts as a dialog in respects to the views and arrangements which it contains. We therefore have a fully nestable architecture in which components (views and arrangments) can be used freely in any context.

The only role of compound views is the delegation of incoming messages to its "children".

3.4 Events and Attached Views

Views must be able to communicate with each other without being too tightly coupled together.

Views are "attached" using a directed connection. The "attached" view serves thus as the message sink and the other view as the message source.

The message source does not know which views are attached to it. A method is used to send messages to all connected views.

When the message sink receives a message, it is also informed of the identity of the sending view.

We make use of the Subject-View protocol for the transmission of data and messages. Therefore, aspect sets are sent in the same manner as we have seen for the view methods getValue(...) and update(...).

In this way, any number of views can be attached to a given view (concatenation is also possible). It is important that neither the event source nor the event target need possess any information about the other party. The necessary data are transfered in a generic manner using the POETView protocol.

For this purpose, the view class contains additional methods:

```
interface View {
    void attachView (in View view2attach);
    void detachView (in View view2detach);
    void postEvent (in AspectSet values, in Verb verb);
    void handleEvent (in AspectSet values,
                      in Verb verb,
                      in View messageSource);
};
```

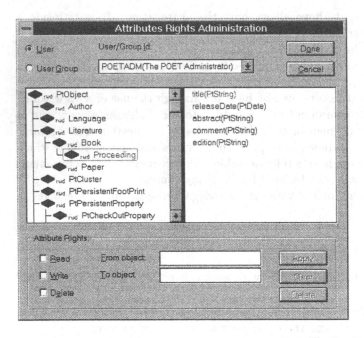

Fig. 1. POET Administrator during the definition of attribute rights in the database

This example shows the POET Administrator during the definition of attribute rights in the database. Different techniques are used. First of all, both of the lists in the center are organised in a compound view, whose output area is managed by a horizontal splitter arrangement. The compound view in turn is a view in the dialog window. However, the dialog window is not aware of the compound view. The views contained in a compound view are only accessible by

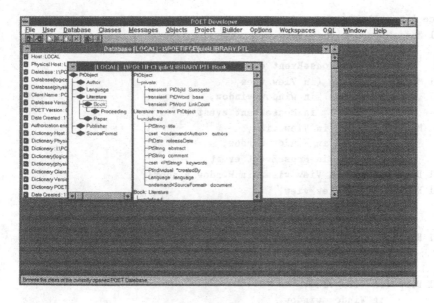

Fig. 2. POET Developer's Class Browser using the same Views and ViewArrangement as the POET Administrator

passing through the compound view itself. The black verticle line in the middle can be moved with the mouse, enabling the user to resize the window as desired. When the user selects an entry in the list on the left side, the right side is informed so that it can adapt its display accordingly. The right window is attached to the left window.

The components described above are used without modification in many other contexts. They need only be combined with other objects in order to yield different types of behavior and appearance.

3.5 Separating Presentation from Contexts: Interactors

Actions performed on a view are often dependent on the context in which it is found. This can affect not only which operations are available, but also the way in which the view is displayed on the screen. If a class browser enables the creation and deletion of classes during the visualization of the dictionary, an object inspector [19] should be able to create and delete objects. The operations may be shown in a menu in the title bar of the frame window or made available to the user in a contextual (pop-up) menu.

Operations on the subject and the display are delegated to an interactor. An interactor is an abstract base class which receives and processes events.

---

[19] A tool for the visualization of instances.

```
interface Interactor {
    bool MouseMove (in View view,
                    in Window window,
                    in MouseEvent event);
    bool MouseButtonDown (in View view,
                          in Window window,
                          in MouseEvent event);
    bool MouseButtonUp (in View view,
                        in Window window,
                        in MouseEvent event);
    bool DoubleClick (in View view, in Window window);
    bool KeyInput (in View view,
                   in Window window,
                   in KeyEvent event);
    bool RequestHelp (in View view,
                      in Window window,
                      in HelpEvent event);
    bool Drop (in View view,
               in Window window,
               in DropEvent event);
    bool QueryDrop (in View view,
                    in Window window,
                    in DropEvent event);
};
```

In addition, any user interface event (mouse, keyboard) can be delegated by the interactor to an arbitrary interactor object. Information relevant to the event, such as mouse coordinates, keyboard codes, view and window, is thus received along with the event itself.

The return value can be used to determine whether the interactor actually handled the event. If, for example, the interactor only uses the right mouse button for the display of a contextual menu and ignores all other events, it returns *true* for a right mouse button event and *false* for all other events. The view can then handle the event itself.

4 Conclusion

POETView has been used for three years for the development of database visualization tools. Over this period, certain of the mechanisms described above have been extended and refined and the software has reached a stable state. Almost no fundamental changes or extensions have been undertaken recently. The use of this framework, besides providing a high level of reusability[20], has also facilitated program maintenance.

---

[20] Components and Design

5   Acknowledgements

Thanks to my colleagues Klaus Blessenohl, Michael Schwieger, Uwe Wittig for the fruitful discussions we have had and to Matthew Gertner for helping me to translate this paper into English.

6   Literature

References

1. Smalltalk-80, The Language and its Implementation Goldberg, A., Robson, D.: Addision-Wesley Publ. 1983
2. The Object Database Standard: ODMG-93 Ed. Cattell, R.G.G, Morgan Kaufman Publ. 1993
3. Software-Werkzeuge in einer Programmierwerkstatt, Ansaetze eines hermeneutisch fundierten Werkzeug- und Maschinenbegriffs Budde, Reinhard; Zuellighoven, Heinz Gesellschaft fuer Mathematik und Datenverarbeitung, GMD-Bericht Nr. 182 R. Oldenburg Verlag, 1990
4. The Art of the Metaobject Protocol Kiczales, Gregor; Des Rivieres, Jim; Bobrow, Daniel G. The MIT Press, Cambridge, Massechusetts, 1991
5. Plug & Play Programming Wong, William M & T Books, New York, 1993
6. The Common Object Request Broker: Architecture and Specification, Resvision 2.0, July 1995, Object Management Group

Large Scale Data Analysis Using AVS5 and POSTGRES*

Ray E. Flanery Jr.** and June M. Donato***

Computer Science and Mathematics Division
Oak Ridge National Laboratory
Oak Ridge, TN 37831–6414
Fax: 423–241–6211

Abstract. In this paper we discuss the use of AVS5 as an interface tool to the public domain database management system POSTGRES. This work is part of ongoing research on data analysis tools for large (terabyte) data sets. Statistical analysis and browsing tools for the data sets are provided via the AVS5 and POSTGRES systems. Graphical interfaces are provided for both the feature extraction stage and the post processing stage of the system. The tools for these interfaces, rather than the statistical tools themselves, are the focus of this paper.

1 Introduction

Data sets in the gigabyte size range are difficult, if not impossible, to analyze with current methods. At Oak Ridge National Laboratory in Tennessee, we are concerned with large data sets from a variety of applications. These applications include:

CHAMMP[4] (Computer Hardware, Advanced Mathematics, and Model Physics)
   program sponsored by DOE, and
ARM[5] (Atmospheric Radiation Measurement) program sponsored by DOE.

The CHAMMP project, which simulates atmospheric global climate models, will eventually be producing data for analysis at the rate of about 1TB (terabyte) per day. The ARM archive for atmospheric water vapor records is maintained at ORNL and currently contains in excess of 350 GB of data distributed in over 50,000 files.

---

* Research sponsored by the Laboratory Directed Research and Development Program of Oak Ridge National Laboratory, managed for the United States Department of Energy by Lockheed Martin Energy Systems, Inc., under Contract No. DE–AC05–84OR21400.

** Director, Advanced Visualization Research Center. E-mail: flaneryrejr@ornl.gov
*** Staff Researcher. E-mail: donatojm@ornl.gov
[4] http://www.esd.ornl.gov/programs/chammp/chammp.html
[5] http://www-armarchive.ornl.gov/

Researchers need tools to analyze these large data sets in a straightforward fashion. The tools must be easy to use. They must present the data in a compact form, yet be able to take advantage of the supercomputers and heterogeneous networks of computers on which the data to be analyzed is created and stored.

The work presented in this paper is part of ongoing research on data analysis tools for large (terabyte) data sets entitled "Analysis of Large Scientific Data Sets." The project utilizes statistical techniques to extract useful or interesting information from data sets too large for normal browsing techniques. AVS5 is used to build the networks for the statistical filters which extract the information. These statistical filters are encapsulated as AVS5 modules. This allows us to interactively update the statistical parameters through the graphical interface. This stage is called the "feature extraction stage." A typical choice of filter parameters could produce filtered information of only a very small (e.g. 0.1%) percentage of the original large data set size. This resulting filtered information is stored and accessed via the POSTGRES DBMS.

In this paper, we will focus on the graphical interface tools between AVS5 and POSTGRES.

AVS5 is the Application Visualization System by Advanced Visual Systems, Inc. which provides an interactive 3D visualization system and a sophisticated graphical user interface. Further information about AVS5 can be obtained via http://www.avs.com/.

POSTGRES is a public domain Data Base Management System. For more information refer to http://s2k-ftp.CS.Berkeley.EDU:8000/postgres/.

The goals of the "Analysis of Large Scientific Data Sets" project were:

- To automate the process of extracting useful or interesting information from the raw data sets.
- To store the resulting data using an appropriate data model for later retrieval and analysis.
- To provide useful tools for browsing the extracted data which are too large and unwieldy to manipulate or browse by current means.
- To implement a Graphical User Interface for the above.

In light of these goals, the following subgoals were also deemed important:

- To have a graphical user interface that even non-experts in statistical analysis techniques, AVS, or POSTGRES could use.
- That information be presented in a compact form, yet allow details to be easily accessed.
- That the tools utilize a client-server structure to allow these large data sets to reside on a large mainframe or supercomputer, yet allow the users to perform analysis and visualization at their workstations.

2 Overview of the System

The system interface consists of two main phases:

– Feature Extraction, and
– Visualization and Analysis.

In the feature extraction phase, the user supplies the system with specifications necessary to create a filtered representation of the large data set. At minimal, the user specifies the following information:

– the input file containing the raw scientific data sets;
– the feature extractor to use in filtering the data.

The system then begins to read the raw data in intervals, applying the feature extractor to chunks of data, and writing a representation of the filtered data to the database. During this process histogram and box-plots of the raw data sections are displayed allowing the user to tailor parameters to better reduce or filter the resulting data representation.

In the visualization and analysis phase, the power of scientific visualization is used to discover unusual or interesting features of the original large data set in an easily comprehensible yet compact format. Through the visual interface the user displays one of the filtered representations of the original data. The system generates the necessary query language commands to the database system to load the appropriate filtered data.

By clicking a button in the user interface, the user may select different views of the filtered data representation. For example, the user might view "statistical value" versus "event time" using a color schema to depict variations in the "time between intervals." This technique gives a visually compact representation of three dimensional relationships in a two dimensional display where color variations represent the third dimension of data information.

Other views of the data are easily selected by a click of an interface button.

3 Technical Issues

The technical approach to the overall system just described contained a number of interesting, and sometimes difficult, implementation issues.

We use AVS5 to create the Graphical User Interface (GUI) as well as to create many of the analysis tools for the process. AVS5 was chosen because it provides a useful GUI, two and three dimensional renderers, and it is easily portable as well as user-extendible.

The database management system chosen was POSTGRES. POSTGRES is a public domain, easily portable, system. It allows back-end functions to better utilize the CPUs of the host machine, and provides object oriented extensions that allow useful Large Objects to be stored with the data.

However, interfacing these two systems presented the interesting challenge.

For example, during the visualization and analysis phase, the user selects some point of interest. The selection is then used to determine and load the corresponding raw data. Unfortunately, AVS5 did not easily allow access to the point location information. Hence a separate module implementing an interactive two-dimensional browser and graphic display was created to provide this crucial information via the user interface.

Due to the size of these scientific data sets, they are typically stored on large mainframes or supercomputers. It is crucial to minimize the amount of data down-loaded and processed on the client workstation. Hence, another aspect of this project was utilizing POSTGRES' back-end function capability to do as much processing on the back-end server machine as possible.

4 Example System Usage

In this section we present and describe a number of typical system screens as seen from the user's viewpoint. Due to the dark background of the original color pictures from AVS, the screen pictures shown in this paper are in reversed video grey scale color.

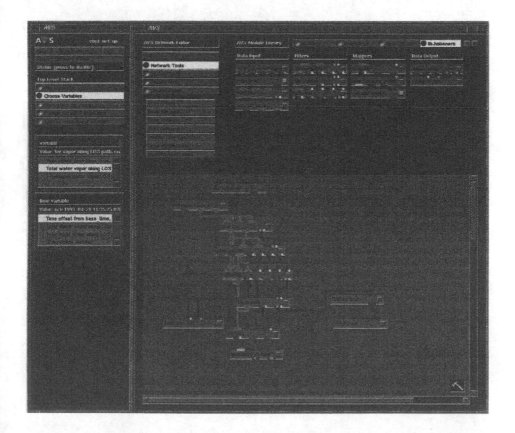

Fig. 1. AVS Network for Filter Pre-Processing

The user starts AVS, selects the "Network Editor", then "Network Tools", and then selects "Read Network" in order to supply the name of the AVS network to load. It is at this stage that the user can select to either pre-process (filter) data from a large data set or may choose to post-process (visualize filtered) meta-data from a previous filtering run.

In this case, the user has selected to pre-process using the change-point filter. The user specifies any desired system characteristics (such as the name of the output database to create or to which to add data). The screen setup for this filter process is shown in Figure 1. This figure shows the actual AVS network for the filter along with parameters available for user specification. Here the user has specified that the variable to monitor is the "Total water vapor along LOS" where LOS stands for "line-of-sight." The time variable is chosen to be the "Time offset from base time." There are also default ranges of variables prearranged within the filter code. These ranges can be changed by the user.

Once the user is satisfied with the setup parameters and files, the user selects "Extract Feature and Monitor" in order to begin pre-processing the data with the filter (in this case, the change-point filter) and to be able to watch this filtering process. Figure 2 is a snapshot during the pre-processing phase. The

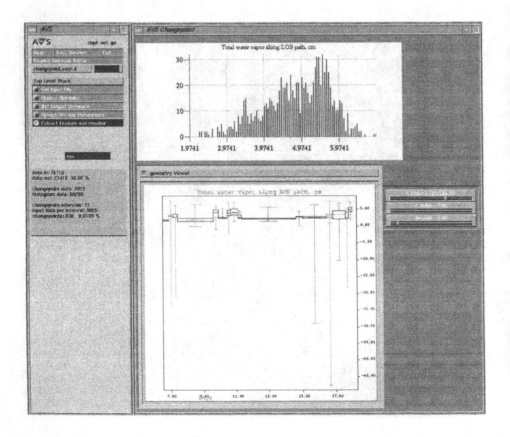

Fig. 2. Snapshot of the Pre-Processing Phase

screen is updated as the data are processed. The user can watch the box-plots and histogram data being displayed in order to select new variables ranges of interest. This is particularly useful when the user wants to insure a particular amount of data filtering. The pre-processing stage may be rerun once the user is satisfied with the variables and ranges selected and the level of data filtering achieved. The pre-processing may also be run for a different set of variables, ranges or filtering process. The filters generate meta-data about the raw data which is stored in the POSTGRES database.

Once the pre-processing is completed, the meta-data is available to the the user via the AVS network interface immediately or for use at a later time.

In the post-processing phase, the goal is to actually utilize the now existent filter generated meta-data to examine relationships or trends. The user is also able to selectively examine the original raw data for features within the meta-data.

To utilize a post-processing module of the system, the user returns to the AVS Network Editor screen and again selects "Network Tools" and then "Read Network." This time the user specifies one of the post-processing systems. Figure 3 shows the AVS network for the situation where the user has selected the "newer changept postgres" post-processor. The database, class names, and variable names are specified as part of the module "New_Read_Postgres_DB."

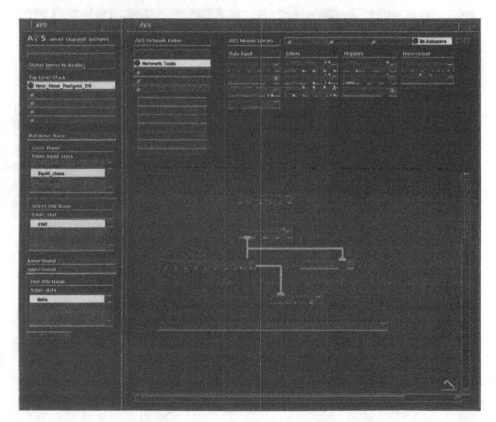

Fig. 3. AVS Network for Post-Processor

The user selects the button "new_choose_point" to begin the post-processing. In Figure 4 the output from the module is depicted (normally in color, but for this paper in grey scale). Different colors/shades represent levels of values for the second variable. Here the user is viewing "Statistical" value versus "Event Time" where the colors/shadings relate to the values for the third variable "Time Between Events." There is a slider that allows the user to browse through the display window. There is also a "Swap Axes" button that allows the user to swap which variable values will be used for the x-axis. By selecting the button, we switch the plot to view "Statistical" value versus "Time Between Intervals" where the colors/shadings relate to the values for the variable "Event Time." This view is shown in Figure 5.

The user may examine the raw data that generated a particular point simply by clicking on that point. For example, in Figure 5 there is a very unusual point in the upper right hand corner of the window. We click on this point and are shown the view in Figure 6. When the user clicked on the point, the module generated appropriate POSTGRES commands to query the database for location information of the raw data. This location information is used to access and view the corresponding original raw data which may have resided in a different database or in a large file of some format.

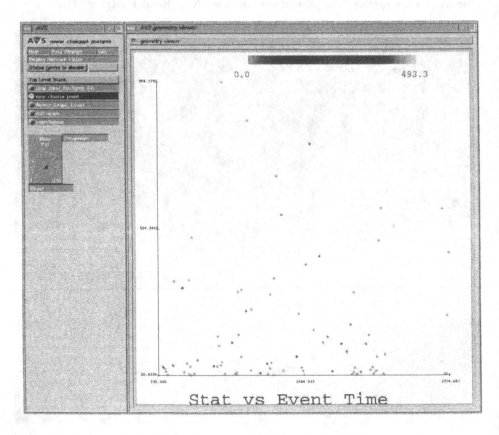

Fig. 4. One View of Post-Processing Output

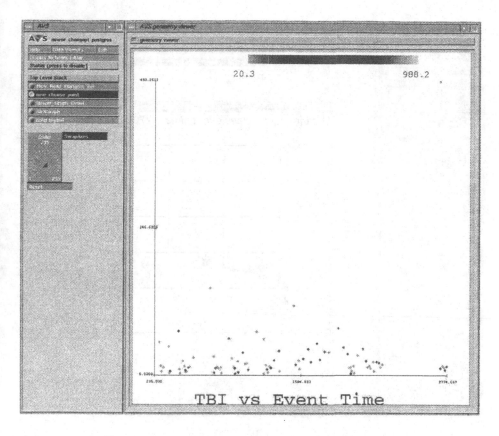

Fig. 5. An Alternate View of Post-Processing Output

This is the power point of the system, in that the user may peruse a small percentage of data and yet still be able to examine interesting or unusual events from the raw data itself without having to download the entire large data set (which may not even be physically possible).

5   Summary and Future Goals

In the statistical analysis and visual representation of large scientific data sets this project has already made a number of successful steps. However, this system is still an initial prototype. There are a number of features still to be designed and implemented. In some cases, we would like to completely revamp certain mechanisms. In particular, we would like to replace AVS5 by the more recent AVS/EXPRESS system in order to gain a number of interface and module implementation features.

We would also like to implement a PVM (Parallel Virtual Machine) or MPI (Message Passing Interface) version of this system to generically provide parallel processing of the filtering and analysis tools. This would allow the system to be

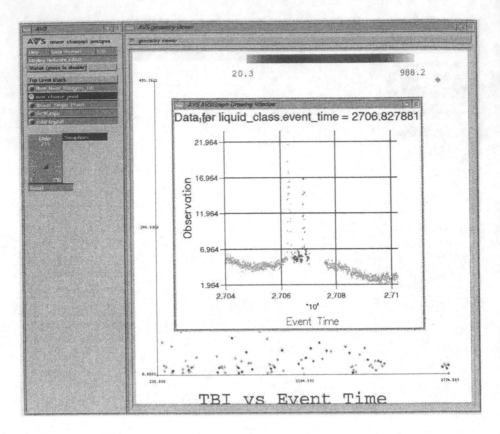

Fig. 6. View of Raw Data Represented by Chosen Data Point

used on parallel and heterogeneous distributed machines, including the currently available parallel supercomputers, such as the Intel Paragon.

Most of all, we would like to extend the system, both in terms of feature extraction and visual capabilities, to more complex data sets, such as three-dimensional data, and to multivariate statistical analyses.

Acknowledgments

This project was initially funded as a Laboratory Director's Research and Development (LDRD) project under the direction of Darryl J. Downing. Members of the statistical analysis team for this project are Darryl J. Downing, V.V. Fedorov, W.F. Lawkins, M.D. Morris, and G. Ostrouchov.

We also take this moment to remember Toby Mitchell.

References

1. Advanced Visual Systems, Inc. *AVS Developer's Guide*, 1992, Waltham, MA.
2. D.J. Downing, W.J. Lawkins, M.D. Morris, and G. Ostrouchov, *FEaTureS - Feature Extraction for Long Time Series: User's Guide*, Oak Ridge National Lab, technical report.
3. P. Kochevar, Z. Ahmed, J. Shade, and C. Sharp, *A Simple Visualization Management System: Bridging the Gap Between Visualization and Data Management*, San Diego Supercomputer Center, in Proceedings Visualization '93, edited by G.M. Nielson, April 30, 1993.
4. M. Stonebraker and G. Kemnitz, *The POSTGRES Next Generation DBMS*, EECS Department, University of California, Berkeley.
5. M. Stonebraker and L.A. Rowe, *The Design of POSTGRES*, EECS Department, University of California, Berkeley.

FAN - An Array-Oriented Query Language

Harvey Davies

CSIRO Division of Atmospheric Research,
Private Bag No. 1, Mordialloc 3195, Australia. email: hld@dar.csiro.au

Abstract. *FAN (File Array Notation)* is an array-oriented language for identifying data items in files for the purpose of extraction (e.g. for visualization) or modification. FAN specifications consist of
- one or more filenames
- one or more variable (array) identifiers
- attribute identifiers (optional)
- dimension identifiers (optional)
- subscripts in various possible forms (optional).

These identifiers can be names or numbers. FAN is intended to be generic and could be applied to any file format, even relational databases. However netCDF is the only such format currently supported. The use of FAN can greatly simplify access to array-oriented data.

1 Introduction

As pointed out by Pratt [Pra75, p57] "Homogeneous fixed-size arrays are perhaps the most common data structures encountered in programming." This applies even more strongly to the data processed by visualization software. This ubiquity of arrays makes it most surprising that array-oriented file formats (e.g. CDF [GM94], HDF [NCS93] and netCDF [RDED96]) were not developed until the 1980s.

A recent survey of database issues for data visualization [B+94b, p25] stated "Interaction with most database systems is still via simple relational languages such as SQL, ...".

FAN is based largely on the subscripting concepts in the array-oriented languages Fortran 90 ([ABM+92]) and APL ([BPP94]). It is also influenced by netCDF and its associated language CDL. These concepts are more relevant to array-oriented data than those associated with traditional (typically relational) databases and associated languages such as SQL.

Dejesus [Dej95, p148] states: "Some people predict the emergence of a standard MDQL (multidimensional query language)." It is hoped that FAN can provide the basis for such a language.

Many authors (e.g. [BFG94]) seem to assume that the best user interface for visualization of array-oriented data is a GUI (graphical user interface). It would

---

* This work is supported by Unidata Program Center, University Corporation for Atmospheric Research, P.O. Box 3000, Boulder, Colorado 80307-3000, USA.

indeed be possible to use a GUI to specify the data to be accessed. For example, there could be a pair of *slider widgets* for each dimension, corresponding to the lower and upper index values. However a language such as FAN provides a communication tool which is more convenient to use and has much more functionality. Of course there is no reason why a GUI interface could not provide an *entry widget* for the purpose of entering FAN specifications.

2 Terminology

The author uses the word *array* in preference to adjectives for data such as *spatiotemporal*, *scientific* and *multidimensional* (see [B+94a, p5]), none of which capture the essential concept. Another possible (though somewhat more general) term is *lattice*, as used by [KBS94].

An *array* is considered to be a k-dimensional rectangular structure containing data items which all have the same *data type* (e.g. character, 32-bit integer).

Subscript values can be specified as integer *indices* commencing at a value called the *index origin* (typically 0 or 1). There can be a *coordinate variable* associated with the subscript. For example, a geographic matrix may have a latitude corresponding to each row and a longitude corresponding to each column. In this case it is useful to provide operations (e.g. find closest to) which map from coordinate variables to indices.

The concept of an array can be generalized to include scalars by treating them as 0-dimensional arrays. The number of subscripts (dimensions) is called the *rank*.

The term *file array* is used to refer to an array stored in a file, especially one with an array-oriented format such as netCDF. Such files will be termed *array files*.

3 Data Model

Kao, et. al. ([KBS94, p71] distinguish between conceptual and physical data models as follows: "*Conceptual data models* provide concepts that are close to the way users perceive data. ... *Physical data models* provide concepts that describe the low level details of how data is stored in the computer."

The FAN conceptual data model is primarily based on Iverson's array model, as implemented in his languages APL and J ([Ive96]). This model allows subscripts to have vector values.

It also allows arrays as elements of arrays. Such *nested* or *boxed* arrays provide a convenient way of representing more complex data structures such as trees and ragged (non-rectangular) arrays.

The physical model for a nested array is an array of pointers to entries in a symbol table, as described by Hui [Hui92]. Nested arrays are not currently implemented in FAN or netCDF. Section 8 mentions preliminary plans for such implementation.

The FAN conceptual data model also includes much of that for netCDF. This includes *dimensions*, *attributes* and *coordinate variables*. It allows multiple arrays within files and each array is identified by its *variable name* or *variable ID number*.

Typically (as in netCDF) the physical data model includes a symbol table containing variable names, data types, ranks, dimensions and starting addresses. Each element is stored at an address which is a linear function of its indices. This obviates the need for indices to be stored, either as fields within records, or in an index to the records (as in a relational database). This provides a very fast and compact storage method, unless there are many missing values.

4 Nature of FAN

As suggested by its third letter 'N' (for 'Notation'), FAN specifications tend to be quite short; typically only ten or twenty characters. However it is by no means a trivial language. The source code for the FAN interpreter includes 242 lines of *yacc* grammar definition, 119 lines of *lex* code (See [LMB92]), as well as about 2000 lines of C.

There is a simple API for reading and writing simple streams of data elements. More complex situations require reference to a C structure created by the interpreter.

The simplest FAN specification consists of just a filename and a variable name. A specification may include multiple filenames and multiple variable names, as well as attributes and dimensions. There are several ways of designating parts of arrays. Specifications are often provided as command-line arguments and FAN is designed to take advantage of shell *wildcarding (globbing)* facilities.

A FAN specification can

- concatenate data from multiple arrays (typically in different files)
- select array sections using *subscripts* in the form of vectors of indices
- specify index values directly, or indirectly via *coordinate variables*
- transpose dimensions

4.1 Comparison with Conventional API

The conventional means of accessing data in array-oriented file formats requires a great deal of coding. Even high-level languages such as IDL use essentially the same low-level API (application programmer interface) as Fortran and C. The IDL interfaces to CDF, HDF and netCDF are described by [Res95].

For example, a simple program to select and print data from a typical netCDF file involves separate operations to open the file, open the variable, inquire about the size of each dimension, extract each relevant attribute and read the data. Then a loop is needed to print the data after testing for missing values and performing any required transformations due to scaling and units attributes. This could easily require a hundred lines of code!

The FAN interface automates these tasks. The user does not even have to know what data type is used in the file. As shown in Section 6.1, the above task can be done by the utility nc2text with one simple command; while Sections 6.2 and 6.3 show that just two lines are needed using either IDL or J with FAN.

5 Software incorporating FAN Interface

Some programs in which FAN is currently incorporated, are

nc2text Utility to print data from netCDF arrays.
text2nc Utility to read ASCII data into netCDF arrays.
ncrob   Utility to reduce or broadcast from netCDF arrays to netCDF array.
con_cif Contouring program based on NCAR graphics.
IDL   Standard IDL using FAN dynamic library.
J   Interpreter for J, with FAN interface modification.

The first three are available as unsupported beta release software in the contrib netCDF library at
<URL:ftp://ftp.unidata.ucar.edu/pub/netcdf/contrib/fan.tar.Z>.
The author and Unidata plan to make them and the FAN library a part of the standard distributed netCDF system.

IDL is an array-oriented programming language, intended for the analysis and visualization of scientific data. It is documented by [Res95]. Further information is available from
<URL:http://sslab.colorado.edu:2222/projects/IDL/idl_ssl_home.html>.

J is an even more array-oriented language. It was developed by Ken Iverson (well-known as the creator of APL) and Roger Hui. Further information is available from [Ive96], [Bur96], [Dav94] and <URL:http://www.jsoftware.com/>. The netCDF API for J involves just two simple verbs, one for input and one for output.

6 Simple Examples

These are based on the FAN command-line utilities nc2text, text2nc and ncrob, together with IDL and J. These provide simpler examples than graphics programs such as con_cif (which use FAN in exactly the same way).

First, the command-line utilities are used to display selected data, change existing data, append new data and calculate a mean. Then IDL (with and without FAN) and J are used for the tasks of reading selected data, displaying it and calculating its mean.

6.1 Using FAN Command-line Utilities

The utility nc2text prints selected data from netCDF arrays.

One can use text2nc to read small volumes (say up to a few thousand lines) of ASCII data and copy it into netCDF arrays, thus modifying existing elements or appending new ones. It is also possible to use text2nc to create, modify and delete attributes.

The utility ncrob reads data from one or more netCDF arrays, performs some process on it and then writes the result to a netCDF array. The letters 'rob' in 'ncrob' stand for *Reduce Or Broadcast*. *Reduce* means to produce an array (e.g. sum, mean, maximum) with lower rank than the original. *Broadcast* means to (repeatedly if necessary) copy an array to another with at least the same rank. An example would be copying the same vector to each row of a matrix. It is practical to process large volumes of data (e.g. 100 MB) using ncrob.

Let us start with a simple netCDF file vec.nc which is printed (in CDL) as follows:

```
$ ncdump vec.nc
netcdf vec {
dimensions:
         n = UNLIMITED ; // (5 currently)
variables:
         float v(n) ;
data:
  v = 10 , 20.3 , 30.2 , 40.9 , 50  ;
}
```

Here '$' is the UNIX command-line prompt.
The following uses nc2text to print the whole array v:

```
$ nc2text vec.nc v
10 20.3 30.2 40.9 50
```

Individual elements can be selected using subscripts. For example:

```
$ nc2text vec.nc 'v[0]'
10
$ nc2text vec.nc 'v[3]'
40.9
```

Several can be selected using a subscript consisting of a list (vector) of indices such as:

```
$ nc2text vec.nc 'v[0 3 1 3]'
10 40.9 20.3 40.9
```

We can write to a netCDF file using text2nc. The following changes the third element from 30.2 to 30.7 and then prints v:

```
$ echo 30.7 | text2nc vec.nc 'v[2]'
$ nc2text vec.nc v
10 20.3 30.7 40.9 50
```

Text2nc reads ASCII text data from standard input, which in this case is a pipe connected to the standard output of echo. Since the dimension has UNLIMITED size, we can append values as follows:

```
$ echo 60.5 70.2 | text2nc vec.nc 'v[5 6]'
$ nc2text vec.nc v
10 20.3 30.7 40.9 50 60.5 70.2
```

Next we use ncrob to calculate the arithmetic mean of v, which is written to a new variable v_mean. Then nc2text is used to print this mean.

```
$ ncrob -r am -c 0 'vec.nc v' 'vec.nc v_mean'
$ nc2text vec.nc v_mean
40.3
```

The option -r am specifies that an *arithmetic mean* is to be calculated. The option -c 0 requests creation of a new variable with rank 0 (i.e. a scalar). The argument 'vec.nc v' specifies the source (input) array and 'vec.nc v_mean' specifies the destination (output) array.

6.2   Using IDL

First, let's use IDL *without* FAN to read this same data, display it and calculate its mean:

```
$ idl
IDL> ncid = ncdf_open( 'vec.nc' )
IDL> varid = ncdf_varid( ncid, 'v' )
IDL> ncdf_varget, ncid, varid, data
IDL> print, format='(7F5.1)', data
 10.0 20.3 30.2 40.9 50.0 60.5 70.2
IDL> ;Following prints mean, variance, skewness, kurtosis
IDL> print, moment(data)
      40.3000      469.433   -0.0135147      -1.71131
IDL> exit
```

Next we use IDL *with* FAN:

```
$ idl
IDL> data = ncget( 'vec.nc v' )
IDL> print, format='(7F5.1)', data
 10.0 20.3 30.2 40.9 50.0 60.5 70.2
IDL> print, (moment(data))(0); Element 0 is mean
      40.300000
IDL> exit
```

6.3   Using J

Finally, we do the same task using J (with FAN).

```
$ j
    data =. ncget 'vec.nc v'
    data
10 20.3 30.2 40.9 50 60.5 70.2
    am data
40.3
```

Note that J sentences (commands) are indented, but results are not. It is assumed that the verbs ncget (netCDF input) and am (arithmetic mean) are defined by the default initialization process.

7 FAN Language

7.1 High-level Syntax

Let *vas* denote a *variable or attribute specification*. A *vas* can have any of the following forms:

```
var
var[subscript, subscript, subscript, ...]
var[subscript, subscript, subscript, ...)
var(subscript, subscript, subscript, ...]
var(subscript, subscript, subscript, ...)
var: att
: att
```

where *var* is a variable name or ID number and *att* is an attribute name or ID number. It is usually more convenient to identify variables, attributes and dimensions by name rather than ID number. The use of ID numbers is discussed in Section 7.4. Attributes are discussed in Section 7.3.

Pairs and Command-line Arguments There are some situations (e.g. J and destination of ncrob) where a FAN specification must be in a single argument. In other cases a FAN specification can span any number of arguments.
Each argument has the form:

```
pair ; pair ; pair ; ...
```

A semicolon (';') has the same effect as a new argument. This allows a FAN specification to contain any number of pairs even if only one argument is allowed. Each *pair* can have any of the following forms:

```
filename vas
vas filename
filename
vas
```

A *filename* must contain at least one period ('.') so it can be distinguished from a variable name. This will be the case if netCDF filenames have a conventional suffix such as the recommended .nc. (In any case it is always possible to prefix a redundant './' directory as in './unconventional' or '/usr/./IdidItMyWay'!) A pair without a *filename* or *vas* uses that of the previous pair. The first pair has no effect by itself unless it contains both a *filename* and a *vas*.
Here is an example of how these are used. It demonstrates concatenation of data from different files.

```
$ cp vec.nc vec_new.nc
$ nc2text v vec.nc vec_new.nc
```

```
10 20.3 30.7 40.9 50 60.5 70.2
10 20.3 30.7 40.9 50 60.5 70.2
$ nc2text v vec*.nc
10 20.3 30.7 40.9 50 60.5 70.2
10 20.3 30.7 40.9 50 60.5 70.2
```

Note the use of UNIX *wildcarding* (or *globbing*) facilities in the latter example using the *metacharacter* '*' matches both vec.nc and vec_new.nc.

7.2   Subscripts

As mentioned above, subscripts are enclosed by either '[' or '(' on the left and either ']' or ')' on the right.

A left bracket '[' sets the *index origin* origin to 0; while a left parenthesis '(' sets it to 1. A mnemonic to associate *left* with *index origin* is an *x-axis with the origin on the left*.

The right hand delimiter controls the relative significance of multiple dimensions. A ']' implies conventional *row-major* (or *lexicographic*) order in which the rightmost subscript varies fastest; while a ')' implies the Fortran convention of *column-major* order in which the leftmost subscript varies fastest.

So far our examples have involved only a single dimension. Now consider a netCDF file mat.nc containing a 2-dimensional array (matrix), which is printed as follows:

```
$ ncdump mat.nc
netcdf mat {
dimensions:
        row = 2 ;
        col = 3 ;
variables:
        short M(row, col) ;
data:
  M =
   11, 12, 13,
    21, 22, 23 ;
}
```

The following are equivalent ways of printing the final element:

```
$ nc2text 'mat.nc M[1,2]'
23
$ nc2text 'mat.nc M(2,3)'
23
$ nc2text 'mat.nc M(3,2)'
23
$ nc2text 'mat.nc M[2,1)'
23
```

Subscript values can be less than the index origin and are then relative to the end. So the final element could also be accessed by:

```
$ nc2text 'mat.nc M[-1,-1]'
23
$ nc2text 'mat.nc M(0,0]'
23
```

As we have seen before, a subscript can contain a vector of indices. Thus one could use any of the following to select all rows but exclude the middle column:

```
$ nc2text mat.nc 'M[0 1,0 2]'
11 13
21 23
$ nc2text mat.nc 'M(1 2,1 3]'
11 13
21 23
$ nc2text mat.nc 'M(1 3,1 2)'
11 13
21 23
```

Triplet Notation A sequence of indices forming an *arithmetic progression* as in

```
$ nc2text vec.nc 'v[0 2 4 6]'
10 30.7 50 70.2
```

can be specified as follows, using a generalization of Fortran 90 *triplet notation*:

```
$ nc2text vec.nc 'v[0:6:2]'
10 30.7 50 70.2
```

The triplet 0:6:2 means *0 to 6 in steps of 2*.
A triplet can take two forms:

start:*finish*:*stride*
start:*finish*

The second form implies a stride of 1. It is possible to omit *start* and/or *finish*. Let I be the index-origin (0 or 1). If the stride is positive then *start* defaults to I (i.e. first element) and *finish* to $I-1$ (i.e. final element). These are reversed for a negative stride; *start* defaults to $I-1$ and *finish* to I. E.g.

```
$ nc2text vec.nc 'v[:6:2]'
10 30.7 50 70.2
$ nc2text vec.nc 'v[::2]'
10 30.7 50 70.2
$ nc2text vec.nc 'v[2:]'
30.7 40.9 50 60.5 70.2
$ nc2text vec.nc 'v[::-1]'
70.2 60.5 50 40.9 30.7 20.3 10
```

Note how the latter example reverses the order.
A triplet can wrap-around the start or end. This is useful with cyclic dimensions such as longitude. Wrap-around is shown by:

```
$ nc2text vec.nc 'v[3:1]'
```

```
40.9 50 60.5 70.2 10 20.3
$ nc2text vec.nc 'v[1:3:-1]'
20.3 10 70.2 60.5 50 40.9
```

But the following does not imply wrap-around:

```
$ nc2text vec.nc 'v[0:-1:1]'
10 20.3 30.7 40.9 50 60.5 70.2
```

since -1 is treated as the end (6). Each subscript can contain any number of triplets and individual values. The colon (:) operator has higher precedence than concatenation. However parentheses can be used to override this precedence rule.

Omitting Subscripts An omitted subscript implies the whole dimension. Thus we can print the first row of mat as follows:

```
$ nc2text mat.nc 'M[0]'
11 12 13
```

and exclude the middle column by:

```
$ nc2text mat.nc 'M[,0 -1]'
11 13
21 23
```

Dimension Names Dimension names play an important role in FAN. Instead of:

```
$ nc2text mat.nc 'M(2 1,1 3]'
21 23
11 13
```

one could write:

```
$ nc2text mat.nc 'M(row=2 1,col=1 3]'
21 23
11 13
```

This is clearer for human readers. But specifying dimension names also provides the important facility of transposing dimensions. For example, this allows ncrob to produce statistics (e.g. means) for rows as well as the normal columns. To transpose the above matrix, one could specify:

```
$ nc2text mat.nc 'M(col=1 3,row=2 1]'
21 11
23 13
```

since the order in which dimensions are specified, controls their order in the output. To transpose a whole matrix, one need only specify the dimension names as in the following:

```
$ nc2text mat.nc 'M[col,row]'
11 21
12 22
13 23
```

or using column-major order

```
$ nc2text mat.nc 'M(row,col)'
11 21
```

```
12 22
13 23
```

In fact only one dimension name is needed, since any not mentioned are appended in their input order. So:

```
$ nc2text mat.nc 'M[col]'
11 21
12 22
13 23
```

Indirect Indexing So far we have located elements using direct index values. FAN also allows an indirect method using *coordinate variables* (i.e. variables with the same names as dimensions).

Consider the following geographic netCDF file geog.nc:

```
$ ncdump geog.nc
netcdf geog {
dimensions:
        lat = 3 ;
        lon = 4 ;
variables:
        float lat(lat) ;
                lat:units = "degrees_north" ;
        float lon(lon) ;
                lon:units = "degrees_east" ;
        double tsur(lat, lon) ;
data:
 lat = -45 , 0 , 45  ;
 lon = -180 , -90 , 0 , 90  ;
 tsur =
   11, 12, 13, 14,
   21, 22, 23, 24,
   31, 32, 33, 34 ;
}
```

FAN provides several *indirect indexing operators*. Perhaps the most useful of these is '~', which gives the index of the coordinate value *closest to* its argument. Thus:

```
$ nc2text geog.nc 'lat[~-40]'
-45
```

prints the latitude closest to 40°S and

```
$ nc2text geog.nc 'tsur[~-40,~10]'
13
```

prints the element of tsur closest to the point 40°S, 10°E. The following shows how indirect indexing can be used within triplets:

```
$ nc2text geog.nc 'tsur[ lat = ~90:~-90:-2 , lon = ~10: ]'
33 34
13 14
```

This gives every second latitude from that closest the north pole to that closest the south pole, and all longitudes from that closest to 10°E to the final one. The other indirect indexing operators are as follows:

@ max <	index value corresponding to max. coordinate value < argument
@ max <=	index value corresponding to max. coordinate value ≤ argument
@ min >	index value corresponding to min. coordinate value > argument
@ min >=	index value corresponding to min. coordinate value ≥ argument

Thus the following prints the minimum longitude greater than 10°E:

```
$ nc2text geog.nc 'lon[@ min > 10]'
90
```

and the following retrieves the rows from the *maximum latitude less than or equal to 30° N* to the *closest latitude to 90° N*, and the columns from the second (i.e 1 with respect to index origin 0) to *minimum longitude greater than 0*.

```
$ nc2text geog.nc 'tsur[lat=@max<=30:~90, lon=1:@min>0]'
22 23 24
32 33 34
```

Offsets It is possible to specify *offsets* using an expression of the form
index + offset
where *offset* is an integer constant (which can be negative). The offset must be the right hand argument of '+'. This '+' operator has even higher precedence than ':'.

One use for offsets is to append along the unlimited dimension without needing to know its current size. The expression '-1+1' represents the index value for appending immediately after the current final record (assuming the index origin is 0). Thus we could append to variable v in file vec_new.nc (whose unlimited-dimension n has the current size 7) by:

```
$ echo 80 | text2nc 'vec_new.nc v[-1 + 1]'
$ nc2text 'vec_new.nc v'
10 20.3 30.7 40.9 50 60.5 70.2 80
```

Coordinate Variable Unit Conversion In file geog.nc the units attribute is degrees_north for lat and degrees_east for lon. One may want to specify coordinate values in some other units. The following shows how this can be done by appending the unit (enclosed in braces i.e. '{}') to the value:

```
$ nc2text geog.nc 'tsur[lat=~0.8{radian}, lon=~-1.5{radian}]'
32
```

giving the value at the point closest to latitude 0.8 radians north and longitude 1.5 radians west. This unit conversion (like that during FAN input and output) is done using the Unidata units library discussed in Appendix C of [RDED96].

7.3 Attributes

As noted in Section 7.1 an attribute *vas* can take two forms:

```
    var: att
     : att
```

As in CDL, the latter denotes a global attribute. The following writes the global attribute title and then reads and prints it:
```
$ echo 'Sample geographic file' | text2nc 'geog.nc :title'
$ nc2text 'geog.nc :title'
Sample geographic file
```
Attributes cannot have subscripts, so there is no way of accessing only part of an attribute. Attributes (unlike variables) are automatically created if they do not exist and their type and size can be changed. The following gives variable lat the new attribute valid_range (with type float) and then prints it:
```
$ echo -90 90 | text2nc -t float 'geog.nc lat:valid_range'
$ nc2text 'geog.nc lat:valid_range'
-90 90
```
One can delete attributes by changing their size to 0. The following example deletes an attribute by reading from the standard UNIX empty pseudo-file /dev/null.
```
$ text2nc 'geog.nc lat:valid_range' < /dev/null
```

7.4 Using ID Numbers for Variables, Dimensions and Attributes

It is possible to use ID numbers in place of names for variables, dimensions and attributes. However dimension ID numbers must be followed by = so they can be distinguished from index values.

The author plans to implement FAN interfaces for some file formats which do not support names. In this case ID numbers will provide the only means of identifying variables, etc.

ID numbers begin at 0 regardless of the index origin. Negative values are relative to the end, which is represented by -1.

There are some situations where ID numbers are more convenient than names. For example, one might have many files (similar to geog.nc) all of whose variables except the final one are coordinate variables. A shell-script to process these files can refer to the main final variable as -1. The following shows the use of such a variable ID number:
```
$ nc2text geog.nc -1
11 12 13 14
21 22 23 24
31 32 33 34
```
The following prints the first attribute of the second variable:
```
$ nc2text geog.nc '1:0'
degrees_east
```
The following Korn shell script pratts prints all the non-global attributes in the file specified by its argument.
```
$ cat pratts
#!/bin/ksh
```

```
integer VARID=0
  # following true if variable VARID exists
while nc2text -s $1 $VARID > /dev/null
do
  integer ATTID=0
    # following true if attribute ATTID exists
  while nc2text -s $1 $VARID:$ATTID > /dev/null
  do
    print -n "variable $VARID, attribute $ATTID, "
    nc2text $1 $VARID:$ATTID
    (( ATTID += 1 ))
  done
    (( VARID += 1 ))
done
```
We can use pratts on file geog.nc as follows:
```
$ pratts geog.nc
variable 0, attribute 0, degrees_north
variable 0, attribute 1, -90 90
variable 1, attribute 0, degrees_east
```
Note that the output from nc2text on lines 3 and 6 is discarded (by redirecting it to the sink pseudo file /dev/null) because we are only interested in the exit status which is zero (true) normally and non-zero (false) if an error occurs.

8 Plans for Future

FAN was developed by the author, quite independently of Unidata, the developers of netCDF. However a close relationship has since developed between him and the group at Unidata. He has been involved with them in planning the future development of netCDF. It has become clear that FAN is likely to play an important role in these developments. In particular the proposed *link variables* for importing foreign data (among other things) will use a generalization of both FAN and URLs.

Several new features of FAN will provide the means for regridding. These include fractional indices, coordinate-space arithmetic progressions and a new '@' operator which will interpolate at specified coordinate values.

The introduction of nested arrays will require new facilities in CDL and FAN. Planning for these is still in the early stages.

The author also has close links with the developers of J. It is planned to make the author's FAN interface available as an optional module. This will be especially useful after the implementation in FAN of nested arrays, which are used extensively in J.

A serious limitation of the current version of FAN is its support of only one file format, netCDF. It is hoped to support CDF, HDF, certain types of text files and certain types of Fortran unformatted files.

9 Conclusions

FAN provides a convenient and natural way of identifying elements of file arrays for a variety of purposes including visualization. It is currently implemented only for netCDF and is likely to play an important role in future versions of netCDF. However FAN is suitable for many types of array-oriented file access and it is hoped to implement FAN interfaces to a variety of file formats.

Acknowledgements

I wish to thank Russ Rew and Dave Fulker of Unidata, for their assistance and encouragement in the development of FAN. I would also like to thank my colleague Martin Dix for his comments on this paper, which has been greatly improved by them.

References

[ABM+92] Jeanne C. Adams, Walter S. Brainerd, Jeanne T. Martin, Brian T. Smith, and Jerrold L. Wagener. *Fortran 90 Handbook*. McGraw-Hill, New York, 1992.

[B+94a] R. D. Bergeron et al. Database Issues for Data Visualization: Developing a Data Model. In J. Lee and G. Grinstein, editors, *Database Issues for Data Visualization: IEEE Visualization Workshop, San Jose, USA, Oct 1993*, pages 3–15. Springer-Verlag, 1994. Lecture Notes in Computer Science 871.

[B+94b] J. Boyle et al. Database Issues for Data Visualization: Interaction, User Interfaces, and Presentation. In J. Lee and G. Grinstein, editors, *Database Issues for Data Visualization: IEEE Visualization Workshop, San Jose, USA, Oct 1993*, pages 25–34. Springer-Verlag, 1994. Lecture Notes in Computer Science 871.

[BFG94] J. Boyle, J. E. Fothergill, and P. M. D. Gray. Design of a 3D Interface to a Database. In J. Lee and G. Grinstein, editors, *Database Issues for Data Visualization: IEEE Visualization Workshop, San Jose, USA, Oct 1993*, pages 173–183. Springer-Verlag, 1994. Lecture Notes in Computer Science 871.

[BPP94] James A. Brown, Sandra Pakin, and Raymond P Polivka. *APL2 at a glance*. Prentice Hall, Englewood Cliffs, N.J., 1994.

[Bur96] Chris Burke. *J User Manual*. Iverson Software Inc., Toronto, 1996.

[Dav94] Harvey L. Davies. Introduction to J. In Alain Delmotte, editor, *APL94 International Conference on APL, Antwerp Belgium, Proceedings Companion*. ACM SIGAPL, 1994.

[Dej95] Edmund X. Dejesus. Dimensions of Data. *Byte*, 20(4):139–148, 1995.

[GM94] G. W. Goucher and G. J. Mathews. A Comprehensive Look at CDF. Technical Report NSSDC/WDC-A-R&S 94-07, NASA/Goddard Space Flight Center, August 1994.

[Hui92] Roger K.W. Hui. *An Implementation of J*. Iverson Software Inc., Toronto, 1992.

[Ive96] Kenneth E. Iverson. *J Introduction and Dictionary*. Iverson Software Inc., Toronto, 1996.

[KBS94] D. T. Kao, R. D. Bergeron, and T. M. Sparr. An Extended Schema Model
for Scientific Data. In J. Lee and G. Grinstein, editors, *Database Issues for
Data Visualization: IEEE Visualization Workshop, San Jose, USA, Oct 1993*,
pages 69–82. Springer-Verlag, 1994. Lecture Notes in Computer Science 871.

[LMB92] John R. Levine, Tony Mason, and Doug Brown. *lex & yacc*. O'Reilly and
Asssociates, Sebastopol Calif., 2nd edition, 1992.

[NCS93] NCSA. HDF 3.3 Reference Manual. Technical report, NCSA, University of
Illinois at Urbana-Champaign, 1993.

[Pra75] Terrance W. Pratt. *Programming Languages: design and implementation*.
Prentice-Hall, Englewood Cliffs, N.J., 1975.

[RDED96] Russ K. Rew, Glenn P. Davis, Steve Emmerson, and Harvey L. Davies.
NetCDF User's Guide. Unidata, University Corporation for Atmospheric Research, Boulder, CO, USA, 2.4 edition, Ferurary 1996.

[Res95] Research Systems, Inc. *IDL User's Guide, Interactive Data Language, Version
4*. Research Systems, Inc., Boulder, Colorada, 1995.

LadMan

A Large Data Management System

Walter Schmeing
VISTEC Software GmbH
Rudower Chaussee 5
12489 Berlin, Germany
Phone: +49 30/6392-6061
Fax: +49 30/6392-6062
E-Mail: walt@vistec.fta-berlin.de
www: http://www.vistec.fta-berlin.de

Abstract. More and more of our customers have to deal with very large datasets like elevation data and digital roadmaps covering Europe or even the entire world, very large images e.g. from satellites or CT-Scans both medical and industrial. In this paper we describe how we tried to solve the problems of storing and especially of accessing those large datasets by developing *LadMan*, a Large Data Management System. We will explain *LadMan's* design and architecture, we will give a short overview of *LadMan's* API and will look at the implementation of *LadMan* as an important part of RUVIS, a Broadcasting Planning and Visualization System developed for German Telekom by VISTEC Software GmbH.

1 Introduction

Today's science, engineering and business are producing increasingly large datasets from different sources which include:

- CFD-, FEA- and simulation packages using large-scale models
- medical scanners using high resolutions (CAT, MRI, ...)
- remote sensing devices (radar, satellites ...)
- GIS-Applications
- Statistics-Applications (political, economic, financial data ...)

To save such large datasets, so they become accessible for further processing or visualization from various tools and applications, one needs to invest in ever increasing storage capacity (disk space). Even worse many of the access tools are only capable of reading the complete dataset; very quickly one reaches the limits of physical and virtual memory in attempting to process these large datasets.

Almost all data are compressible thereby reducing their size dramatically. One can use standard compression tools like compress, pack or gzip to save the large data files.

This reduces the required disk space but then requires decompression of the complete file to access the data for further processing even if only a small part of it is needed.

We defined the following requirements to be implemented by a Large Data Management System:

- most important is an easy and fast access to the data
- subsampling like cropping, downsizing, zooming, slicing etc. should be done while reading, to make accessing possible independently of the available memory
- the data should be stored in compressed and platform independent form
- there should be no limit in the dimensionality (1D, 2D,3D,4D,..nD, time varying) and any dimension should be dynamically extensible.
- the System should support "all common" data types (char, short, int, long, float, double) (scalar, vector, tensor)

To reach these goals we designed *LadMan,* a Large Data Management System, that divides the original datasets into smaller pieces and stores these regions in compressed format. Smart readers access and decompress only those regions of interest at any time. The access tools have to keep in memory only one region at a time parsing the data region by region for the application.

This approach leads to applications preserving disk and memory resources making them available for examining extremely large datasets.

2 *LadMan*: A Large Data Management System

2.1 Overview

LadMan permits the storage of huge datasets of any dimension, type and size in compressed format and gives you access to those data via smart readers. *LadMan* divides large n-dimensional datasets into smaller pieces and saves the generated regions in compressed and system independent format to the storage media.

The regions have the same number of dimensions as the complete dataset itself. The user can define the size of the regions (region dimensions) separately for each region or more globally for each dimension. While accessing the data *LadMan* only reads or writes one region at a time.

Suppose one has a large 3D-dataset of 1024x1024x1024 elements, one could divide it into regions of 32x32x32 in size to let you easily generate isosurfaces by reading in only a few interesting regions. If examining this data means slicing through the 3rd dimension, you would be better to divide it into regions of 1024x1024x1 in size for *LadMan* to get one complete z-slice while reading one region.

By default the system uses for each region the compression algorithm with the best compression rate out of the five already integrated algorithms. *LadMan* allows the user to select a favorite one or can even link in a new algorithm or bind to a hardware compression chip.

LadMan can manage the following data types:

- char, unsigned char
- short, unsigned short
- int, unsigned int
- long, unsigned long
- float
- double

combined as scalar, vector or tensor data.

The simple *LadMan*-API provides access to the compressed data via smart readers capable of doing subsampling like cropping, downsizing, interpolating, mirroring, stretching, slicing, etc. while reading the data.

Using *LadMan* one can have a quick look at a complete large dataset reading it in at a low resolution. Then one can decide which small part of the data one wants to see in detail by reading it in at a higher resolution.

2.2 The Data Manager

The Data Manager is the kernel of *LadMan* responsible for accessing the requested regions of the complete data set. It accesses only one region at a time sending the region data through the proper de/encryption and (de)compression filter and the data converter to make it available in a system usable format.

In read mode the Data Manager has to perform the following steps for each requested region:

- read in the compressed data of the current region
- decrypt the data using the proper user defined password
- decompress the data using the corresponding algorithm
- convert the data from *LadMan* representation to the native machine one
- copy the data into the user data buffer (doing subsampling if necessary)

The compression filter of *LadMan* uses five built-in run length compression algorithms. One can explicitly define the algorithm *LadMan* should use or let the Data Manager optimize the compression rate by dynamically testing the result of the different algorithms. One can easily integrate another particular algorithm not built-in or use any hardware compression chip.

The Data Manager stores the data in a system independent format. This allows one to access the same *LadMan*-Databases from every supported system.

A memory manager allows the user to define how many megabytes of memory *LadMan* shall use. The Data Manager keeps as many region data in memory as it can hold in the user defined memory limit. If the system reaches this limit it will free the oldest region.

Data Model

LadMan uses a Logical
Hierarchical Data Model

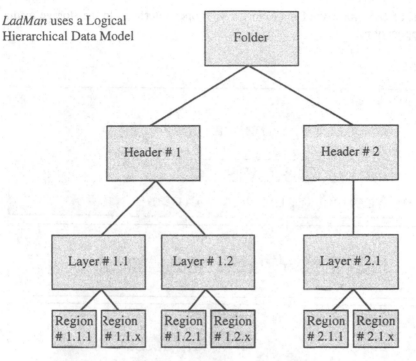

LadMan is like a library holding books of different sizes and content.
The books have pages of the same paper size with text or images.

Header	The Header determines the data and coord space (dimensions, solutions)	Books
Folder	The Folder describes the relation of the different data	Library
Layer	The Layer defines the data structure (type, veclen, etc.)	Pages
Region	The Region holds parts of the data in compressed format	Text/Images

Architecture

The kernel of *LadMan* is the Data Manager with open interfaces to the storage media and the applications.

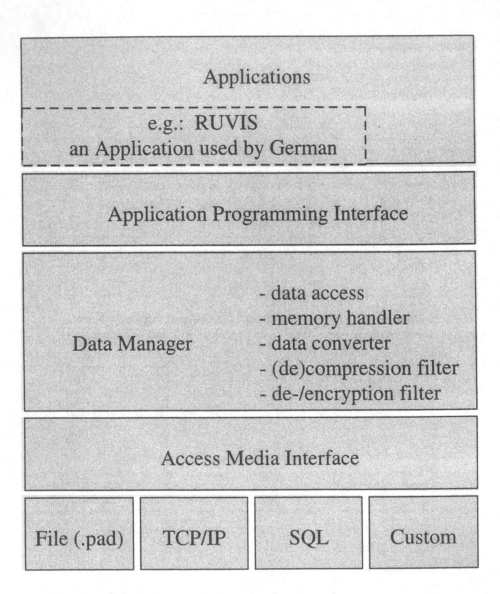

2.3 The Access Media Interface

LadMan has an open interface to access the storage media. By default it uses the built-in Pad-File. Pad stands for Packed Data and the Pad-File-Media stores *LadMan*-Data to disk files. You can store one *LadMan*-Database into one or more disk files even on different filesystems.

Due to the simple interface one can define and use a different media (e.g. DAT-Tapes). Already integrated is a TCP/IP-Interface, so one can install LadMan-server and -clients and an SQL-Interface, that lets you store the *LadMan* data into a commercial data base. One *LadMan* data base can be stored on several media of different types.

The Data Manager uses the following four pseudo functions only:

- OpenMedia ()
- CloseMedia ()
- ReadMediaData ()
- WriteMediaData ()

In the case of the integrated Pad-File-Media the interface sets these functions as follows:

- OpenPadFile ()
- ClosePadFile ()
- ReadPadFile ()
- WritePadFile ()

and internally these use the following System-Calls:

- open ()
- close ()
- lseek ()
- read ()
- write ()

To add a different media one writes new versions of the four interface functions in consideration of the defined parameter list and media-structure.

2.4 The Application Programming Interface (API)

LadMan has a simple Application Programming Interface (API). In the following you will find an excerpt of the important calls:

- data_id = DBFLD_OpenData (media_id, header_name, data_name,
  password) opens data and returns a unique data_id used by the API Access
  Routines
- DBFLD_ReadData (data_id, data, minIndices, maxIndices)
  reads data of data_id from min- to maxIndices into data buffer (every value)
- DBFLD_GetData (data_id, data, minIndices, maxIndices, dimensions)
  reads data of data_id from min- to maxIndices into data buffer of dimensions
- DBFLD_ExtractData (data_id, data, minCoords, maxCoords, dimensions)
  reads data of data_id from min- to maxCoords into data buffer of dimensions,
  where min- and maxCoords reside in the User Coordinate System.

- DBFLD_WriteData (data_id, data, minIndices, maxIndices)
  writes data of data_id from min- to maxIndices to a *LadMan*-Database
- DBFLD_FillData (data_id, data, minCoords, maxCoords)
  writes data of data_id from min- to maxCoords to a *LadMan*-Database ,
  where min- and maxCoords reside in the User Coordinate System.
- DBFLD_CloseData (data_id)
  closes and frees the data and its associated structures

To understand the access mechanism we give a more detailed description of :

DBFLD_**GetData** (data_id, data, minIndices, maxIndices, dimensions)

minIndices, maxIndices and dimensions are integer buffers with entries for each dimension. By defining minIndices and maxIndices one crops the data. Setting the size value for each dimension lets one downsize or interpolate the data. If the size of a dimension equals to one, *LadMan* cuts e.g. a time step or a slice or a line. If maxIndex is less than minIndex, *LadMan* mirrors the data in this dimension.

The application programmer can use a single function call to access the data with all possible subsampling features.

2.5 Extended Features of *LadMan* (in a nutshell)

User Coordinates:	The user can link each dimension to their coordinates to realize mapping of indices into user coordinate space (e.g. latitude and longitude)
Data Encryption:	All data can be encrypted by a user defined password preventing unauthorized users to access or "debug" the data. To accelerate the access speed *LadMan* lets one encrypt the higher level hierarchies but leaves the data itself uncrypted.
Data Storage:	*LadMan* stores its data in a platform independent way so a data base is identical on all platforms and accessible from each platform.
Memory Handler:	The user can define the amount of memory *LadMan* should use causing the system to keep already read data in memory till the defined limit is reached. Then the oldest data are freed.
LOD's: (level of details)	*LadMan* lets you store a dataset in different resolutions and automatically reads the data from the best fitting LOD accelerating the access speed dramatically and minimally increasing the storage capacity.

3 Experiences Using *LadMan*

Using the simple Application Programming Interface (API) it has been simple to write interfaces or converter to create *LadMan*-Databases from different input formats (e.g.: TIFF, JPEG, DICOM, ...).

Developing such a converter one should take in consideration that *LadMan* always stores a complete region to the data base, even if the data to be stored covers only a part of that region. (*LadMan* first reads the old region data, if already present). It is recommended to develop a converter so that it writes a region only once to the newly created data base avoiding updating of this region. If the new size of a compressed region exceeds the old one, *LadMan* has to append the region data to the end of the data base increasing the data base size and leaving gaps in the data base.

Suppose you want to store an image and have defined the region size to 50x50 pixel. If the new converter would store the image pixel by pixel to a data base, *LadMan* has to write this region 2500 times and probably has to expand the data base each time. So one better fills the region data buffer first pixel by pixel and then writes the completely filled region data buffer to the data base. If it cannot be avoided to produce gaps one can of course use the REORG-utility to pack a data base filling the gaps.

If a user creates a *LadMan*-Database he should have in mind, how he wants to access the data in order to define the optimal region sizes.

E.g.: to store a 3D-dataset for slicing through the Z-dimension one should set the region size of that dimension to 1 for *LadMan* to read a complete Z-slice with one Database-Access. But if instead one wants to read a complete X-slice from this data base, *LadMan* has to access every region in the data base.

So the user should carefully plan the definable region sizes.

One can also store the same data set with different region sizes to one data base. We applied this for example to the Data of the National Library of Medicine's Visible Human Project, which we stored in four different data layers each one optimized for different access (X-slice, Y-slice, Z-slice, 3D-access for e.g. isosurface). Although we stored the same data four times, the size of the data base is still only less than 70% of the original data due to the compression.

In almost all cases *LadMan*-Access is faster than "traditional" readers (like file access) probably because *LadMan* reads compressed data and therefore far less data from disk.

Using *Ladman* in different projects we have developed a higher level API, that automatically reads the best fitting level of detail or the right "slice layer" or reads in advance the regions the application probably will demand next while panning through a dataset.

4 *LadMan* as Part of the RUVIS-Application

RUVIS is a VHF/UHF-Broadcasting Planning and Visualization System developed by VISTEC for Deutsche Telekom AG (German Telecom) to simplify and accelerate the planning of broadcasting transmitters. The system helps to optimize technical parameters of the transmitter station like power and frequency and to find its best location.

RUVIS supports the planning engineer by providing access to several different data:

- elevation data
- land usage data
- digital road maps in various resolutions
- vector data like state and district borders
- political data like inhabitants or households etc.
- economic data
- coverage data generated by a wave propagation model

The RUVIS-Application makes this data visible to the engineer.

RUVIS can blend different data such as transmitter coverage with district borders and road maps generating images which will be visualized in a 2D-display or as textures mapped over the terrain.

The data are available as 2D-*LadMan*-Fields using geographical latitude and longitude as user coordinates. Most of the data cover a large part of Europe (at least the complete area of Germany). The digital road maps alone would consume more than 6 Gigabytes of disk space if stored in uncompressed format. Using *LadMan* the same data require less then 800 Megabytes saving more than 5.5 Gigabytes of storage capacity.

Furthermore the smart readers of *LadMan* in conjunction with RUVIS provide the planning engineer easy access to the available data. It allows him data to be read at different resolutions into buffers of the same size used for blending. Zooming in and out for getting new views or switching between road maps of different scale is a very easy task now.

5 Conclusions

Scientists and engineers are increasingly concerned with large datasets. They want to be able to examine these sets. Tools are necessary for storing and accessing their large datasets. Such tools must be easily integrated into existing applications.

LadMan implements these demands by its design:

- large n-dimensional datasets become divided into smaller regions
- these regions are being stored in compressed format saving much disk space
- smart readers give easy access to the data (regions)
- a simple API allows a fast integration into applications
- higher level interfaces (e.g. to AVS or DX) make it immediately available to the user
- new storage media can be added very easily

This open design lets *LadMan* manage very different data supporting scientists and engineers working in various fields.

The integration of *LadMan* into an existing Visualization-Application (RUVIS of German Telecom) has proved useful to the planning engineers and the application programmers.

6 References

[1] Treinish, Lloyd A., Unifying principles of data management for scientific visualization. In *Animation and Scientific Visualization Tools & Applications*, pp. 141-170, Academic Press, 1993

[2] Nielsen, G., Brunet, P., Gorss, M., Hagen, H. et al., Chapter III: Visualizing Large Data Sets, in *Scientific Visualization Advances and Challenges*. L. Rosenblum et al. (Eds.), pp. 143-198, Academic Press, 1994

[3] ACM Siggraph94 Course #27: Visualizing and Examining Large Scientific Data Sets, Chair: Theresa Marie Rhyne, Instructors: Hibbard, Treinish, Hussey, 1994

[4] Samet, Hanan, Applications of Spatial Data Structures. Computer Graphics, Image Processing, and GIS, Addison-Wesley Publishing, 1990

[5] Frank, Andrew U., Kuhn, Werner (Eds.), Spatial Information Theory: A theoretical Basis for GIS, International Conference COSIT'95, Semmering, Austria, September 1995, Proceedings, Springer-Verlag, 1995

The Tioga-2 Database Visualization Environment

Alexander Aiken*, Jolly Chen, Mark Lin, Mybrid Spalding,
Michael Stonebraker and Allison Woodruff

Department of Electrical Engineering and Computer Sciences
University of California, Berkeley
email: tioga@postgres.berkeley.edu

Abstract. This paper reports on user experience with Tioga, a DBMS-centric visualization tool developed at Berkeley. Based on this experience, we have designed Tioga-2 as a direct manipulation system that is more powerful and much easier to program. We present a detailed design of the revised system together with an extensive example of its application. We also give a progress report on a Tioga-2 implementation.

1 Introduction

Database system performance—as measured by either processing speed or the quantity of data that can be managed—has grown by an order of magnitude in recent years, making increasingly sophisticated applications feasible on ever-larger data sets. However, database query languages have changed relatively little and are difficult for non-experts to use. The vast majority of database users are unable to customize applications to their own needs, let alone develop their own custom applications. Thus, at present the expanding capabilities of database systems can be exploited fully only by expert programmers. Making databases easier to use and program, and thereby more accessible, is an important issue today and will become more important as database technology becomes faster, cheaper, and more powerful [11].

This paper reports on the design of Tioga-2, a new database visualization environment. We use the term "visualization environment" rather than "programming environment" to emphasize that most programming operations in Tioga-2 are performed by manipulating graphical representations of either programs or data. Tioga-2 is based on a small set of primitive operations for transforming data and its visualization. These primitives have been chosen carefully to have clear, simple semantics and to be composable. Thus, Tioga-2 users can build sophisticated applications—or modify existing applications—by successive composition of the primitives. We believe that by providing a small set of general "building blocks", minimum language syntax, and immediate feedback on the effect of incremental program modifications, Tioga-2 makes it much easier for database users to develop database applications.

* This research was sponsored by NSF under grants IRI-9400773 and IRI-9411334.

Tioga-2 has not been designed in a vacuum. Previously, we reported on the design and implementation of Tioga, a visualization system that is coupled closely with the POSTGRES DBMS [12]. The design of Tioga-2 has been influenced heavily by what we learned from user experiences with Tioga and a companion commercial product, Illustra Object-Knowledge, based on the same ideas. In the rest of this introduction, we first discuss the problems and lessons from Tioga and then outline our solution to those problems in Tioga-2.

1.1   Tioga

Tioga adopts the "boxes-and-arrows" programming paradigm popularized by AVS [13], Data Explorer [7], and Khoros [9]. Every box is a user-defined function, which has been registered with POSTGRES. A programmer constructs a Tioga program using a drag and drop editor to move and connect boxes on the screen.

Every Tioga program has a designated *viewer* connected to the output of a specified box. The viewer provides the user with a two-dimensional *canvas* onto which the programmer places renderable objects. In addition, the viewer provides a *pan* feature whereby the user can "fly over" the canvas viewing areas of interest. Furthermore, the user can *zoom* into areas of the canvas to see more detail. Zoom is a powerful construct, as it supports so-called *drill-down*—the ability to change the visual representation of data. For example, a state map of the United States could become a county map upon suitable zooming. In addition, we specified but never implemented the features of multiple viewers, viewers within viewers, cloning of viewers, slaving of viewers, and wormholes [14].

Experience with Tioga and Illustra Object-Knowledge can be summarized as follows:

1. Programmer model
   Tioga is based on the idea that an expert programmer constructs POSTGRES user-defined functions (boxes) and that a second programmer uses an editor to "wire up" visualizations. In this way, Tioga implements a "big programmer / little programmer" environment.
   It has been sufficiently hard to construct boxes-and-arrows programs that the little programmer must, in fact, be a big programmer. The key problem is that simplifying the specification of control logic through a boxes-and-arrows notation does not simplify programming sufficiently. For example, to construct Tioga applications, the little programmer must understand locating objects on a canvas and turning objects into graphical representations. It turns out that even expert programmers find these tasks difficult. As a result, little programmers have not been able to program in Tioga because it is not nearly easy enough to use.

2. Programming environment
   Tioga has the familiar notion of building a program, compiling it, and then running the compiled result. Novices have difficulty learning how to program effectively in this paradigm. For example, if nothing appears on the screen,

then there is a "bug" in the program. Bugs are hard for the programmer to find because Tioga provides a viewer only for the final result; it is not possible to place a viewer on any edge in a diagram to visualize the data that is flowing along that edge.

3. Expressive power

   As a result of trying to provide a simple programming model, Tioga is in some ways oversimplified. To select only a single example, because every box must be a user-defined function, a box has a single output, which must be of a specific type. This makes it difficult to implement functionality of the form:

   if condition **then** deliver data to box i **else** deliver data to box j

1.2 Tioga-2: Guiding Principles

Based on our experiences, we are redesigning Tioga completely from scratch, and the result is Tioga-2, described in this paper. We begin with the principles that have guided the redesign.

Much of the problem with the original Tioga system is that there is no way to specify some aspects of a visualization except via ordinary statement- and expression-oriented programming. Learning to write procedural code is a high hurdle for non-programmers, and some visualization aspects—such as writing functions to position data in a multi–dimensional space—are difficult even for expert programmers.

There is an alternative way to specify data visualizations. Non-programmers intuitively understand how to specify desired computations "by example"—by manipulating sample data. Instead of writing in a standard programming syntax, the programmer begins with very simple displays of data and composes them directly on the screen to construct elaborate visualizations. In moving from the boxes-and-arrows notation of Tioga to the direct manipulation programming paradigm of Tioga-2, we have identified a number of principles we believe to be important to a usable, flexible, and powerful direct manipulation visualization system:

1. Every result of a user action has a valid visual representation.
   All data types constructible by Tioga-2 programs have a well-defined screen representation. As such, the programmer obtains immediate visual feedback on the effect of any change to a Tioga-2 program and can visually inspect intermediate results. This principle facilitates debugging activities and solves problem (2) noted above.

2. Programming is incremental.
   Visualizations are constructed incrementally by successive composition of a small number of simple primitives. Combined with the ability to visualize results of incremental changes immediately, we believe that we can empower the little programmer to construct Tioga-2 programs. In Tioga-2, there is no distinction between constructing a program, modifying an existing program, and using an existing program.

3. To the extent possible, programming is specified visually by direct manipulation of visualized data.

   A boxes-and-arrows representation of the user's program is available and must be used for certain operations. However, considerable programming is done by direct manipulation of the screen without reference to this data structure.

4. Every operation has a clear, well-specified semantics.

   Unlike many previous direct manipulation systems there is no inference procedure to synthesize a program from a user's examples [4]. Instead, every Tioga-2 operation has a straightforward, unambiguous meaning as a step in a program.

5. Retain the "big programmer/little programmer" model.

   We recognize that there are computations that cannot be specified in Tioga-2. For example, while Tioga-2 has the equivalent of an if-then-else construct, it does not have arbitrary recursion. Thus, we expect that big programmers will construct additional Tioga-2 boxes as in the original Tioga system.

The remainder of this paper is organized as follows. We begin in Section 2 with a quick tour of the structure of Tioga-2. This section introduces terminology and notation used throughout the paper. Section 3 presents the user's view of Tioga-2, the user interface. The description of Tioga-2 programming begins in Section 4 with the primitive operations for editing boxes-and-arrows diagrams and performing standard database operations. Section 5 presents primitives for defining visualizations of database relations. Section 6 describes three sets of primitives for defining alternative views of data and connections between related data: (a) *drill down*, in which a user moves from a coarse visualization (e.g., a state map) to a more refined visualization of the same data (e.g., a county map), (b) *wormholes*, in which a user can move from a visualization of one data set to a visualization of a different data set, and (c) *rear view mirrors*, which allow users to keep track of "where they came from" (i.e., wormholes through which they have travelled). Section 7 continues with mechanisms to link multiple visualizations together. Section 8 discusses database updates. A progress report on an implementation of Tioga-2 together is given in Section 9; this section also covers a few additional features we have found either necessary or convenient to add based on early experience with Tioga-2. Finally, Sections 10 and 11 cover future and related work respectively, and Section 12 presents a few conclusions.

2 The Model

Before presenting the Tioga-2 system in detail, we define some basic terminology and concepts. The reader may wish to skim this section on a first reading.

Tioga-2 programs are represented by dataflow graphs with boxes and arrows. A *box* is a primitive procedure with some number of *inputs* and *outputs* (see Figure 1). The output of one box may be connected to the input of another box by an *edge* (also called an *arrow*). Box inputs and outputs are typed and

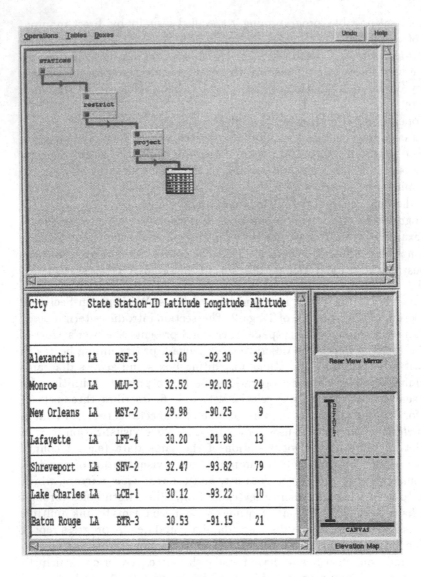

Fig. 1. Weather stations in Louisiana.

edges connect outputs to inputs of compatible types. Any attempt to connect an output to an input of incompatible type is a type error. Tioga-2 programs have dataflow semantics; when data is present on all of a box's inputs, the box can "fire", producing results on one or more outputs. Execution is lazy, evaluating only what is required to produce the demanded visualization.

A box input or output may be a scalar value (e.g., a runtime parameter supplied by the user) or a *displayable*, described below. Displayables define visualizations. Most Tioga-2 boxes compute displayable outputs from one or more displayable inputs. Tioga-2 has three displayable types: *extended relations*, *composites*, and *groups*.

The first displayable type is an extended database relation R. In Tioga-2, the visualization of R is defined by R's attributes. Intuitively, R "knows" how to display itself. We assume an object-relational DBMS in which a relation has stored attributes as well as methods defining additional attributes. For each tuple t of R, *location attributes* define the position of t on the screen and a *display attribute* defines the screen representation of t. Tioga-2 visualizations are constructed "tuple-wise"—the visualization R is the sum of the visualizations of each tuple of R.

Every visualization has at least the two screen dimensions and a representation for every tuple. Therefore, an extended relation has at least x and y location attributes, corresponding to the two screen dimensions, and an attribute *display*. A relation R may have additional location attributes; the *dimension* of R is the number of R's location attributes. A relation may also have multiple display attributes defining alternative representations of the data. We adopt a uniform notation and write $t.l$ to denote attribute l of tuple t, whether l is a stored or computed attribute. We stress that the location and display attributes used to define visualizations are computed attributes and are not stored in the database.

The second displayable type is a composite of relations $C = Composite(R_1, \ldots, R_n)$. A composite visualization is the overlay of the composite's components— the visualizations are simply superimposed. Thus, composites provide a way to combine visualizations of different relations in the same viewing space.

The third type of displayable is a group of composites $G = Group(C_1, \ldots, C_n)$. A group visualization is the visualization of each of the composites C_i arranged either side-by-side, top-to-bottom, or in a tabular fashion according to the user's specification. Groups allow visualizations of different viewing spaces to be combined. To render $Group(C_1, \ldots, C_n)$, a viewer displays each of the C_i in the specified layout. The viewer has a position for each of the n displayables—the user may independently pan and zoom in each of the grouped visualizations.

In summary, there are three kinds of displayable types, described as follows:

$$G = Group(C_1, \ldots, C_n)$$
$$C = Composite(R_1, \ldots, R_n)$$
$$R = \text{relations with attributes } x, y, display$$

Many Tioga-2 operations presented in subsequent sections are defined only for R or C inputs. To make programming easier, Tioga-2 extends such operations to work on "higher" types. For example, the **Restrict** operation filters a relation; it is a box that takes an R input and produces an R output. Given a group G input to **Restrict**, Tioga-2 asks the user for the composite within the group, and the relation within that composite, to which the **Restrict** applies. After applying the **Restrict** to the selected relation, Tioga-2 reassembles the composite and the group in the obvious way. This is all done graphically with point-and-click operations, so that the user need not be aware explicitly of how **Restrict** is overloaded to work on group and composite displayables.

Displayable types are translated into screen output by *viewer* boxes. If an n-dimensional relation R is the input to a viewer, then the viewer has an $n + 1$-dimensional *position* specifying the location of the viewer for each of the n dimensions and the *elevation*. The user controls the position by panning in the n viewing dimensions and by zooming, which changes the elevation, moving the user "closer to" or "further from" the data. A viewer displays the x and y dimensions of R on the 2-D canvas; the remaining $n - 2$ dimensions are available as sliders. If R has location attributes $x, y, l_1, \ldots, l_{n-2}$ each tuple t of R is rendered by drawing $t.display$ at position $\langle t.x, t.y, t.l_1, \ldots, t.l_{n-2} \rangle$ in n-space. Because a visualization space may be larger than the canvas, the viewer filters tuples to the ranges specified by the sliders for dimensions $l_1, \ldots, l_{n-2}$, filters tuples to the visible area on the screen for dimensions x and y, and then renders the tuples' *display* attribute to the screen.

3 User Interface

The Tioga-2 user interface contains several main windows. All may be visible on the screen or iconified. There is a single user interface both for building and for using programs, but a user browsing a previously constructed visualization will not require all of the windows available. A screen dump of the interface is shown in Figure 1. The user interface windows are: a *program* window, containing a boxes-and-arrows representation of a Tioga-2 program, a *canvas* window for each viewer in the current program, and a *menu bar* containing the pull-down menus to invoke primitive operations.

A canvas window shows data visible in a viewer at the current position. In addition, each canvas window includes: a *rear view mirror*, zero or more *slider* bars, an *elevation map*, and an *elevation control* (a dashed line through the elevation map).

The menu bar includes menus of all operations, tables, and boxes available, an *undo* button to undo the last operation performed, and a *help* button.

A Tioga-2 program is constructed incrementally by applying program editing operations to the program window (thereby modifying the boxes-and-arrows diagram) and rendering and/or drill down operations to a canvas window (thereby making modifications via direct manipulation). At any stage in the construction of a program the current result is displayed on all non-iconified canvases.

Since a canvas may be much larger than the available screen real estate, we allow the user to change the viewer's position, altering the area visible in the viewer. Scroll bars control panning in the screen dimensions x and y; canvas slider bars control panning in any remaining dimensions. The elevation control allows the user to drill down into data displayed on the screen. Elevation maps are an interface for programming drill down (Section 6).

4 Program and Data Management Operations

This section discusses the operations available in the program window and Tioga-2's database operations. These operations allow the incremental construction of a boxes-and-arrows program specifying data the user wishes to visualize. Operations for constructing visualizations themselves are discussed beginning in Section 5.

We use the following example to illustrate Tioga-2 programming. An agricultural specialist wishes to construct a visualization of temperature and precipitation data for various sites in Louisiana. The data is stored in two relations: *Stations*, which contains a tuple describing each weather station, and *Observations*, which contains all observations (e.g., date, time, conditions) from all stations. The data covers all of North America and contains a great deal of information besides temperature and precipitation.

As a first step toward constructing a temperature and precipitation visualization for Louisiana, the user limits the *Stations* relation to the stations of interest. For every relation known to the Tioga-2 system there is a box of the same name that takes no inputs and produces as output the tuples of the relation. Beginning with the *Stations* box, the user incrementally adds boxes to perform standard database operations such as restricting the data to tuples satisfying a predicate (e.g., stations in Louisiana) and projecting out unneeded fields (e.g., date of construction). Figure 1 shows a boxes-and-arrows diagram and canvas. The last box in Figure 1 is a viewer, which in this case displays data using a default two-dimensional table format. The user can also inspect any of the partial results. If the user discovers that any step produces unexpected results, he can inspect, delete, and replace boxes as necessary to fix the program.

For convenience, the operations in this section are subdivided into operations that manipulate program structure and database operations.

4.1 Program Operations

This group of primitives permits the initialization, loading, and saving of programs, as well as the deletion, insertion, and connection of boxes into an existing program. There are also primitives that provide familiar language abstractions analogous to procedures and macros. The operations are listed in Figure 2; we briefly discuss the most interesting.

If the user clicks on one or more edges in the current program, **Apply Box** gives the user a menu of all boxes whose inputs match the types of the selected edges. This is a shorthand way to identify those boxes in the database that could possibly take the indicated edges as input.

A design principle of Tioga-2 is that every operation preserves a visual representation. The thesis is that users are most likely to understand their programs and recognize errors if the results of every small, incremental change can be visualized and inspected. Deleting boxes from a program is dangerous, because inputs of other boxes may be left dangling and, therefore, their results unavailable for visualization. To preserve the property that "everything is always visualizable", arbitrary box deletions are not allowed in Tioga-2. A box may deleted if it has no outputs connected to other boxes (in which case no box inputs are left dangling), or if it has a single input and output of the same type (in which case the system connects the deleted box's predecessor to its successor). A box may also be **Replaced** by another box with compatible types.

A **T** box simply passes its input unchanged to both outputs, and allows another box, for example a viewer, to be connected to the **T**.

Encapsulate permits the user to define new boxes. The user specifies a portion of the program to be encapsulated by drawing a closed curve around a region of the program. Edges cut by the curve are the inputs and outputs of the new box. The new box may be used like any other primitive box.

Encapsulated boxes may also be parameterized to create something akin to a macro or (more accurately) a higher-order function. The user draws additional closed areas within the program region to be encapsulated. These areas become "holes"—they are not included in the encapsulated box, and edges cut by a hole are unconnected. To use an encapsulated box with holes, the user must specify a box—with compatible types—that can be plugged into each hole.

Operation	Effect
New Program	Erase the program canvas.
Add Program	Add a named program to the program canvas.
Load Program	Shorthand for **New Program** followed by **Add Program**.
Save Program	Save the current program in the database.
Apply Box	see discussion
Delete Box	see discussion
Replace Box	Replace one box by a different box with compatible types.
T	Add a T-node to a designated edge.
Encapsulate	see discussion

Fig. 2. Operations that manipulate the boxes-and-arrows diagram.

4.2 Database Operations

The primitives in this group provide database operations, which are listed in Figure 3. Each operation adds a new box to the program. The type of the introduced box is indicated in Figure 3. Note that all input/output types are R. As discussed in Section 2, these operations are extended to apply to composite (C) and group (G) types as well.

As mentioned above, the **Add Table** operation adds a new "source" box to the current program. The box is named for a table in the database and has a single output edge. The parameters of many Tioga-2 operations can be specified in several ways; usually there is at least one textual and one graphical method. For example, the user may specify the table to add to the program by either typing the name or selecting it from a menu of available relations. Note that **Add Table** is a special case of **Apply Box** with zero inputs.

A **Restrict** box filters its input, retaining only tuples that satisfy a restriction predicate. The user is prompted for the predicate to be applied. A **Sample** box produces a random subset of an input relation on its output. Each input is retained with a user-specified probability. **Sample** is useful for improving interactive response by reducing the size of data sets to be processed.

Operation	Box Type	Effect
Add Table	$\emptyset \rightarrow R$	Add the box producing a specified relation as output.
Project	$R \rightarrow R'$	Standard database projection; user is prompted for fields.
Restrict	$R \rightarrow R$	Filter a relation to tuples satisfying a predicate.
Sample	$R \rightarrow R$	Randomly sample a relation.
Join	$R \times R' \rightarrow R''$	Standard join of two relations; user is prompted for join predicate.

Fig. 3. Operations on relations.

The result of applying these operations is to iteratively build up a boxes-and-arrows program in the program window. We now turn to the visualization of the result of such programs.

5   Rendering Operations

The previous section has indicated how a Tioga-2 program can be built to retrieve complex computations (relations) from the database. Now we must deal with two additional questions:

- How are tuples positioned on the canvas?
- How are tuples rendered as screen pixels?

As discussed in Section 2, these questions are addressed by location attributes specifying the position of tuples in n-space and display attributes that specify tuples' screen representations. This section describes location and display attributes, default displays, and their associated operations.

5.1   Location and Display Attributes

Figure 4 shows a visualization of the Louisiana weather station data produced by the diagram shown in Figure 1. Each station in the state is represented by one tuple in the relation. The visualization shows a circle and the name of each station at its *(longitude, latitude)* coordinate. To position representations

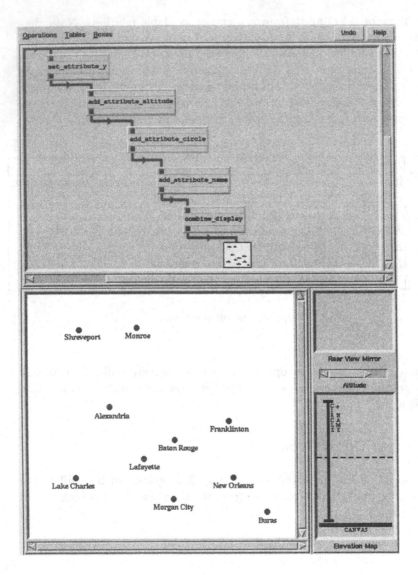

Fig. 4. A visualization of weather station locations.

of tuples on the screen, relations have location attributes. Every relation must have x and y location attributes to specify the x and y dimensions of a 2-D canvas; in Figure 4, the x dimension is longitude and the y dimension is latitude. There may be additional location attributes, which specify slider dimensions. In Figure 4, there is a slider dimension *Altitude*. By setting the range of altitude values that are visible using the slider, the user can see any appropriate subset of the stations. Location attributes are represented by floating point numbers.

Tioga-2 requires that every relation have at least one *display* attribute. A display attribute is a list of primitive *drawable* objects. Intuitively, a viewer renders a tuple by simply painting each drawable in its *display* attribute on the screen. In Figure 4, the display attribute is a list containing the text of the name of the station and a circle. There may be additional display attributes to provide alternative visualizations of the data.

The primitive drawables include: point, line, rectangle, circle, polygon, text, and viewer. Each primitive drawable has an *offset*, a *color*, and a *style*. The offset gives a position relative to the location attributes of the tuple; thus, multiple drawables need not be stacked directly one atop the other. In Figure 4, the name is positioned below the circle. Of the primitives listed above, all but viewers are standard primitives for graphics hardware. Viewers are used to implement wormholes (Section 6). The list of primitive drawables is preliminary and more may be added in the future.

In Tioga-2, every relation is augmented with location and display attributes. Actually computing the values of these attributes should be avoided except where necessary. As discussed in Section 2, display and location attributes, along with any other "extra" attributes, are specified by functions of the base tuple.

5.2   Defaults

To guarantee that boxes produce relations with initial valid displays, Tioga-2 provides default location and display attributes. There is a default display for each atomic type (i.e., each type of a column of a relation). The default display for a relation renders each field in the tuple, side by side, using the default display for each column type to produce a screen representation. The default space has two dimensions: the x-location is 0 and the y-location is the sequence number of the tuple. Typically, the default attributes define a display consisting of a sequence of tuples in ASCII. The major relational DBMS vendors all have so-called *terminal monitors*, which produce a display of this form for the result of any possible query.

Just as the user may incrementally modify the data management operations to change the data to be visualized, so may the user incrementally modify the location and display attributes of a relation to change the visualization. Initially, every **Add Table** operation introduces a box that produces a relation with the default display and location. The user may then incrementally modify the defaults, or replace them altogether, by adding boxes to the diagram or by manipulating data on the canvas. In Figure 4, the default viewer of Figure 1 has been changed by modifying location functions (to associate *(longitude, latitude)* with (x, y) canvas coordinates) and the display function (changed to the combination of station name and a circle).

5.3   Operations

In the remainder of this section we discuss the operations for modifying location and display attributes listed in Figure 5. Most of these operations apply to all attributes, not just location or display attributes.

Operation	Box Type	Effect
Add Attribute	$R \to R'$	Add an attribute to a relation; user is prompted for definition.
Remove Attribute	$R \to R'$	Remove an attribute; cannot remove attributes x, y, or *display*.
Set Attribute	$R \to R'$	Change the value of an existing attribute.
Swap Attributes	$R \to R'$	Interchange two attributes.
Scale Attribute	$R \to R'$	Multiply numerical attribute by a number.
Translate Attribute	$R \to R'$	Add a number to a numerical attribute.
Combine Displays	$R \to R'$	Combine two display attributes.

Fig. 5. Location and display operations.

The user may add new attributes, including new location and display attributes. Adding a location attribute adds a new dimension to the visualization. Adding a display attribute creates an alternative visualization of the data. **Add Attribute** prompts for the type and definition of the new attribute; the definition may depend only on other attributes of the relation. **Set Attribute** changes the type and definition of an existing attribute.

In both **Add** and **Set Attribute**, an attribute's definition may be given in a general query language. However, the preferred method is to begin with a very simple definition (e.g., a copy of another field, or a single primitive drawable) and then refine it using the other operations.

Swap Attributes is handy for interchanging two dimensions (two location attributes), thereby "rotating" the canvas, or interchanging the display attribute with one of the alternative displays, thereby changing the visualization of the data.

Scale and **Translate Attribute** are defined only for numeric fields. These operations are convenient shorthands for more complex **Set Attribute** commands. **Scale** and **Translate** are useful for changing location attributes, thereby scaling or translating dimensions of a visualization.

Combine Display is the mechanism for combining primitive drawables to form more complex displays. The user positions the displays on top of one another graphically to establish the relative position; alternatively, an explicit offset of one display to the other can be entered. The combined display becomes a new display attribute. The user may combine any of the display attributes of the relation. In Figure 4, a circle display has been combined with a text display showing the name of the station.

6 Drill Down

Drill down allows users to see more details in data of interest. There are two distinct, useful notions of drill down. The first provides a more refined view of the same data in the same visualization space (e.g., switching from a state to a

Operation	Box Type
Set Range	$R \to R$
Overlay	$Composite(R_1, \ldots, R_n) \times Composite(R_{n+1}, \ldots, R_m) \to$
	$Composite(R_1, \ldots, R_m)$
Shuffle	$Composite(R_1, \ldots, R_{i-1}, R_i, R_{i+1}, \ldots) \to$
	$Composite(R_i, R_1, \ldots, R_{i-1}, R_{i+1}, \ldots)$

Fig. 6. Primitives for drill down.

county map). The second allows movement between one space and a different, but semantically related, space (e.g., after finding a weather station, switch to look at its temperature/precipitation data).

Two mechanisms provide drill down in Tioga-2. First, the user can specify that additional detail about screen objects becomes available as the user zooms in. Second, we have a notion of *wormholes*, by which a user can move from one canvas to another canvas.

6.1 Additional Detail

The first form of drill down is defined as operations on relations R and composites C. There are three operations:

- **Set Range**
  This operation specifies the maximum and minimum elevations at which a relation's display is defined. Outside of this range, the relation contributes nothing to the canvas.
- **Overlay**
  Two composites may be overlaid. The relative position of one overlay to another may be given either by an explicit n-dimensional offset, or by dragging one canvas over the other. If the component displays are defined with different elevation ranges, then it is possible to program drill down by having the displayable at the lower elevation provide a specialization of the displayable at the higher elevation.
- **Shuffle**
  It may be desirable to change the drawing order of the relations within a composite. The **Shuffle** command moves a relation to the "top" of the drawing order.

Figure 7 illustrates overlay and setting ranges. Weather stations are now shown together with a map of Louisiana; this is achieved by overlaying the map (derived from a relation of lines defining the map) with the result of Figure 4. In addition, a third display is overlaid to give less detail at higher elevations. This display shows only a circle at the station's location. The programmer has set the ranges of the two weather station displays so that station names disappear at high elevations, where they would be illegible. The range of the Lousiana map is all elevations (the default).

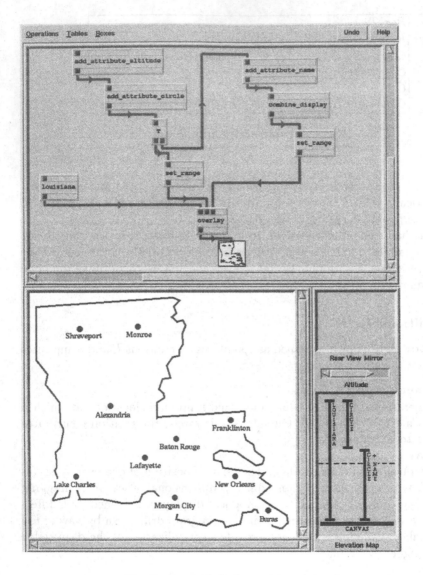

Fig. 7. Overlaid displays with restricted ranges.

There is a small difficulty with the overlay in Figure 7. The visualization of the state map of Louisiana has no *Altitude* dimension, and such a dimension makes no sense for a flat map. However, the composite has an *Altitude* slider; how are changes in Altitude to be interpreted for the Louisiana map? If the user attempts to overlay relations with different dimensions, Tioga-2 warns about the mismatch. If the user wishes, the underlying relations are treated as invariant in the "extra" dimensions. This achieves the desired effect in Figure 7: the user can change the *Altitude* slider to see different subsets of the stations, but the Louisiana map remains in place for reference.

The *elevation map* is a bar-chart display of the maximum/minimum elevations and drawing order of all elements of a composite on the current canvas (see Figure 7). The elevation map can be manipulated directly by the user to adjust the ranges and drawing order of overlaid relations. For a group displayable, a viewer shows an elevation map for only one member of the group at a time. In this case, the user can explicitly cycle through all of the elevation maps.

6.2 Wormholes

It is often desirable to associate objects in one visualization space directly with objects in a different visualization space. A *wormhole* is a viewer onto another canvas, i.e., what is visible inside a wormhole is a point on another canvas from some elevation. Figure 8 shows an example application of wormholes. Upon zooming into an individual station s, a wormhole appears (achieved by a combination of modifying display functions and overlaying and setting ranges) that takes the user to a canvas displaying temperature data for each station as a function of time. The user is initially positioned viewing the data for station s.

Providing wormholes is technically straightforward. Viewers are primitive drawable objects; thus, Tioga-2 programs may produce displays containing viewers (wormholes). A viewer drawable requires several parameters, including the size for the viewer, a destination canvas, the elevation from which the canvas is viewed, and the initial location; the user defines these values as part of the display attribute. As with any drawables, wormholes can be overlaid with other drawables. In Figure 8, the axes labels are the result of overlaying text at an offset from the wormhole (for brevity, these boxes are not shown).

When a user zooms in on a wormhole and reaches zero elevation he passes through the wormhole and moves from the original canvas to the destination canvas. Needless to say, the user can pan and zoom on this second canvas, as well as move to a third canvas. After changing canvases several times, there is a definite possibility the user will get lost. For this reason, we introduce the notion of a rear view mirror.

6.3 Rear View Mirrors

For each canvas, we introduce an additional window called a *rear view mirror*. This window shows the "bottom side" of the canvas through which the user last moved. Hence, immediately after going through a wormhole, the user is looking down at a new canvas from some specific elevation and is at negative ground level for the canvas he just left. As the user descends toward the new canvas, the distance from the previous canvas increases. In Figure 9, the rear view mirror shows that the user came through the wormhole at New Orleans in Figure 8.

Every Tioga-2 displayable has a minimum and maximum elevation. If both are positive, then the viewer only shows objects on the top side of the canvas. If the minimum and maximum elevations are both negative, then the viewer places objects only on the underside of the canvas, and they are visible only in

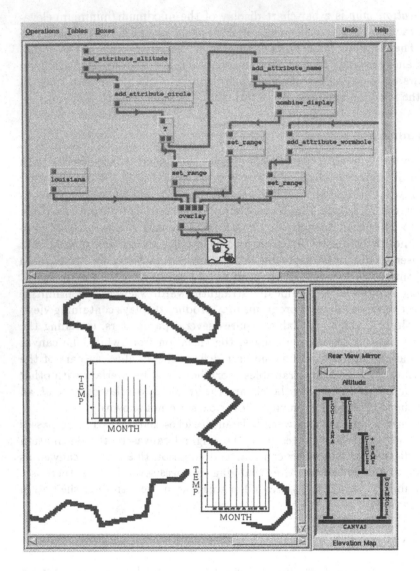

Fig. 8. A visualization with wormholes.

the rear view mirror after the user proceeds through a wormhole. If the minimum elevation is negative and the maximum is positive, then the objects can be seen on both sides of the canvas. Thus, the programmer can create overlays in such a way that the top side and the underside of the canvas both have meaning. One is visible from above in the viewer window and one is visible from below in the rear view mirror.

A natural use of the rear view mirror is to illuminate the wormholes back to the canvas from which the user came to this canvas. In this way, the user can "find the way home" if he is lost. As such, the rear view mirror is a generalization of the notion of "back" in a hypertext system.

7 Additional Operations

This section discusses the remaining Tioga-2 features, with the exception of updates (Section 8) and a few user-interface features discussed in Section 9. *Slaving* constrains two viewers to move together. *Magnifying glasses* provide hierarchical viewers (viewers within viewers). As discussed below, magnifying glasses are quite different from wormholes. *Stitch* and *replicate* produce group displays. Slaving and magnifying glasses are operations on viewers, while stitch and replicate are operations on displayables.

7.1 Slaving

Two viewers may be *slaved* together, in which case the system maintains the relative offset between the two viewers. When a viewer is deleted, all of its slaving relationships are also deleted. Slaving is only defined for two viewers with the same dimensions.

7.2 Magnifying Glasses

A user may create a *magnifying glass* by placing a viewer inside another viewer. Typically, a user places a copy of the current viewer inside itself and then zooms the inner viewer to magnify what is in the outer viewer. A magnifying glass must have the same dimensions as its containing viewer. The inner and outer viewers may be slaved; magnifying glasses may also be deleted.

A simple technique for correlating temperature and precipitation uses a magnifying glass in Figure 9. The user begins with a temperature vs. time display. The underlying relation that is being visualized has more information—in particular, the precipitation data—that is not being utilized. An alternative display attribute shows precipitation vs. time (the boxes defining the precipitation display are not shown). By creating a magnifying glass using this alternative display, the user sees the precipitation data for points underneath the magnifying glass. In Figure 9, the magnifying glass is realized by making the precipitation display the *display* attribute (done by the **Swap Attribute** box) and then viewing the result.

7.3 Stitch

Any number of composites can be *stitched* to form a group displayable. Groups can be displayed side-by-side, arranged vertically, or laid out in a tabular fashion. If the user performs a window operation on one of the group members, such as moving the window on the screen or iconifying it, then the same operation is performed on the other members. Zooming and panning is defined for each of

199

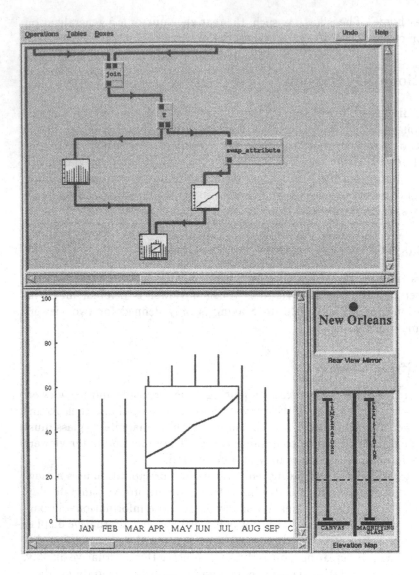

Fig. 9. Using a magnifying glass.

the constituent displays. That is, there is a separate focus for all components, as well as separate x, y, slider, and zoom dimensions. Components may be slaved.

In Figure 10, a display showing temperature vs. time is stitched to a display showing precipitation vs. time. The precipitation display is slaved to the temperature display, so that whenever the user changes the date range under temperature, the precipitation display changes to display the same date range.

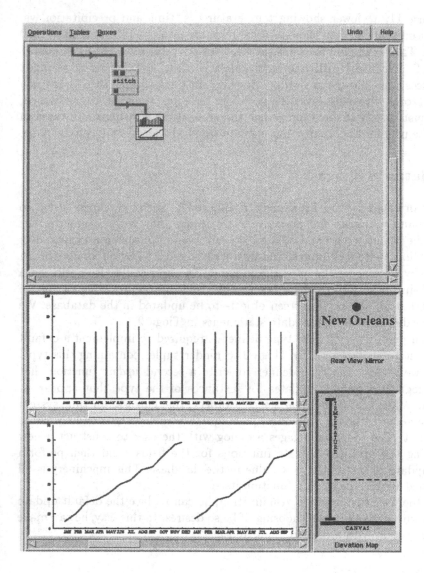

Fig. 10. An example of stitched viewers.

7.4 Replicate

A relation can be *replicated* by specifying a partition. Replicated displays for each partition are stitched together into a group. The user must specify the area to be given to each display and the initial point of focus.

The partitioning predicate is specified by giving a collection of predicates in the underlying query language or an enumerated type. For example, the specification may be that replication is tabular, with predicates **salary** ≤ **5000** and **salary** > **5000** in the horizontal dimension and the enumerated type **department** in the vertical dimension.

In Figure 11, a viewer showing temperature vs. time and precipitation vs. time has been replicated to show records for years prior to 1990 and after 1990 separately. This example motivates the need for operator overloading discussed in Section 2. Because **Replicate** partitions a relation, it takes an R as input and produces multiple R's as output. However, in this example the display is a G type (a group of two displays). Thus, before the replication can be performed, the user must specify the relation. When the user selects **Replicate**, the system prompts the user for the group component on which the replication is to be done.

8   Updates in Tioga-2

Tioga-2 is oriented toward browsing a database. As such, we expect users to wander around a canvas and possibly notice things they wish to update. For example, the quantity on hand of specific items could appear on a canvas. The user would find an item of interest and then wish to order a certain number of the item, thereby decreasing the quantity on hand. The user could also notice data errors and simply wish to fix them. As a result, we focus on providing an update capability that allows specific screen objects to be updated in the database. We do not consider general SQL update statements in Tioga-2.

For each primitive type, the type definer is required to implement a default display function that is used by Tioga-2 to render tuples containing this type. Similarly, we require the type definer to write a second *update* function that enables Tioga-2 to provide updates for instances of the type that appear on the screen. When a user clicks on a screen object, the Tioga-2 run time system activates a generic update procedure, passing it the tuple corresponding to the screen object. The function engages a dialog with the user to construct a new tuple—using the primitive update functions for the fields—and then perform an SQL update to install the new value in the database. This machinery is all encapsulated within the update function itself.

When the user customizes a visualization, he can replace the default update command with one of his own choosing, if he so desires. In this way, he can make an update system with a desired "look and feel".

9   Implementation

In this section we discuss briefly how the design is evolving to address issues encountered during implementation. The changes described here result from observations about how users progressively render data in a multi-dimensional space. The changes include a paint program window to provide more intuitive rendering and two new object types for displaying objects that are not associated with database data.

The current implementation of Tioga-2 is being developed on DEC Alpha workstations using Postgres95 for the database engine, Tcl/Tk for the boxes-and-arrows editor, and OpenGL for the 3D graphic visualization.

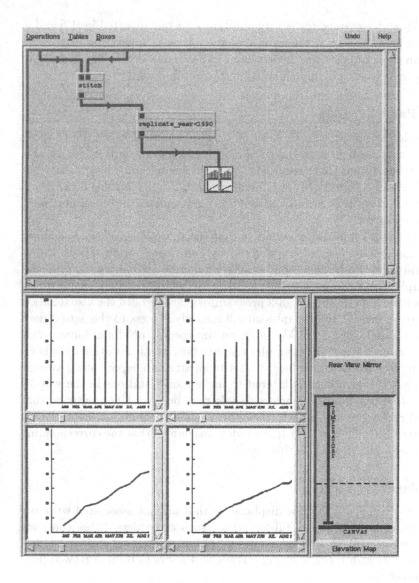

Fig. 11. A replicated viewer.

9.1 Overall Design

Tioga-2 is currently being constructed as four major modules:

- a boxes-and-arrows editor for data programming (Section 4),
- a new paint program window for rendering display attributes and specifying wormholes (Sections 5 and 6.2),
- a composite and group editor for additional operations (Section 7),
- and a menu bar.

The boxes-and-arrows editor is very similar to the one reported in [12] and is not discussed here. The paint program implementation is largely complete, with the exception of wormholes, and is described in Sections 9.2–9.5. The composite and group editor is not yet implemented and is not discussed.

9.2 The Paint Program

To make rendering intuitive for the user of Tioga-2, an interface similar to those in *paint programs* has been constructed. This window has a palette of displayable primitive objects (point, line, rectangle, circle, polygon, and text) on the left side of the screen.[2] Like conventional paint programs, a displayable primitive is rendered by selecting that primitive from the paint palette and then placing it in the canvas window.

The paint program includes a window that shows tuples from the visualized relation in the default format, constructed by converting all objects to a textual representation. Postgres95 requires such a function for every valid type and Tioga-2 simply uses it. Note that this display is in addition to any visualization the user constructs; thus, the Tioga-2 programmer can see both the visualization and attribute values of sample tuples simultaneously. Access to the actual data being visualized helps users quickly interpret unexpected results of incremental changes to a visualization. For example, suppose that weather station data is visualized using a rectangle whose height is set to an attribute representing average annual rainfall. If the relation is filtered to include only stations in the world's driest areas, then the height of each rectangle may be zero. Upon noticing that all displayed rectangles are, in fact, lines, the Tioga-2 programmer instantly can check the attribute values in the tuple window to confirm that the corresponding attribute values indeed produce this result.

9.3 Displayable Objects

The paint program can also draw displayables that are not associated with any tuple. These displayables are useful for "trim" such as borders, titles, company logos, etc. Semantically, these displayables are objects associated with an overlay. We introduce two such types of objects: *static* and *sticky* (a term borrowed from the Pad project [8]).

An example static object is a scale for the (x, y) dimensions with tick marks on the axes. These objects are static because they have constant position in the (x, y) dimensions. Panning and zooming of a static object has the same visual effect as panning and zooming in the rendered data.

An example sticky object is a window title. The object sticks to a particular position in the window and does not have an (x, y) position. As such, panning has no effect on a sticky object. Zooming on a sticky object produces a screen representation so long as the sticky object's overlay is visible at a particular viewing elevation.

---

[2] Thus, the appearance of the current interface has evolved to look somewhat different from the screenshots shown in this paper.

9.4 Dimensia Disorientation

Early in our implementation efforts we noticed an unanticipated problem: certain operations could leave the Tioga-2 user suddenly visualizing a region with no data in it, resulting in a blank screen. The most important case arises when the' user changes the dimensions of the visualization space. For example, suppose that employee tuples are being viewed and the fields are salary, name and age. Further suppose that the tuple (10000, john, 18) appears on the screen and that the x dimension is set to the salary attribute (i.e., the x location of the viewer is approximately 10,000). Now suppose that the programmer changes the x dimension to age. In all likelihood the tuple disappears from the viewer—in fact, all data disappears from the viewer—and the Tioga-2 programmer suffers from *dimensia disorientation*.

To allow the user to keep the focus of a visualization in an area of interest when performing dimension operations, we have added *sticky tuple mode* to Tioga-2. This mode ensures that a particular tuple remains on the screen when the dimensions of the visualization space are altered.

9.5 Painting Displayables

A Tioga-2 visualization of a relation is the sum of the visualizations of each tuple of the relation. Each time the programmer modifies the display it is potentially necessary to recalculate the visualization of each tuple of the relation. This is especially expensive when the user is actively modifying the visualization instead of simply browsing—in this case the underlying relation and the desired visualization may both change.

To make visual programming as interactive as possible, we have added *one tuple mode*, a restriction of sticky tuple mode. In this mode, only the single sticky tuple appears on the screen and, therefore, the screen can be painted without access to the database. The user edits the visualization of the single example tuple to his liking and then switches to viewing the entire relation to confirm that the visualization is as desired.

The sticky tuple is specified by the programmer by selecting an example tuple in the default data window and then clicking on a One Tuple Mode button in the paint program.

10 Future Work

Tioga-2 raises several interesting issues that we plan to address in future work. A few of these problems are discussed briefly in this section.

10.1 Caching Data vs. Caching Graphics

Tioga-2 is designed for visualizing large databases, and thus not all data can be held in memory at any one time. For this reason, and because browsing has locality (i.e., panning and zooming move to nearby points in the viewing space), caching both the database data that is being graphically represented as well as the actual graphical representation appears to be beneficial. However, given that there is limited space available for all caches, any space used for caching data is not available for caching graphics and vice versa. This is not a trivial optimization problem because the graphical representation is typically much larger than the data representation. As a result the graphical coverage will likely be much smaller than the data coverage; on the other hand, fast response time to panning operations is only possible with a graphical cache. We expect to explore these multi-cache issues in detail.

10.2   Sampling

When programming a visualization from a very large data base, it may be desirable to construct a visualization for a random sample of the data. In this way, the programmer can move from initial rendering to a final product on a small data set. Only when he is satisfied with the result should he move to execution on the complete data set. Hence, a possible extension (or alternative) to Tioga-2's "one tuple mode" is the seamless integration of random sampling.

10.3   Clutter

In many cases data is very non-uniform when placed on the canvas. For example, if the population of the United States is rendered at the (x, y) coordinates of each citizen's home address, then the spacing appropriate in Montana yields incredible clutter in New York City. Conversely, a spacing appropriate in New York City places people much too far apart in Montana. We plan to search for solutions to the problem of intelligently displaying non-uniform or "cluttered" data.

10.4   Foreign Systems

It is possible that a Tioga-2 application would entail some browsing of a canvas, along with the display of reports, spreadsheets, and forms. How Tioga-2 should interact with other subsystems, such as spreadsheets, is a topic for future investigation.

11   Related Work

While developing browsers for exploring data is a relatively new research area, the literature is already substantial. This section surveys a cross-section of related work.

As discussed in Section 1, Tioga-2 retains the boxes-and-arrows notation for programs originally developed for dataflow languages and popularized for visualization by AVS [13], Data Explorer [7], and Khoros [9]. These systems are similar to Tioga in their reliance on simplifying programming by using dataflow graphs. Thus, these systems share Tioga's basic problem that boxes-and-arrows notation alone does not simplify programming sufficiently for novice programmers (see Section 1.1). *Weaves* is another boxes-and-arrows system [3]. Weaves are intended to support visual programming, so the boxes-and-arrows program is itself the only visualization of interest. An extension of weaves supports limited drill down [5].

Many browsing systems are based on a "paradigm". A classic example is the Fisheye interface, which magnifies data in the center of focus to a greater degree than data at the periphery [10]. Another example is Magic Lenses, which provides a set of primitive lenses (windows akin to our magnifying glasses) that can be placed over data and over each other to modify a visualization [1]. While we find paradigms appealing, we suspect a flaw in the assumption that the space of possible visualizations can or must be greatly restricted in advance.[3] In our experience, paradigms serve a class of users well and frustrate users with other applications. To be generally useful—as Tioga-2 aims to be—it is important that users be able to construct arbitrary *ad hoc* visualizations of their own, even inventing their own paradigms if necessary. In short, visualizations should be as programmable as possible.

A different approach has been taken by the ambitious Pad project [8]. In Pad, all data lives on a two-dimensional plane. As in our system, every entity (an object in Pad, a tuple in Tioga-2) has a position and "knows" how to draw itself. Pad also provides facilities for overlay and drill down that are in some ways richer than the facilities in Tioga-2. Pad allows a very large class of visualizations to be built. However, Pad is not end-user programmable; it is designed as a toolkit for expert programmers and provides a traditional programming interface.

Within the area of browsers for databases, the work of Krishnamurthy and Zloof on Rendering By Example (RBE) is closest to our own. In particular, RBE shares our view on the importance of a system that is both highly programmable and easy to program [6]. RBE provides a more declarative programming interface than Tioga-2, but RBE can construct a much less general class of visualizations.

Finally, a database-centric visualization system raises the issue of how browsing queries are implemented with tolerable performance. This question is beyond the scope of this paper; the interested reader is referred to [2] for related work on the optimization and efficient implementation of browsing queries.

12 Conclusions

We are now hard at work implementing Tioga-2. An initial version of the system is functional, and we expect to have a complete prototype by summer 1996. We plan to systematically test the implementation on little programmers to ascertain whether it lives up to its goals.

---

[3] In fairness, Magic Lenses is not intended strictly as a browsing paradigm, but as a general user interface paradigm.

References

1. E. Bier, M. Stone, K. Pier, W. Buxton, and T. DeRose. Toolglass and magic lenses: The see-through interface. In *Proc. of SIGGRAPH 1993*, pages 73–80, Anaheim, CA, August 1993.

2. J. Chen. Optimizing interactive browsing queries. Unpublished manuscript, University of California, Berkeley, June 1995.

3. P. Cox, M. Gorlick, and R. Razouk. Using weaves for software construction and analysis. In *Proc. of the 13th International Conference on Software Engineering*, pages 23–34, Austin, TX, May 1991.

4. Allen Cypher. *Watch What I Do: Programming by Demonstration*. MIT Press, Cambridge, MA, 1993.

5. M. Gorlick and A. Quilici. Visual programming-in-the-large versus visual programming-in-the-small. In *Proc. of the IEEE Symposium on Visual Languages*, pages 137–144, St. Louis, MO, October 1994.

6. R. Krishnamurthy and M. Zloof. RBE: Rendering by example. In *Proc. of the 11th International Conference on Data Engineeering*, pages 288–297, Taipei, Taiwan, March 1995.

7. B. Lucas, G.D. Abram, N.S. Collins, D.A. Epstein, et al. An architecture for a scientific visualization system. In *Proc. of the IEEE Visualization Conference*, pages 107–114, Boston, MA, October 1992.

8. K. Perlin and D. Fox. Pad: An alternative approach to the computer interface. In *Proc. of SIGGRAPH*, pages 57–64, Anaheim, CA, August 1993.

9. J. Rasure and M. Young. An open environment for image processing software development. In *Proc. of the SPIE Symposium on Electronic Image Processing*, pages 300–310, San Jose, CA, February 1992.

10. M. Sarkar and M.H. Brown. Graphical fisheye views. *Communications of the ACM*, pages 73–84, December 1994.

11. M. Stonebraker, R. Agrawal, U. Dayal, E. Neuhold, and A. Reuter. DBMS research at a crossroads: The Vienna update. In *Proc. of the 19th International Conference on Very Large Data Bases*, pages 688–692, Dublin, Ireland, August 1993.

12. M. Stonebraker, J. Chen, N. Nathan, C. Paxson, and J. Wu. Tioga: Providing data management support for scientific visualization applications. In *Proc. of the 19th International Conference on Very Large Data Bases*, pages 25–38, Dublin, Ireland, August 1993.

13. C. Upson et al. The application visualization system. *IEEE Computer Graphics and Applications*, 9(4):30–42, July 1989.

14. A. Woodruff, P. Wisnovsky, C. Taylor, M. Stonebraker, C. Paxson, J. Chen, and A. Aiken. Zooming and tunneling in Tioga: Supporting navigation in multidimensional space. In *Proc. of the IEEE Symposium on Visual Languages*, pages 191–193, St. Louis, MO, October 1994.

Collaborative Visualization Based on Distributed Data Objects

A. Wierse

Computer Centre University of Stuttgart (RUS)

Abstract: The COllaborative VIsualization and Simulation Environment (COVISE) has been designed for a distributed and collaborative scenario in a high-performance computing and networking environment. Special emphasis has been put on the handling of the data in the whole system. Its concept though is sufficiently flexible that even the (more common) scenario of desktop workstation and slower WAN-connections can benefit from the advantages of a collaborative working environment. We will give an overview of the system and its architecture, explain its advantages and present our experiences, including performance measurements.

1   Introduction

Most visualization systems currently available focus on the visual programming paradigm in an algorithm oriented way. Data itself cannot be accessed by the user directly, but exists only internally. Means are provided to connect modules to networks which perform certain visualization tasks, but the access to the underlying data mostly is limited to providing a filename for the input-module.

There is no explicit control of data by users within most of the current dataflow based visualization systems. Thus either data produced by intermediate steps is kept, even if it is not needed any more, or this caching mechanism can be switched off globally. As data does not exist as directly accessible data objects a selective handling is not possible. On the other hand a user who wants to examine a certain interval in time repeatedly would be delayed by the application creating the same temporary objects over and over again instead of creating the sequence once and then displaying just out of „cache".

The supercomputers that are available today are able to solve numerical problems that result in amounts of data to be measured in Gigabytes. Solutions of time dependent problems in fluid dynamics can easily consist of several hundred timesteps, each several Megabytes in size. The efficient visualization of these solutions puts significant weight on the organization of compute resources as well as storage resources.

Think for example of a massively parallel computer system with 512 nodes, each with 128 MBytes of memory, which is used to solve a time dependent fluid dynamical problem via domain decomposition. The transfer of the final solution to a workstation would be very inefficient if possible at all, even if high-performance networks were available. The obvious solution for this problem is to do as much of the visualization work on the parallel system and then transfer the least possible amount of data to the workstation.

Usually the simulation and visualization steps are part of the so-called visualization pipeline (see figure 1). The output of an on-line numerical computation is reduced in a filtering step like sampling or cropping. In the next stage the data is mapped from the computational domain to a geometry (e.g. the calculation of an isosurface). Depending on the geometry the rendering step computes the pixel image which finally is displayed.

Fig. 1. The Visualization Pipeline

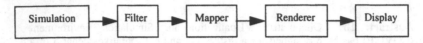

To make all this even more complex we are now focussing on a collaborative working scenario. Two engineers located at remote sites want to discuss the results of such a computation, simulating the normal situation of two engineers sitting in front of the same workstation and discussing a problem. Therefore both must see the same image, need to be able to communicate (talk) with each other and be able to point to something of interest. Of course the networks must be fast enough to allow a sufficiently fast communication between the two partners. Delays of a second or more make it very difficult to communicate (think of the delay apparent in transatlantic satellite telephone calls).

2 Data objects

2.1 The Problems

Most visualization systems available today follow the visual programming paradigm. Usually the visualization pipeline is assembled based on functional modules. The output of one module will be used as input for the module that follows next in the execution. The data that flows (hence the widely used name „Data Flow Model") from one module to the next is usually sent via a socket connection or exchanged via shared memory provided the two modules are running on the same machine.

But for most of these visualization systems the data only has a temporary characteristic. One module creates the data, sends it through a connection to the next module and forgets about it. In the best case a kind of caching is available: the data is not deleted but will be saved until the next execution; if the inputs have not changed since the last execution, a recomputation is not necessary and the saved data object can be send to the next module immediately.

Another inefficiency occurs when modules are distributed between several computers. The result of a numerical simulation on a supercomputer could for example be processed by two or more modules on a workstation. If the module on the supercomputer and the modules on the workstation communicate directly, a copy of the results will be sent to each of the two modules, thus wasting precious memory resources.

When numerical computations are performed on supercomputers in many cases several runs with varying parameters (boundary conditions, material coefficients, etc.) are performed (parameter studies). The results of these studies will be compared to find the optimal solution for a given problem. This requires that the data will be saved in a way that allows easy access to the different results and that different data sets can be displayed using the same visualization scenario.

In the case of a wide area distributed scenario other problems occur: usually the connections between remote locations are significantly slower than local area networks. Access to remote supercomputers today for example is usually not faster than 2 MBit/ s. Regarding the amount of data that is produced by a numerical computation on such a computer, the time needed to bring the data from the supercomputer back to the user is far from interactive speeds, even if pre-processing steps reduce the amount of data that has to be transferred. When a collaborative session is running, either the data has to be distributed somewhere in the execution pipeline (preferably at the point where the amount of data is the least) or it must be available on both sites and will be processed synchronously.

All these problems make it obvious that the handling of data is a non trivial task. A high-performance visualization system must be able to take care of these problems. There must be a way to deal with the data objects to make an overall system performance possible. This cannot be reached without an efficient data management.

Visualization systems like IRIS Explorer or AVS have no dedicated data management. Data is just something that flows from on module to the next. The situation with IBMs Data Explorer is better but still far from an overall data management.

2.2   A Solution

In a multi process environment, where data has to be exchanged between modules, shared memory is the most efficient way to do this if the modules are running on the same computer. This means that the data has to be written into the shared memory by one module; the module that wants to read the data must know the address and can then read it directly. Since shared memory is not available on all computers (e.g. Windows NT) we refer to this as „shared data space". Of course the storage of data in this shared data space must be coordinated or administrated.

A natural way to achieve this is the introduction of a data manager. It plays the role of an administrator for the data stored in the shared data space. If a module wants to store an object in the shared data space, it sends a request with its requirements to the data manager. The data manager then reserves a chunk of memory and sends the address back to the module. When another module wants to read this data object, it simply asks the data manager for the address and can then access the data directly in the shared data space.

If two modules (C and D in figure 2) reside on different computers, each computer has its own shared data space. This means that the data manager on the remote computer where the second module runs has no knowledge about the existence of the desired data. If now the second (D) module requests the data (3), the remote data manager cannot find it in its list and in turn asks the other data manager whether it can provide the data. The data manager which holds the desired data object now sends the data and the requesting data manager creates a copy of the data object in its shared data space (3'). Finally it sends the address of this copy to the module which initially asked for the data (D).

For the problem of identifying the objects in the shared data space several possibilities exist: for example one could use unique numerical object identifiers or a simple naming scheme. In COVISE (COllaborative VIsualization and Simulation Environment) we decided to use both: every data object that is stored in the shared data space has a unique object id. It is composed of the address of the computer where it was created on and the time (but it has no further meaning, i.e. the id should not be used to refer to creation time or location). In addition each data object has a name, consisting of a string of arbitrary length.

Fig. 2. COVISE system architecture

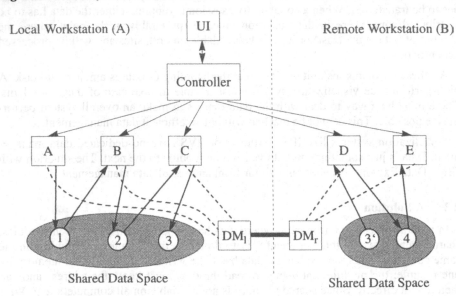

Local Workstation (A)   Remote Workstation (B)

The reason for having such a name points to a significant difference between COVISE and other visualization programs following the visual programming paradigm: in COVISE the user can access all data objects that exist in the shared data space. A data object that is created as the output of one module and will be used as the input to the next module in the execution pipeline has a life beyond the pure execution of the pipeline. After it has been created the user can take a look at it.

2.3   The Advantages

It is obvious that the introduction of a dedicated data management introduces additional overhead in the visualization process. So there have to be some good reasons and the overhead should not be too large.

Let us first take a look at the communication overhead: Measurements have shown that the overhead for the creation of a new data object (this means sending a message with the request for the creation to the datamanager, the allocation of memory there and sending the message with the address back to the module) is in the range of one millisecond. This is not negligible. But if we again take into account that we are talking about a distributed collaborative visualization system this millisecond is very small compared to the time needed to send for example 3 MB of data across a network (even via HIPPI this will take about 50 ms (based on the transfer rates that we actually measured in our configuration)). In other words this means, that for a completely local execution the overhead is significant, but in the situation that COVISE has been designed for, it is bearable to insignificant (if you think about remote supercomputer access at 2 Mbit/s).

Another source for overhead is the creation of intermediate objects for the data exchange between modules. Every data item that will be exchanged between modules will be occupying space in the shared data space. But this is more related to the usage of the visual programming paradigm than to that of such a shared data space. In an optimal environment the data is processed in small pieces; the complete visualization pipeline is applied to each of these pieces at once, thus the required intermediate storage is very small. In the case of a data-flow network every module boundary induces the creation of an intermediate data object for the data exchange.

Let us now take a look at the advantages: the first advantage has already been mentioned: the user can take a look at the data itself. Not only its visual representation, but also to all the intermediate results that were created executing the visualization pipeline. This can be very useful during the debugging of either the numerical code or of visualization modules.

Related to this is the idea of keeping the data beyond the current session (this is not yet implemented in COVISE, but everything is prepared for it). If parameter studies are performed, many similar runs of the numerical simulation will be evaluated. Instead of saving the direct results of the computation one could simply store the most recent intermediate representation of this data in the visualization pipeline and thus save a significant amount of processing time upon the start-up of the next session.

This goes hand in hand with the concept of persistent objects. Since we already deal with data objects residing in a shared data space, one could extend this scenario and view the shared data space as a cache to a larger persistent data space on disk. This would improve the overall system in several ways:

- The separation between numerical computation, the resulting data and the visualization would vanish. All this would exist in a single environment, thus allowing an integrated view for the user.

- The mechanism could be used to allow a paging/swapping mechanism. Once the shared data space is not sufficient to hold the data and the limit of physical memory is reached, the oldest data objects could be written out to disk and the freed space would be available again.

- Upon start-up of a session it is very easily possible to create exactly the same situation when the session was interrupted. This includes all modules as well as the intermediate and final data objects in the visualization pipeline. If necessary even the parameters of the module could be included.

A very important consequence of this dedicated data management is that the transfer of data is completely controlled. To illustrate the advantage of this, let us take a look at the following scenario: we have two workstations, connected via Ethernet and FDDI. Although FDDI is significantly faster, its characteristic of using tokens for the synchronization of transports gives it potentially higher latency than Ethernet. Thus it could well make sense to send short messages via Ethernet while the transfer of larger objects is definitely more efficient via FDDI. To make such a scenario possible, the data transfer between data managers is done over two connections in such a case: ordinary messages will be sent via the Ethernet connection while there is a dedicated FDDI connection only for the transfer of complete (and usually large) data objects. This would also avoid filling up the FDDI with many small messages, saturating the net with an effective transfer rate well below what is possible. This problem is partly resolved by using ATM. The small packet size of ATM basically makes the difference in message size insignificant.

In the problem section (see "2.1 The Problems") the case of two modules requesting the same data object of a remote computer has already been mentioned. It is obvious that our data manager concept solves this problem. After the first request has been received the data manager asks the other datamanager for the transfer, copies the data object into the shared data space and sends the address back to the requesting module. The request of the second module that arrived in the mean time can be answered immediately by returning the same address. Not only that the second transfer of the same data object across the network could be avoided; also there is only one copy of this data object in the shared data space instead of two in the local memory of each module.

3 The Implementation

In figure 2 you find the overview of the COVISE system architecture as it will be found in a simple distributed case. COVISE has been implemented using C++. Fixed components of the system are the data manager, the controller and the map editor (user interface). A special role, especially in a collaborative scenario play the renderers. For the renderers we currently use OpenInventor and Performer, both from Silicon Graphics; we plan to integrate a simple OpenGL renderer which would allow us to support a variety of platforms for the final display. The user interface is written in Motif (making it available on UNIX platforms in general), and we are currently trying to port it to Windows NT. We already have COVISE running on SGI (complete), HP (complete) Cray (remote modules only), the NEC SX4 (remote modules only) and Windows NT (remote modules only). We will port it with appropriate functionality to Sun and Cray T3E in the future.

3.1 The Controller, Map Editor and Renderer

Although our approach is very data oriented the controller plays the main role for the execution of a visualization pipeline. It launches every process, establishes the connections between them and organizes the execution of the visualization modules. The map editor is driven by user events, while the data manager responds to requests, either from modules, other datamanagers or the controller itself.

After the user has started COVISE, the datamanager for the local shared data space and the map editor will be started. The controller reads all information about the available modules (including input and output ports and parameters) and sends it to the map editor for display to the user. Now the user can start modules by clicking on the list of available modules. The new module is started, first connected to the controller and then to the data manager which provides the information to access the shared data space. After the user has constructed a complete visualization pipeline the execution can be issued.

Based upon the information about input and output ports the controller constructs names for the corresponding data objects and sends them together with the current parameter settings in the map editor to the module for execution. After the module completes, the controller informs the next modules similarly. So the whole pipeline will be executed.

If the user decides to make use of a remote computer, the map editor offers the option *add host*. The user provides the host name, the user and a password. Via a call to rexec now a so called mini controller is started on the remote machine, which immediately sends the information about the modules that are available on this host back to the controller; in addition to this the data manager is started on the remote machine, connected to the other already existing data managers and the shared data space is initialized. If a module is selected to run on this machine, this module is started via rexec and connected to the controller and its local data manager.

In cases where no shared data space is available (e.g. on earlier Cray operating systems) each module is integrated with a data manager (messages from the module to the datamanager are handed through a simple function call) and treated as if it were a module running on its own computer.

Due to the distributed nature of this architecture the case of collaborative working is not very different. Currently the user has to provide the participating partners at start time. For each of the participating partners the same procedure as initiated by the *add host* command in the map editor is performed. In addition a map editor will be displayed on each screen, where the others can follow the actions of the master. All the other map editors are not functional, i.e. no commands can be issued except the request to become the master. The commands that are executed on the masters map editor will be sent to the controller which executes them and in turn forwards them to all the other map editors (slaves). They can then mimic the master map editor.

While all modules work the same as in the non-collaborative working mode, the renderer is handled similar to the map editor. Since all users shall see the same resulting image, it is necessary, that transformations done by the user in the master renderer are propagated to the slave renderers. Again the data management concept comes in very handy: all renderers will be provided the name of the data object that has to be displayed and access it via their data manager (which gets the data object from the computer where it has been created if necessary). All that has to be exchanged between the master and the slave renderers are the transformation matrix and such things as lights and drawing mode. Since this information does not need much bandwidth, COVISE runs well even over slow connections when the data is available on both sides.

3.2   The Datamanager

All data objects that are exchanged between modules will be stored in the shared data space. In order to allow the extension of the available types of data objects through the user, we decided to choose a representation in the shared data space that makes it easy for the data manager to handle these objects without the exact knowledge of their structure. This is especially important when the representation of numbers is different between computers (e.g. IEEE floating point format and the Cray format). So each data item that is stored in the shared data space is preceded by a type information.

Types can be (amongst others): char, short, int, float, double, chararray, intarray, floatarray, etc. Furthermore there are arrays of strings and most important it is possible to define structures. These structures are identified by a type that is different from all other types. To assure this, the type is a simple encoding of a six letter word that is somehow related to the type (e.g. GEOMET for geometry). This is followed by a header which consists of the object id, the number of elements in the structure, the name of this object, its reference count, its version number and an attribute field. This is then followed by the elements which can be basic data types or pointers to other data objects. Together with a data type SET which contains an arbitrary number of data objects, this allows to build every data structure, allowing the data manager to do every processing that is necessary.

When a connection between processes is created, it is checked, whether conversion will be necessary. Since the IEEE floating point format is widely used in the workstation market and even most of the newer supercomputers use this format we chose it as network default. The fact that the Crays (which are the only computers that run COVISE using another format right now) are also doing the conversions fastest supports this decision. The problem of byte swapping (MIPS and Intel processors use a different byte order) is related and can be handled in the same routines automatically.

Upon the creation request for a data object the desired space is allocated in the shared data space. The address of this space in the form of a segment identifier and the offset into this segment is sent to the requesting module. The information about this data object is held in an internal structure and includes the name of the data object, its address, a pointer to the connection to the creating module, to accessing modules, their access rights and connections to the data managers that have a copy of it (or the connection to the data manager that holds the original object).

The names for the data objects in a visualization pipeline are constructed by the controller. This assures that the names created during such an execution are unique. The data manager though still checks for the uniqueness of the names. Only the object id is guaranteed to be unique. Currently the names of existing objects are not forwarded to the other data managers automatically. This will change though: after a data object is created, its name will be forwarded to the other data managers in the time where the data manager waits for the next request, thus reducing the time for the search of a data object.

As stated above we will include persistency into our data management. Similar to this, one could use the data manager as an interface to a full blown data base management system. This would combine the efficient handling of the data that is created during the execution of the visualization pipeline with the possibilities of a modern DBMS.

3.3 The Modules

The actual work of the visualization is done in the modules. Here the actual access to the data stored in the shared data space happens. Objects are created in the modules and the whole information about the type and access methods is available. Although object oriented techniques are accepted and widely used, we hesitated to use the plain object oriented approach.

The main reason for this is related to the main application area: the visualization process is usually described in terms of procedures: the three dimensional result of a numerical computation will be sliced, the data on this hyperplane will be mapped as colors on this slice and the result will be displayed. Of course this could be expressed in a more object oriented manner: we take the resulting object, out of this object we create a cutting surface, together with the data on this surface we create a colored geometry and this geometry will finally be converted into a pixel representation.

It is obvious that both representations lead to the same result. Therefore we decided to use an approach where the data objects and the procedures are standing equally besides each other. We handle data object as entities, but allow the user to build the visualization pipeline out of modules that represent what he actually has in his mind. On the other hand all the data that is created during this visualization can be accessed by the user in a straightforward fashion.

For the module programmer the situation is very easy. The communication with the data manager is completely hidden inside the class that is used as a base class for objects that will be stored in the shared data space. The user simply creates an object by providing the name that comes from the controller and the information that is necessary to create an object of the appropriate size:

```
new_object = new Polygon(„Poly_name", no_of_points, no_of_lines);
```

Each class now provides the routines that are necessary to access the data. Either one can use complete routines that do the error checking or it is possible to get access to the pointers and access the data directly (but with the risk of corrupting the shared data space). When the module no longer needs the data object it simply uses the C++ destructor. In this destructor all the communication with the data manager is done to inform it about the no longer existing access.

Due to this encapsulation the module programmer has no need at all to know such things as where the module runs, where the data resides, what are the preceding or following modules, conversion of data, etc.

If the module programmer wants to create a custom data type, this will work by deriving a new class from the class *DistributedObject*, the base class for all data objects in the shared data space. Here some basic initialization and access routines must be defined. This however can be done really easy by using an already existing class as a template and modifying only what is different. All access mechanisms are provided by the appropriate classes for the basic data types (Int, Floatarray, etc.).

This approach and the concentration of all system calls into a special communication library makes it possible that the same module source code is used on the Cray, the SGI workstation and a Windows NT PC. All that is necessary is a recompilation on the desired computer. If for example the vectorization of a Cray shall be used for the module code, it is of course mandatory to modify the source appropriately though.

4   Experiences

The COVISE system is now in its fourth year of development. Some decisions taken in the first phase of the conception have been revised, but the main structure is still the same. A major rewrite in the code for the transfer of data objects (especially the packing and unpacking of objects for transfer via a socket) lead to some significant improvements.

Important for the effective test of the system is the availability of real world problems. Although we worked for three years with data sets from project partners, reaching up to 100 MB, some serious performance problems showed up in the data management as well as in the renderers when we used a different data set, provided by a car manufacturer. Although the size was only moderately larger (300 MB) the different structure with a strongly hierarchical form pushed the current data handling to its limits. By modifying some routines and restructuring the process of packing and unpacking of data objects, some parts of the communication ran up to 30 times faster. Of course we didn't have the impression that our implementation was slow until we tried this different data set.

COVISE is the base communication software for several large projects currently going on or starting in the near future at RUS. This includes things as different as distributed virtual reality, international collaborative working in the design phase of a car manufacturer, rapid prototyping or improving the preprocessing-computation-postprocessing time of a complex engine computation.

Fig. 3. Parallel execution on two hosts

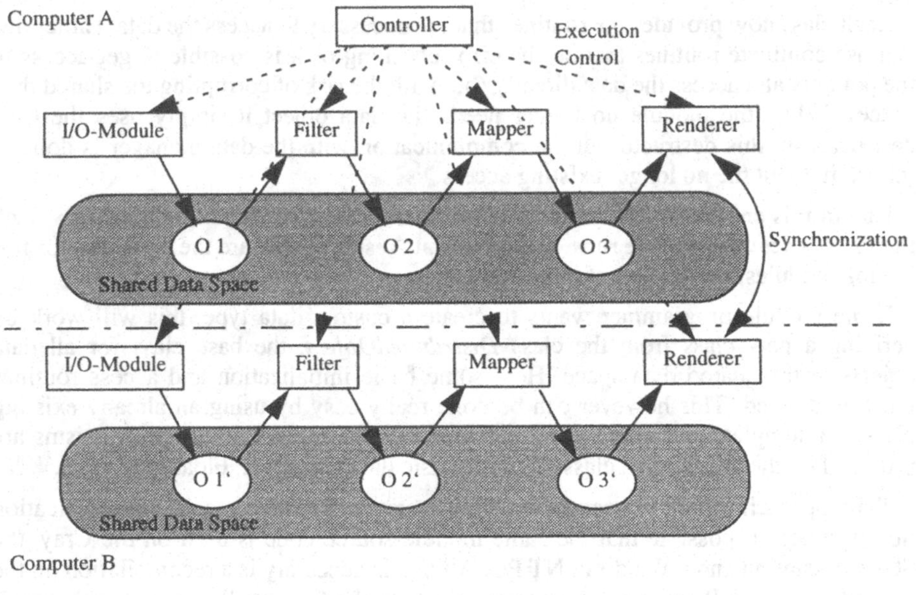

The special requirements in a high performance computing and networking environment make it necessary that the configuration can be adapted to the actual scenario. This includes the routing between the computers (which is independent from the application) as well as the optimal setting for communication parameters such as buffer sizes for TCP sockets (which is absolutely impossible for commercially available packages). If we look at the HIPPI connection between our two Crays this becomes obvious: without optimization the peak rate was approximately 13 MB/s. By simply increasing the socket buffers this could be improved to more than 55 MB/s (see [15] for the exact measurements).

Although the COVISE software has been developed with a high performance scenario in mind, only few modifications were necessary to work efficiently with a low bandwidth connection (2 Mbit/s). The main problem here is that the link is to slow to transfer the data in an interactive timescale. Therefore we modified the controller so that it is possible to have two copies of the visualization pipeline, one on each of the two participating computers (see figure 3). The data is transferred asynchronously and only the execution of the two pipelines is synchronized. Once the result is displayed in the renderers everything works as in the normal collaborative working mode.

5 Conclusions

The development of a new visualization system is a significant effort. There must be good reasons to justify the amount of work that has to be invested in such a system. In this paper we tried to show the problems that we faced and that we could not solve by using commercially available visualization packages.

Due to the fact that we aimed at a distributed high-performance environment many decisions have been made that lead to a non-optimal performance under non distributed environments or slower network conditions. But even in these cases the advantages of a database oriented data management are still obvious and improve the overall performance in comparison to other packages that are less flexible.

Given the fact, that the amount of data that is produced by the increasingly complex numerical calculations run on todays supercomputers grows continuously, we think that our kind of data management and its openness with regard to full blown database management systems is an important tool for the scientists who perform those computations. It allows them to handle the data efficiently and to utilize the costly hardware in an optimal way.

6 References

[1] IRIS Explorer 2.0, Technical Report, Silicon Graphics Computer Systems, Mountain View 1992

[2] Al Stevens, "C++ Database Development", New York, 1992

[3] S. Mullender (Ed.), "Distributed Systems, Second Edition", Addison Wesley, New York, 1993

[4] A. Wierse, U. Lang, R. Rühle, "Architectures of Distributed Visualization Systems and their Enhancements", *Workshop Papers of the Fourth Eurographics Workshop on Visualization in Scientific Computing*, Abingdon, UK, April 1993

[5] M. Arya, D. Swanberg, V. Vasudevan, A. Wierse, "Database and Visualization: System Integration Issues", "Database Issues for Data Visualization", *Lecture Notes in Computer Science*, Volume 871, p. 16 - 24, Lee, Grinstein (Eds.), Springer, 1994

[6] J. Gray, A. Reuter, "Transaction Processing: Concepts and Techniques", Morgan Kaufmann Publishers, San Mateo, 1994

[7] P. Haas, P. Christ, "Networking Issues in PAGEIN: The "N" of "HPCN" ", *Lecture Notes in Computer Science*, W. Gentzsch, U. Harms, Vol. 797, pp. 86 - 93, Springer Berlin, 1994

[8] R. Khanna (Ed.),"Distributed Computing, Implementation and Management Strategies", Prentice Hall, Englewood Cliffs, 1994

[9] S. Rill, R. Grosso, "Future Aerospace Working Scenarios Using High Speed Networks and Supercomputers Applied to Flow Simulation for Complete Aircraft", *Lecture Notes in Computer Science*, W. Gentzsch, U. Harms, Vol. 797, pp. 60 - 69, Springer Berlin, 1994

[10]M. Sloman (Ed.), "Network and Distributed Systems Management",Addison Wesley, Workingham England, 1994

[11]A. Wierse, U. Lang, R. Rühle, "A System Architecture for Data-oriented Visualization", "Database Issues for Data Visualization", *Lecture Notes in Computer Science*, Volume 871, pp. 148 - 159, Lee, Grinstein (Eds.), Springer, 1994

[12]G. Abram, L. Treinish, "An Extended Data-Flow Architecture for Data Analysis and Visualization", Proceedings Visualization '95, G. Nielson, D. Silver (Eds.), pp. 263-270, IEEE Computer Society Press, Los Alamitos, 1995

[13]AVS/Express, Developer's Reference, Advanced Visual Systems, Waltham, MA, Aug. 1995

[14]User Guide, AIX/Visualization Data Explorer/6000, Version 3.1, IBM Corporation, Yorktown Heights, 1995

[15]A. Wierse, "Performance of the COVISE visualization system under different conditions", in *Visual Data Exploration and Analysis II*, Georges G. Grinstein, Robert F. Erbacher, Editors, Proc. SPIE 2410, 218-229, 1995

[16]W. Schroeder, K. Martin, B. Lorensen, "The Visualization Toolkit: An Object-Oriented Approach to 3D-Graphics", Prentice Hall, Upper Saddle River, NJ, 1996

[17]A. Wierse, R. Lang, U. Lang, H. Nebel, D. Rantzau, "The Performance of a Distributed Visualization system", *Proceedings of the International Workshop on Visualization, held January 18 - 20 1994 in Paderborn*, W. Borchers, G. Domik, D. Kröner, R. Rautmann, D. Saupe, VSP-International Science Publishers, to appear

Springer and the environment

At Springer we firmly believe that an international science publisher has a special obligation to the environment, and our corporate policies consistently reflect this conviction.

We also expect our business partners – paper mills, printers, packaging manufacturers, etc. – to commit themselves to using materials and production processes that do not harm the environment. The paper in this book is made from low- or no-chlorine pulp and is acid free, in conformance with international standards for paper permanency.

Springer

Lecture Notes in Computer Science

For information about Vols. 1–1107

please contact your bookseller or Springer-Verlag